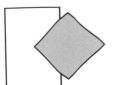

Introduction to clinical health psychology

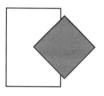

Introduction to clinical health psychology

Paul Bennett

Open University Press
Maidenhead · Philadelphia

Open University Press
McGraw-Hill Education
McGraw-Hill House
Shoppenhangers Road
Maidenhead
Berkshire
England
SL6 2QL

email: enquiries@openup.co.uk
world wide web: www.openup.co.uk

and
325 Chestnut Street
Philadelphia, PA 19106, USA

First Published 2000

Reprinted 2003

A catalogue record of this book is available from the British Library

ISBN 0 335 20497 X (pb)   0 335 20498 8 (hb)

Library of Congress Cataloging-in-Publication Data
Bennett, Paul, 1955–
    Introduction to clinical health psychology / Paul Bennett.
        p.   cm.
    Includes bibliographical references and index.
    ISBN 0-335-20498-8 – ISBN 0-335-20497-X (pbk.)
        1. Clinical health psychology.   I. Title.
R726.7.B457 2000

616′.001′9–dc21   00-037365

Typeset by Graphicraft Limited, Hong Kong
Printed in Great Britain by Biddles Ltd, www.biddles.co.uk

To Gill, Tom, Christina and Jenna

Contents

Introduction

Why a book on clinical health psychology?

The term 'clinical health psychology' stems from two strands of psychology, each with a different history and focus. Clinical psychology has moved from its historical roots of the 1950s, when practitioners worked almost exclusively in psychiatric settings, to the provision of therapy in a wide variety of settings and with a range of patients, including those who are physically ill. Underlying this move has been a more subtle shift in therapeutic approach. The focus of clinical interventions is no longer solely the remediation of mental health problems. Many clinical psychologists work in settings such as pain clinics or on cardiac rehabilitation programmes, where the majority of patients cannot be considered 'mentally ill'. The rationale for this shift is that the behavioural changes required by participants in such programmes can be facilitated by practitioners with a theoretical understanding of factors that influence behaviour change and the skills to work with individuals or groups to facilitate this process. Clinical psychologists have also moved from an almost exclusively patient focus to one that encompasses a wide variety of roles, including teaching and training, the supervision of others engaged in psychological therapy, and working at an organizational level in a variety of ways.

Those that have made the move to working with physically ill patients have necessarily had to encounter and use a different set of theories and principles from those that guide practice in psychiatry or other specialisms. They have encountered the scientific discipline of health psychology.

Health psychology is an applied discipline. As such, it draws predominantly on theoretical models developed in a wide variety of psychological disciplines, including cognitive psychology, social psychology, and the study of emotions. In the UK, for example, its development began in the mid-1980s, when it was first recognized as an area of academic interest by the British Psychological Society (BPS), which in 1986 established a health psychology section, led by Professor Marie Johnston. Since then, this group has gained divisional status within the BPS. This change in status is not trivial. It indicates that the status of health psychology has shifted from one of a shared scientific interest to that of an applied profession. Health psychologists, with appropriate training, can now achieve chartered status and work autonomously within the health service and other settings. Health psychologists are already working in areas such as health promotion, health-related research, and as consultants to a variety of organizations. An increasing number are also more directly involved in the provision of health care.

The delineation of the roles of the two professional groups in this setting has already resulted in forests of paper being consumed in consultation documents and lively debate. At present the boundaries between the two professions are blurred. A crude position statement would indicate that clinical psychologists will maintain the patient as their primary focus, while health psychologists work at other levels: teaching, training, working at an organizational level, and so on. Those who have both clinical skills and the knowledge and practice base of health psychology, and who may truly be called clinical health psychologists, may adopt any or all these roles. However, this simple categorization fails to take account of the training in non-patient issues that clinical psychologists receive, and will surely be challenged by clinicians who are skilled in working at an organizational level, by health psychologists who prove to have excellent therapeutic skills, and so on.

Whatever the final, probably overlapping roles, adopted by each profession, what is clear is that psychologists working in medical settings need to be aware of both health and clinical psychology theory and how it can be applied to maximize the effectiveness of health care delivery. This book provides an introduction to the knowledge base, theory, and the practice of both health and clinical psychology as applied to health, and is relevant to professionals, trainees or students wishing to gain an understanding of health and clinical psychology as applied to the care of the physically ill. It is divided into four parts:

◆ Part I: Behaviour, stress and health
◆ Part II: Understanding health-related behaviour
◆ Part III: Applied health psychology
◆ Part IV: Clinical interventions

Part I: Behaviour, stress and health

The two chapters in Part I consider the relationship between behaviour, stress and health. Chapter 1 firstly considers the risk for disease associated with a number of individual behaviours such as smoking or poor diet, before moving to consider more 'social' causes of ill health such as low socio-economic status or poor working conditions. It also considers how the effects of gender on health may be behaviourally mediated and not simply a function of biology. Each section considers some of the controversies that have been associated with the relevant area of research as well as what we know about the associations between each risk factor and disease. Chapter 2 focuses on social, psychological and physiological theories of stress. It considers the relationship between theories that consider stress to be 'in the eye of the beholder' (for example Lazarus and Folkman 1984) and those that consider stress to be a more direct function of environmental demands and resources (for example Hobfoll (1989)). It then describes the physiological processes that underlie the stress response, considering the cortical, sympathetic and immune systems.

Part II: Understanding health-related behaviour

The second part also comprises two chapters. The first provides a critical overview of some of the most influential theories of behavioural decision making used and developed by health psychologists. These social cognition theories attempt to identify key variables (attitudes, social norms, cost/benefit analyses and so on) that underpin choices related to health behaviours. They have not been without their critics, however, and the chapter explores some of the strengths of other approaches to the study of health-related behavioural choices. The second chapter in Part II examines children's and adults' concepts of both health and illness and how these concepts influence their response to illness. It also considers how cognitions form an important part of our response to one particular symptom: pain.

Part III: Applied health psychology

This part has three chapters. The first identifies a number of elements of the care system that impact on how people cope with illness and react to hospitalization. The second considers how these may be influenced by psychologists and other health professionals to maximize the effectiveness of the health care system and minimize its adverse psychological consequences on the individuals who enter it. The chapters cover issues such as the experience of hospitalization, how people cope with a diagnosis of severe or chronic illness, staff/patient interactions, adherence to medication and behavioural programmes, factors that influence medical decision making, and stress and the hospital system. The second chapter includes examples of the work currently conducted by health psychologists within the health care system.

The third chapter in Part III adopts a critical stance in relation to health promotion. It argues that while educational and community-wide programmes based on psychological principles have proven effective in changing behaviour in the past, future initiatives should focus on changing new risk factors and social and structural moderators of disease, including socio-economic inequalities and work factors, rather than focusing exclusively on changing individual behaviour. In doing so, the chapter refers back to some of the risk factors discussed in the Chapter 1 and social cognition theories discussed in Chapter 3.

Part IV: Clinical interventions

The final part has four chapters. The first provides a brief description of the clinical interventions that are conducted with patients who are physically ill. The types of intervention selected for inclusion in this chapter are those most commonly used with patients in acute medical settings. They include interventions that have been developed specifically for use with patients with chronic health problems, and others that are in more general use. The effectiveness of these approaches in the management of disease states, reducing risk for disease progression, and helping people to cope with the emotional sequelae to their illness is considered in the final two chapters. Sitting between these chapters is one that focuses on the assessment of health and psychological status in physically ill patients. This interrupts the flow between the chapters describing therapeutic approaches and their application in health care settings. This was done for two reasons. First, to emphasize the importance of assessment and not to make it the final, 'add-on', chapter. Secondly, some of the assessment instruments described in this chapter contribute to the evaluative research reported in the following two chapters.

And finally . . .

Writing this text has encouraged (nay, forced!) me to read in areas of health and clinical psychology about which I previously knew very little. It has instilled an interest in areas previously hidden from me, some of which I am now actively involved in researching. I hope the book is able to provoke such an interest in you, and that you enjoy reading it.

Paul Bennett

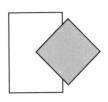

Part I
Behaviour, stress and health

Psychosocial correlates of health

The assumption that behaviour or personality is linked to health is not new. The Ancient Greeks and Romans described associations between personality and health, and this presumptive link has since continued through medical folklore and even psychoanalytic theory. However, the scientific exploration of links between behaviour and health is a relatively young venture. Even 'classic' studies identifying a link between smoking and disease were conducted only in the 1950s and much relevant research is more recent. This research has had three primary foci. The first has been the link between behaviours, such as smoking or eating habits, that confer risk of disease indirectly. Smoking, for example, may cause disease as a result of the carcinogens inhaled. The behavioural repertoire associated with smoking is not in itself harmful. A second set of research has focused on behaviours that *directly* moderate risk of disease. This includes exercise, but perhaps more excitingly from a psychological perspective has also included individual differences, including Type A and C behaviour. A third strand of research has focused on elements of the social or psychological environment that influence disease rates, including social support and socio-economic status. The latter, in particular, has recently emerged as an extremely important area of research.

Rather than simply report the relationship between these variables and disease rates, this chapter not only reports such data but also looks at some of the issues or controversies raised by each set of research. The chapter considers:

◆ Individual risk factors and disease

◆ Personality and disease

◆ Social and environmental influences on health

Individual risk factors and disease

Investigating the behaviour/disease relationship

Two differing methodologies have been used to measure the association between psychosocial factors and health. The simplest is known as a case-control design, and involves comparing individuals who have a disease with controls matched on important variables such as socio-economic status (SES) and age. Any between-group differences found on other variables of interest are thought to imply causality. This type of approach is fairly cost-effective but has a number of weaknesses. First, it considers only differences between the survivors of illness and controls. Those who die of their disease are excluded from such an analysis, potentially weakening the magnitude of any observed behaviour/disease relationship. Secondly, the method allows associations between variables to be identified but the directions of such relationships have to be assumed. In some cases the direction of any relationship may be obvious: people with lung cancer, for example, are unlikely to start smoking as a consequence of their disease. However, causality can be more difficult to disentangle in other cases. Findings of high levels of stress in individuals with a debilitating disease, for example, may raise the question as to whether the disease or the stress came first.

An alternative approach, known as a **longitudinal design**, involves measurement of behaviour in a cohort of (typically) healthy individuals prior to disease onset. As the study progresses, those that develop disease are identified and comparisons are made between the baseline characteristics of these individuals and those who do not develop the disease. Again, any differences on such measures are thought to imply causality. This method has the benefit that the behavioural variables are measured prior to disease onset, so causality can be assured. However, there are a number of problems inherent in this approach. First, the cohort of individuals has to be sufficiently large to ensure that a statistically significant number of individuals will develop the diseases under investigation. Secondly, the method is based on the assumption that baseline levels of behaviour will remain constant over the period of the study. The long duration of such studies makes this assumption questionable. It is possible that many individuals within the cohort will make considerable lifestyle changes over follow-up periods that may last up to twenty years or even more. Any such changes may attenuate the relationship between behaviour and the initiation of disease. That such studies still find relationships between behaviour and disease attests to the strength of such relationships.

Behaviour and health

Some of the first evidence to substantiate a link between behaviour and health came from the Alameda County Study (Berkman and Syme 1979).

This longitudinal study has followed nearly seven thousand initially healthy individuals for a period of more than 20 years and identified which factors measured at baseline were associated with health or ill health over this period. One of their earlier reports was the first to highlight an association between 'lifestyle factors' and increased longevity. The behaviours, now known as the Alameda Seven, were: sleeping 7–8 hours a day, having breakfast every day, not smoking, rarely eating between meals, being near or at prescribed weight, moderate consumption of alcohol, and regular exercise. Cross-cultural comparisons have also shown an association between behaviour and health. The longevity of the Abraskians, a people who live in a remote part of Russia and who reputedly live to extreme ages, for example, has been attributed to genetics and a variety of behavioural factors, including a low animal fat and high vegetable diet, high levels of social support, no consumption of alcohol or nicotine and vigorous work activity.

Evidence linking behaviour and health is now overwhelming. Peto and Lopez (1990), for example, estimated that 75 per cent of all cancer-related deaths are attributable, at least in part, to behaviour. Others, including the World Bank (1993), have stated that a significant number of chronic diseases and up to half of all premature deaths can be attributed to behavioural factors. Five behaviours in particular are associated with risk for disease: smoking, alcohol misuse, poor nutrition, low levels of exercise and unprotected sexual intercourse.

Smoking

Smoking doubles the risk of premature death. Approximately 3 million people die of tobacco use each year across the world (Peto and Lopez 1990). It is responsible for approximately 30 per cent of cases of coronary heart disease (CHD), 75 per cent of cases of cancer, 80 per cent of cases of chronic obstructive airways disease, and 90 per cent of deaths associated with lung cancer. The risks attributable to passive smoking are also substantial. It is estimated that about 25 per cent of lung cancers that occur in non-smokers are attributable to passive smoking. In Greece, the risk for cancer attributable to passive smoking is considered comparable to that of smoking itself.

Present morbidity levels associated with smoking reflect the cumulative risk of smoking over many years, and historical processes of some decades ago. Increased lung cancer rates in women over the past two decades are thought to be the result of a rapid increase in the numbers of women smoking during and after the Second World War. Reductions in lung cancer rates amongst men may reflect the introduction of cigarette filters at about the same time. In contrast, childhood illnesses represent the more immediate impact of smoking. In the USA, an estimated half million cases of childhood pneumonia and bronchitis are attributed to parental smoking. Smoking cessation decreases risk for all smoking related diseases: former smokers live longer than persistent smokers do.

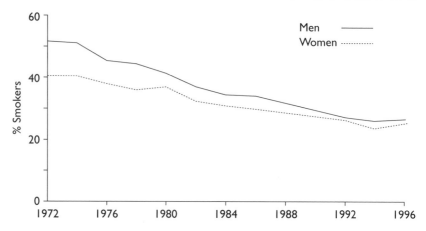

Figure 1.1   Changes in the prevalence of male and female smokers in the UK
(*Source*: Office of National Statistics 1999)

In the West, smokers are now a minority in every age and social group. In the UK, for example, adult smoking rates between 1974 and 1996 fell by 26 per cent among men and 22 per cent in women, to 29 and 28 per cent of the population, respectively (see Figure 1.1). Smoking rates among young people fell consistently between 1974 and 1992. More recently this decline has slowed and there is evidence of increasing smoking rates in this group, particularly among young women, who may soon prove the majority of smokers in a number of countries.

Excessive alcohol consumption

Excessive alcohol consumption may impact adversely on both short- and long-term health. It is thought to contribute to 3 per cent of all cancers. Alcohol also contributes to conditions such as cirrhosis of the liver and hypertension. However, the most damaging effect of alcohol may be behavioural. It is estimated that 20 per cent of psychiatric admissions, 60 per cent of suicide attempts, 30 per cent of divorces, and 40 per cent of incidences of domestic violence are associated to some degree with alcohol misuse.

In general, there is a linear relationship between level of alcohol consumption and disease rates. The one exception to this is that relating to CHD. A number of cross-sectional studies in the 1970s reported a J-shaped relationship between consumption and disease rates. This suggested that moderate consumption of alcohol is associated with lower risk for CHD than total abstinence, while higher levels of consumption increase risk. This unexpected relationship was met initially with some caution, with some suggesting that it may have been an artefact of the populations studied. It was suggested that the higher than expected rates

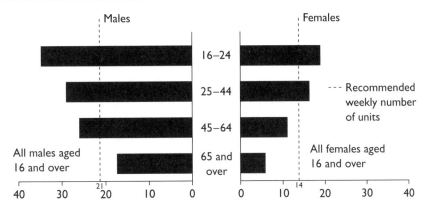

Figure 1.2   Average levels of alcohol consumption in British men and women according to age in 1998
(*Source*: Office of National Statistics 1999)

of CHD among the non-drinkers may have reflected the inclusion of individuals who had stopped drinking as a consequence of drink-related health problems. However, a number of longitudinal studies (see, for example, Shaper *et al.* 1994) have found the J-shaped relationship between alcohol and CHD after following cohorts of individuals free from disease at baseline. A mechanism through which cholesterol reduces risk of CHD has now also been found: moderate consumption appears to reduce harmful cholesterol levels.

Defining what is meant by excess alcohol consumption has proven far from simple. This confusion is illustrated by changes to health advice made by the UK government in 1995. Between 1986 and 1995 the recommended limits for weekly consumption were 21 units of alcohol or less for men, and 14 units or less for women. In 1995, a government committee established to review these guidelines recommended they be increased to 28 and 21 units per week, respectively. These changes caused a furore and much criticism among alcohol experts, particularly as they were not based on any new evidence (see, for example, *British Medical Journal*, vol. 293). Consequently, a number of health promotion and alcohol agencies have been reluctant to adopt these guidelines and there is a lack of clear advice concerning the recommended limits to consumption.

The percentage of the population to exceed the 21/14 unit limits has remained quite stable throughout the past decade, although there has been a slight increase among women: 27 per cent of men and 12 per cent of women exceeded these limits in 1996 (see Figure 1.2). Consumption declines with age: 40 per cent of men aged 18–24 and 18 per cent of those over 64 years report drinking over the recommended limits. The same pattern is found among women, although consumption is lower, with rates of 24 and 7 per cent respectively. Those in the lower socio-economic groups tend to drink more than the more socially advantaged.

Cholesterol

Raised serum cholesterol levels increase risk for CHD. The Multiple Risk
Factor Intervention Trial (MRFIT), for example, followed over 350,000
adults for six years and found a linear relationship between baseline
cholesterol level and the incidence of CHD or stroke (Neaton *et al.* 1992).
Individuals within the top third of cholesterol levels were three and a
half times more likely to develop cardiovascular disease than those in the
lowest third. While there is no threshold level below which there is no
risk for CHD, risk is significantly increased by cholesterol levels above
5.2 mmol/litre for those aged over 30 years, and above 4.7 mmol/litre for
younger people. These margins place about two-thirds of the UK population at some risk for CHD as a consequence of their serum cholesterol
levels (Lewis *et al.* 1986).

   Cholesterol is essential to life. It is a constituent of every cell in the body,
and is implicated in a variety of bodily functions, including the production
of sex hormones and the bile necessary for digestion. A significant percentage of our cholesterol is synthesized by the liver; the rest is absorbed
from food. Circulating levels of cholesterol are also mediated by stress
(see Chapter 2) and exercise levels. Nevertheless, the most frequent method
by which public health authorities have tried to control cholesterol is
through dietary means. Recommended levels of intake are frequently
substantially lower than actual levels. In the USA, for example, approximately 44 per cent of calories are consumed as fat, contrasting with the
recommended level of 30 per cent. Despite these figures, there is some
evidence that the British diet is becoming more healthy (see Figure 1.3).

   The unexpected twist in the cholesterol story is that low cholesterol
levels also confers risk of premature mortality. The MRFIT study found
that individuals with low cholesterol levels carried a risk of suicide or
trauma-related death 1.4 times greater than that of men in the mid-range.
Even more dramatically, a longitudinal study of 52,000 Swedish adults
reported that participants in the low cholesterol range evidenced a rate
of non-illness-related mortality 2.8 times higher than those in the mid-
range: risk for suicide was 4.2 times greater (Lindberg *et al.* 1992).

   The link between low levels of cholesterol, suicide and accident rates
may appear, at first consideration, somewhat surprising. However, there
is considerable evidence from forensic studies that low levels of cholesterol are associated with aggression, personality disorder and low mood.
With these findings in mind, the excess mortality following cholesterol
reduction is perhaps not so surprising. More problematic is finding
an explanation. Current explanations are focusing on a link between
cholesterol and serotonin levels. Low levels of cholesterol are associated
with low serotonergic activity, which, in turn, is linked to aggression and
disinhibition of behaviour. While there is reasonable evidence to support
both these links, the mechanisms through which the effects are mediated
are unclear. One possibility is that low cholesterol levels mediate changes

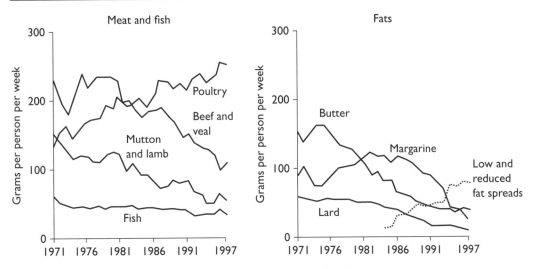

Figure 1.3 Changes in the British diet over the past two decades
(*Source*: Office of National Statistics 1999)

in cell membrane function resulting in alterations to the serotonergic neurotransmission processes.

Exercise

Those who are physically active throughout their adult life live longer than those who are sedentary. One of the earliest studies to report such a relationship compared CHD rates among bus drivers and bus conductors who shared a similar working environment, but engaged in significantly different levels of exercise. Bus conductors evidenced significantly lower rates of CHD. In retrospect, some of these differences may be attributable to differences in stress levels associated with the differing job types (see below). However, these findings have been supported by a number of longitudinal studies. Paffenbarger *et al.* (1986), for example, monitored leisuretime activity in a cohort of Harvard graduates for a period of 16 years. Those who expended more than 2000 kcal of energy in active leisure activities per week lived, on average, two and a half years longer than those who expended less than 500 calories in exercise. How this protection is achieved, whether through short, intense periods of exercise or longer, less intense periods, appears unimportant and no additional health gain is achieved by exceeding these limits. Uptake of exercise is protective against CHD, leading to reductions in resting blood pressure, cholesterol and triglyceride levels. Exercise is also an important aspect of weight control and, particularly in women, is protective against osteoporosis. As a function of the relatively low levels of fat in those who exercise regularly, it may also protect against some cancers.

Forty-five per cent of the UK population report engaging in some form of leisure exercise at least once a month, with the figure rising to 64 per cent if walking is included in these activities. A lesser number of individuals achieve the levels of exercise considered necessary to protect against CHD: here, the figure is nearer to 25 per cent of the adult population (Norman *et al.* 1998). These figures, however, represent a significant rise in exercise participation: in 1985, only 20 per cent of British men and 2 per cent of women engaged in such levels of exercise. Those who engage in exercise are more likely to be young, male, and members of higher socio-economic groups. Participation in leisure exercise among professionals, for example, is virtually double that among unskilled manual workers (80 versus 45 per cent), although the latter may engage in more physically demanding work activity. Those who participated in some form of sport in their youth are almost three times more likely to exercise in adulthood.

Unsafe sex

Estimates of the prevalence of HIV in 1997 suggested that a total of 30.6 million people were infected with HIV worldwide. In the UK, the primary route of infection has been through sex between men, accounting for 72 per cent of all AIDS cases reported by 1998. Eighteen per cent of cases resulted from heterosexual sex. However, the incidence of new cases among gay men is falling slowly while the incidence of HIV infection within the heterosexual community is rising. In addition, young people are at increasing risk of infection: adolescent heterosexuals account for about 20 per cent of all newly reported cases in the USA (Stiff *et al.* 1990).

Nearly half of British adolescents aged between 16 and 17 report having had at least one sexual partner during the previous year. However, they are unlikely to plan intercourse and those using a condom are in the minority. The findings of a large-scale British survey conducted by Wellings *et al.* (1994) indicated that only about half of those whose first sexual experience occurred between the ages of 16 and 24 years used a condom at first intercourse: 31 per cent of men and 24 per cent of women report using no form of contraception. Younger people were less likely to take precautions: over 60 per cent of respondents who had their first sexual experience at the age of 13 reported not using any form of contraception.

Heterosexuals in the general adult population use condoms consistently only about 10–15 per cent of the time with primary partners and 15 per cent of the time with secondary partners (Dolcini *et al.* 1995). Even more concerning from a disease prevention perspective is the choice made by those who are known to be HIV positive not to use a condom. Sobo (1993), for example, was able to identify a group of HIV positive women who did not use a condom with their lover or husband, but did

Table 1.1   The percentage of respondents engaging in one or more key health-related behaviours

No. of health behaviours	Percentage of sample
0	6.2
1	20.6
2	34.3
3	30.9
4	8.1

Source: Norman *et al*. 1998

so with more casual sexual partners (see Chapter 3). The likelihood of an increase in the rate of non-protected intercourse appears to be rising, perhaps because of the wide prevalence of beliefs that new treatments for HIV will be curative (Kalichman *et al*. 1998).

Is there a healthy lifestyle?

In an attempt to answer this question, Norman *et al*. (1998) categorized over 13,000 people in a British survey as either engaging or not engaging in up to four health-related behaviours: not smoking, moderate alcohol use, exercising three or more times a week, and eating fruit or vegetables regularly. While 93 per cent of the sample reported engaging in at least one of these behaviours, only 8 per cent reported that they did them all (Table 1.1).

Personality and disease

Type A behaviour and hostility

First identified by two cardiologists, Rosenman and Friedman, Type A behaviour (TAB) was defined as an excess of competitiveness, time urgency and easily aroused hostility. The absence of such characteristics is referred to as Type B behaviour. Early case-control and longitudinal studies showed significant associations between TAB and CHD. Such was the research consensus achieved that, by the mid-1980s, TAB was considered to confer the same degree of risk for CHD as the more traditional risk factors of high blood pressure and cholesterol. Subsequent, and frequently methodologically flawed, studies failed to find a relationship between TAB and disease progression in men either at high risk of CHD or who had already experienced a myocardial infarction (MI). As a consequence, this degree of consensus is no longer evident. However, one component of TAB, hostility, appears to convey the degree of risk previously ascribed to TAB and this has formed the primary focus of more recent research.

A number of case-control studies have reported significant associations between hostility and CHD, with the strongest relationship being found among those under 50 years of age. Such a finding is not unique: the predictive power of other biological and behavioural risk factors is also strongest among younger people. However, the most convincing evidence linking hostility to CHD has stemmed from longitudinal studies. In one of the earliest such studies, Barefoot et al. (1983) followed 255 physicians for 25 years and found that those who scored above the median on measures of hostility taken while in training were nearly five times more likely to experience an MI over this period than those who scored below the median. These data have been supported by findings in older populations. European studies (for example Everson et al. 1997) following middle-aged men for up to 25 years have found an association between hostility and coronary events. Hostility may also contribute to the development of CHD in women (Lahad et al. 1997). Data from some of these and other studies combined into meta-analysis suggested a significant association between hostility and CHD (Miller et al. 1996).

A second set of studies has measured the association between hostility and the degree of atheroma of the cardiac arteries, measured using angiography. Although there have been a number of positive findings, several studies have failed to find any relationship between hostility and atheroma. One explanation for these disparate findings may be biased sampling. Angiograms are invasive procedures usually conducted only on patients who report some degree of symptomatology. Accordingly, the samples used are likely to be non-representative, and the results of most of these studies should be considered with caution. Two types of study are the exception to this rule: those that track the progression of atheroma over time, and those involving angiograms in representative populations. In the first type, Julkunen et al. (1994) measured the relationship between hostility and the progression of atherosclerosis over a two-year period in a sample of 119 middle-aged men. The progression of atheroma was almost twice as fast in highly hostile participants as in those who were low in hostility. Utilizing the second methodology, Barefoot et al. (1994) took advantage of the need for airline pilots to have routine angiograms to ensure their fitness to fly. They compared the hostility scores of pilots with angiographic evidence of CHD with those having none. Among non-smokers only, pilots found to have evidence of CHD had higher hostility scores than did those in the comparison group.

Type C behaviour

Type C behaviour has been independently described by Greer and Morris (1975) and Temoshok (1987). It is defined as an aggregate of several coping styles, in particular being stoic, cooperative, appeasing, unassertive and inexpressive of negative emotions, particularly anger. It is thought to be linked to the development of cancer.

A number of studies have shown an association between Type C personality and the incidence or progression of cancer. Using a case-control design, Kune *et al.* (1991), for example, compared patients newly diagnosed with colorectal cancer and community controls matched for age and gender. Patients with cancer were significantly more likely to report histories of unhappiness in childhood and recent adult life and to have strong feelings of discomfort when experiencing feelings of anger. These differences may have been influenced by knowledge of a diagnosis of cancer. Accordingly, more weight should be ascribed to the findings of studies where a diagnosis was not known at the time of psychological assessment. A number of such studies (for example Greer and Morris 1975) have found that women who suppressed their anger or had a conforming personality were more likely to have malignant changes than those without these characteristics. Longitudinal studies have also shown Type C characteristics to predict cancer. Shaffer *et al.* (1987), for example, followed 972 physicians for a 30-year period and found that participants characterized by high levels of 'acting out' and emotional expression had a less than 1 per cent risk of developing cancer. Participants characterized as 'loners' and thought to inhibit emotional expression were 16 times more likely to develop cancer than those in this group.

Concordant with the Type C hypothesis is work examining the impact of 'fighting spirit' on cancer progression. This constellation of behaviours is considered to be the opposite of Type C behaviour, and has been associated with longer survival following diagnosis. In the first study to identify this characteristic as a prognostic factor, Derogatis *et al.* (1979) found that women who showed 'fighting spirit' during treatment for metastatic breast cancer lived significantly longer than those who did not. However, many of these women also received less chemotherapy, suggesting that disease severity may have been worse in the poor survival group or that their higher levels of fighting spirit could have been a consequence of being subjected to lower levels of a physically and mentally debilitating treatment. Greer (1991) also found fighting spirit to be an important determinant of survival. In a longitudinal study following 62 women with early non-metastatic breast cancer, he identified five reaction types: denial, fighting spirit, stoic acceptance, helplessness and hopelessness, and anxious preoccupation. Breast cancer recurrences and mortality were recorded 5, 10 and 15 years later. By 15-year follow-up, 45 per cent of the women who were categorized in the fighting spirit group were alive without recurrences; this compared with 17 per cent in all the other groups. Similar evidence has been published in a variety of cancers, including melanoma and lung cancer. However, there have also been some negative findings. In a larger replication study of the original Greer study, for example, Dean and Surtees (1989) found denial measured after surgery was associated with a *favourable* outcome in a group of 125 women with non-metastatic breast cancer followed for up to eight years.

Such contradictory findings have meant that the relationship between Type C behaviour, 'fighting spirit', and cancer remains controversial and far from proven. A related strand of research has focused on the health outcomes following attempts to facilitate active coping with disease and the expression of emotions. These studies are considered in Chapters 7 and 8.

Social and environmental influences on health

Socio-economic status and health

There is strong historical evidence that the more affluent members of society have lived longer than the less well off. More recent evidence of this health gradient can be found in a study of nineteenth century obelisks in Glasgow graveyards. In an imaginative study, Davey Smith *et al.* (1992) measured the height of obelisks in Glasgow graveyards as a proxy for the wealth of the individual buried beneath them. They compared these with the ages of the first generation buried below and found a strong linear relationship between the height of the obelisks and the age of their first occupant, suggesting that the more wealthy lived longer. What is important is not just that this relationship existed, but that the families buried in the graves represented a small and wealthy fraction of the Glasgow population. This is not evidence that the very poor and immiserated did not live as long as the rich did: rather, that the relatively rich did not live as long as the very rich. Such a gradient still exists. It is progressive, and throughout the social classes. It holds for women as well as men and is characteristic of all western countries (Wilkinson, 1992).

A number of explanations have been proposed to account for these differences. People in lower socio-economic groups may be exposed to more environmental insults, low quality and damp accommodation, and air pollution. An alternative explanation may be that less well off individuals engage in more health-damaging behaviours, such as smoking or excessive alcohol consumption. While both these explanations may account for some of the differences in some of the studies, they cannot explain them all. Marmot *et al.* (1984), for example, explored the impact of a number of these variables on the health of British civil servants working in London over a period of ten years. Their findings indicated that while those in the more deprived social groups did engage in more health-damaging behaviours, these did not fully explain the health/SES relationship. When variations in smoking, obesity, plasma cholesterol and blood pressure were statistically partialled out of the risk equation, occupational-status-related differentials in health still remained. Mortality was three times higher among men in the lowest grade than those in the highest.

While people who occupy the lower socio-economic groups may engage in more health-damaging behaviours, the adverse health effects of these behaviours may be overwhelmed by factors associated with their economic position. Hein *et al.* (1992), for example, reported data from a 17-year prospective study of CHD in Danish men. Adjusting for a variety of confounding factors, they found that men who smoked were three and a half times more likely to develop CHD than non-smokers. However, when these data were analysed according to SES, white-collar smokers were six and a half times more likely to experience a cardiac event than the equivalent non-smokers. Amongst blue-collar workers, smoking status conferred no additional risk for CHD. Fewer middle-class people may smoke, but those that do may be particularly vulnerable to its health-damaging effects. Conversely, the impact of smoking on the health of the less well off is seemingly overwhelmed by social factors.

Comparisons of life expectancy across different western countries suggest some intriguing explanations of the relationship between social class and health. Wilkinson (1992) provided powerful evidence that it is not absolute wealth that determines health. He drew on evidence that showed only a weak relationship between the absolute wealth of the society and overall life expectancy. More predictive is the distribution of wealth within a society. The narrower the distribution, whatever its absolute level, the better the overall health of the nation. Accordingly, although Japan and Cuba differ substantially on measures of economic wealth, both have relatively equitable distributions of income and long life expectancies throughout their populations. Of particular interest is evidence from Scotland, which tracked average age of mortality and income distribution over the life of the Thatcher government. As earning differentials rose, so premature mortality among the less well off increased despite their access to material goods, food, clothing and so on remaining relatively constant. These data led Wilkinson to suggest that, for the majority of people in western countries, health hinges on relatively more than absolute living standards.

Wilkinson's explanation of health differentials suggests that we engage in some form of comparison of our living conditions with others in society, and that knowledge of a relative deprivation in some way increases risk of disease. Three different psychological processes may also be implicated in the health gradient. Individuals in the lower socio-economic groups report more stressors than those in higher groups and that these stressors are frequently linked directly to their material conditions. In addition, the less well off have less control over their environment and fewer personal resources to moderate the impact of such stressors than the better off. Finally, social support, a powerful mediator of health status, is less available to those in lower socio-economic groups (Adler *et al.* 1994).

Social isolation and health

There is substantial evidence that both men and women who have a small number of social contacts are more likely to die earlier than those who have more extended networks. Data from the Alameda County Study (Berkman and Syme 1979), for example, showed increased longevity to be associated with relatively high numbers of social ties as a consequence of marriage, contacts with close friends and relatives, church membership and membership of other organizations. The most isolated were the most prone to premature death even after controlling for factors such as smoking, alcohol use and levels of physical activity. In a later study, Reynolds and Kaplan (1990) found that women who had few social contacts and were socially isolated were at double the risk of developing hormone-related cancers and evidenced an almost fivefold increase in risk of dying from them than less isolated women.

Similar results have been reported in European samples. Orth-Gomer and Johnsson (1987), for example, followed a cohort of 17,400 men and women for a period of six years and found that both men and women who had a restricted social network evidenced a 50 per cent greater risk of CHD than those who were socially embedded. However, the relationship between social contact and health was not always linear: those with many social contacts did not always benefit in terms of health. Older women, for example, who had many social contacts evidenced higher mortality than those with medium-sized networks. To explain these apparently anomalous findings, Orth-Gomer and Johnsson analysed their data not simply according to the absolute number of contacts, but taking into account the nature of the contacts. When they did this, they found the strongest predictor of mortality was a lack of social integration, which the authors considered to provide guidance, practical help and a feeling of belonging. They found only a low association between the provision of emotional support and CHD, although a later study by the same group found this to be an important protective factor. In an alternative interpretation of the Type A hypothesis, Orth-Gomer and Unden (1990) suggested that TAB or hostility might confer risk of CHD as a consequence of associated social isolation. In a longitudinal study, following a cohort of men for ten years, they found no differences in mortality between Type A and Type B men. However, over this period, 69 per cent of the socially isolated Type A men in the cohort had experienced an MI, in contrast to the 17 per cent incidence among those who were socially integrated.

Further evidence of the impact of social isolation can be found in studies of populations already experiencing disease. Williams *et al.* (1992), for example, found that patients with CHD who were unmarried and without a confidant experienced a threefold higher risk of mortality over a five-year follow-up period than those who were. Reflecting the subjective nature of social support, some studies that have failed to find a relationship between marital status and mortality following diagnosis of illness have found the *quality* of these relationships and the emotional support within them to be associated with survival.

The mechanisms through which social isolation confers risk are yet to be fully understood. Two primary processes are thought to be through depressed mood and health-compromising behaviours, both of which are associated with social isolation. Broman (1993), for example, reported that a decrease in social ties predicted an increase in health-damaging behaviours, while gains in social ties were associated with increases in health-protective behaviours. Of course, social ties may also serve to maintain unhealthy behaviours: friends may offer cigarettes to fellow smokers and put pressure on individuals not to quit smoking so as to maintain group cohesion. The impact of depression on risk of disease is considered in the next chapter.

Gender and health

Women, on average, live longer than men do. In the UK, life expectancy rates in 1996 were 75 years for men and 80 years for women. The most obvious explanations for these differences are biological. Oestrogen, for example, delays the onset of CHD by reducing clotting tendency and blood cholesterol levels. Not only is there a marked increase in the prevalence of CHD in postmenopausal women, they also become affected by the same influences as men. Lahad *et al.* (1997), for example, found hostility scores were linearly associated with increased risk of MI in postmenopausal women.

Studies of the relationship between disease and factors such as work strain, social support and hostility have rarely been conducted with women. Those that have suggest that men typically evidence greater stress hormone, blood pressure and cholesterol rises in response to stressors than women. However, while there may be some differences in the process of response between the sexes, these differences may not simply reflect biological differences. Work by Lundberg *et al.* (1981), for example, suggested that women in traditionally male occupations exhibit the same level of stress hormones as do men in similar jobs. In addition, where women feel equally or more threatened by the stressor than men their physiological response matches that of men. These findings suggest that social and cultural processes may drive some of these differences.

Societal processes also influence levels of engagement in health-related behaviours. Women exercise less frequently than men, partly as a consequence of family responsibilities and joint home/work responsibilities. In addition, women are frequently disadvantaged in behavioural negotiations. Nowhere is this more stark than in the negotiation of sexual behaviour: nearly 40 per cent of a sample of young Australian women reported having engaged in sexual intercourse at some time when they did not want to do so (Abbott 1988). Whatever the cause, men behave differently from women: they are more likely to smoke cigarettes, and smoke higher nicotine and tar cigarettes than women: they typically eat less healthily, and drink more alcohol than women (Reddy *et al.* 1992). They may also encounter adverse working conditions more frequently than women.

Together, these data suggest that while biological factors may contribute to some of the differentials in health status between men and women, others are behaviourally or societally mediated. Gender differentials in life expectancy arise, to a significant degree, from the cumulative effects of different social worlds that men and women experience from the moment of their birth. As socio-political conditions change and more women enter the workforce, an emerging question is whether they will also take on the excess mortality associated with men. This does not seem to be the case. Indeed, there is increasing evidence that occupying multiple roles, including paid employment, is associated with better health and lower rates of premature mortality (Vagero and Lahelma 1998). However, there may be some important exceptions to this general finding: women who occupy demanding roles both at work and in the home appear at particular risk of disease (see below).

Minority status and health

There is a strong association between ethnicity and health status. In the UK, rates of ill health and premature mortality amongst ethnic minorities are typically higher than those of the white population, although there are also differences in mortality patterns between ethnic minorities. Rates of CHD amongst British men from the Indian sub-continent are 36 per cent higher than the national average and among young people are two to three times higher than that of whites. The Afro-Caribbean population has particularly high rates of hypertension and strokes, while levels of diabetes are high among Asians. In contrast, both groups have lower rates of cancer than the national average. A similar picture is found in the USA, where black people have higher age-adjusted mortality rates than whites for a number of diseases including various cancers, heart disease, liver disease, diabetes and pneumonia.

Some of these variations in health outcomes may be explained by differences in behaviour across ethnic groups. In the UK, for example, alcohol-related morbidity is high amongst African Caribbean men and Asian males of Punjabi origin, while a high dietary fat intake is common among Asians. Ethnicity may also confer different sexual norms and behaviours that may impact on health. The most common exposure route for HIV infection among whites is through sexual intercourse between men: for blacks it is through heterosexual intercourse, whilst for Asians it is mixture of both.

A significant proportion of members of ethnic minorities occupy lower socio-economic groups. Accordingly, explanations of health or behavioural differences between ethnic groups have to take socio-economic factors into account. Stress specifically associated with minority status may also contribute to high disease rates. Ethnic minorities experience wider sources of stress than whites as a consequence of discrimination and racial harassment and the demands of maintaining or shifting culture. They may also experience more problems in gaining access to health services such as cancer screening and antenatal care.

Minority status may also be conferred by behaviour. A number of studies have shown that isolation experienced as a consequence of sexual orientation may impact significantly on health. Cole et al. (1996) found that healthy gay men who concealed their sexual identity were three times more likely to develop cancer or infectious diseases than men who were able to express their sexuality. The same research group found social rejection to influence disease progression in HIV-infected men. Those who experienced social rejection evidenced a significant acceleration towards a critically low CD4+ lymphocyte level (see Chapter 2) and time to diagnosis of AIDS.

Working conditions and health

One of the most widely accepted models of work stress is that of Karasek and Theorell (1990). Their job strain model identified three key influences on work stress: the demands of the job, the latitude the worker has in dealing with these demands, and the support available to them. They suggested that these interact to predict stress and stress-related disease. In contrast to previous theories of work stress, they noted that high job demands are not necessarily stressful; it is when these combine with low job autonomy and low levels of support that the individual is likely to experience stress. Their model suggests that rather than the stereotypical 'stressed executive', those who experience stress are likely to hold blue-collar or supervisory posts. In a review of studies examining the strength of the Karasek model, Kristensen (1995) considered 16 studies measuring the association between job strain and mental and physical health outcomes. Fourteen reported significant associations between conditions of high job strain and the incidence of either CHD or poor mental health. An alternative model has been proposed by Siegrist et al. (1990). This suggests that work stress is a consequence of an imbalance between perceived efforts and rewards. High effort and low reward are thought to result in emotional distress and adverse health effects. In a five-year longitudinal tracking over 10,000 British civil servants both theories received some support (Stansfeld et al.

1998). Age-adjusted analyses showed low decisional latitude, low work social support, and effort/reward imbalance to predict poor physical health.

For men, it appears that job strain is a function of the working environment alone. For women, who may frequently have significant responsibilities beyond the workplace, work strain appears to combine with other areas of stress to confer risk of disease. Haynes and Feinleib (1980), for example, showed working women with three or more children to be more likely to experience CHD than those with no children. Alfredsson *et al.* (1985) compared the risk conferred by work strain and working overtime on men and women in a sample of 100,000 Swedish men and women. As predicted by Karasek's model, higher rates of MI were associated with increased work strain in both men and women. However, working overtime decreased risk for MI among men, while it was associated with an increased risk in women. For women, working overtime of ten hours or more per week was associated with a 30 per cent increase in risk for CHD. One explanation for these contradictory findings is that men may compensate for their increase in working hours by a decrease in demands elsewhere in life. For women, such increases may not be so compensated and simply increase the total demands made on them. This increase in overall demands may constitute the main risk for stress and disease. Support for such a hypothesis can be found in the results of a study by Lundberg *et al.* (1981), who found that female managers' stress hormone levels remained raised following work, while those of male managers typically fell; this effect was particularly marked where the female managers had children.

Summary and conclusions

Since the 1950s there has been irrefutable evidence that certain behaviours contribute to the development of disease. This has led, in part, to a movement towards increasing personal responsibility for health care and significant health promotion programmes and numerous self-help books aimed at promoting individual behaviour change. In the wake of this personal responsibility movement has followed a new wave of research which has emphasized that health is a consequence not simply of one's own behaviour but also of the social, economic and political context in which we live. This has fed criticism of the self-help movement, claiming that this approach leads to a risk of blaming individuals for their own poor health. It has also highlighted the need for public health initiatives to target environmental factors as well as individuals if the health of the population is to be enhanced. Such an agenda has been established by the World Health Organization and is returned to in Chapter 7.

Further reading

Hardey, M. (1998) *The Social Context of Health*. Buckingham: Open University Press.

Orth-Gomer, K., Chesney, M.A. and Wegner, N.K. (eds) (1998) *Women, Stress, and Heart Disease*. New Jersey: Lawrence Erlbaum.

2 Stress and health

There is an enduring and popular belief that stress leads to ill health. Its perceived importance in the aetiology of disease can perhaps best be illustrated by the findings of several studies conducted in different countries and at different times that have consistently shown that a significant majority of cardiac patients identify stress as the most likely cause of their heart attack. In the face of such consistent beliefs, psychology has struggled first to define stress and then to establish its actual relation to disease. This chapter considers some of the evidence amassed. Three differing models of stress are examined: one which considers stress to be a physiological process in response to a variety of external events; one which considers stress to be a function of environmental events; and one which considers stress to be a result of cognitive appraisal of environmental events: stress as 'in the eye of the beholder'. The strengths and weaknesses of these models are considered before the chapter describes the physiological processes that mediate between the experience of stress and the development of disease. Finally, the chapter considers epidemiological evidence linking stress and disease and how stress may influence the development of a number of specific diseases.

The chapter considers:

- Definitions of stress
- The psychophysiological substrates of stress
- The nature of the stress/disease relationship
- Psychophysiological processes mediating between stress and disease

Towards a definition of stress

The earliest coherent model of stress was a physiological model developed by Selye (1956). The General Adaptation Syndrome identified three stages

Table 2.1   Representative items from a life events scale and a hassles scale

Life event	Stress rating 0–100	Daily hassles
Death of a spouse	100	Too many things to do
Divorce	73	Not enough time
Jail term	63	Too many responsibilities
Death of a close family member	63	Troubling thoughts
Marriage	50	Social obligations
Fired at work	47	Concerns about getting ahead
Pregnancy	40	Misplacing or losing things
Change to different line of work	36	Not getting enough sleep
Son or daughter leaving home	29	Problems with children
Change in living conditions	25	Overloaded with family responsibilities
Vacation	13	Job dissatisfaction
Christmas	12	

within the stress process. The initial stage is one of alarm in which the body is activated to cope with a stressor. The nature of this stressor is unimportant: Selye assumed an equivalent response to physical and psychological stimuli. The alarm stage is driven primarily by the sympathetic nervous system, and is followed by the second stage of resistance, mediated by longer-term hormonal processes. Finally, if the stress continues the result is exhaustion and the depletion of bodily resources resulting in illness. If this illness removes the individual from the source of the stress, a recovery phase can follow during which physical resources are renewed and health improves. This has proven an extremely influential model of stress, and is returned to later in the chapter. However, it acknowledges no psychological mechanisms, nor does it attempt to explain the emotional aspects of stress.

In an attempt to address the first of these issues, a strand of research known as life events theory began to consider the social or psychological causes of stress. The theory assumed that stress arose as a consequence of the life events that an individual experienced. The more events experienced, the greater the degree of stress, and the greater the risk of subsequent illness. Holmes and Rahe (1967) believed that the degree of stress associated with these events was both quantifiable and the same for all individuals. Accordingly, on the basis of rankings assigned to a variety of stressors by experimental participants, they developed the Life Events Inventory, which rank-ordered a series of life events, assigning them scores between 0 and 100 according to their severity (Table 2.1).

This approach to the study of stress has been extremely influential and many studies have found an association between the number of life events a person experiences, their severity, and the onset of physical and mental illness. However, the impact of life events on physical health is small and accounts for little of the variance in illness reporting (Lin *et al.* 1979). This may be, in part, a consequence of their infrequency. More important may be the number of more minor stressors, or daily hassles the individual experiences (see Table 2.1). The cumulative effects of such minor events may contribute more to the stress process than the less frequent life events so far considered. Kanner *et al.* (1981), for example, found the frequency of daily hassles to be more strongly associated with physical and mental health problems than major life events.

Two further weaknesses of the life events approach reflect those of the General Adaptation Syndrome. First, it does not attempt to understand the emotional experience of stress. Second, it cannot explain why some people may experience the same number and magnitude of events and have differing emotional and health outcomes. It makes no attempt to explain the processes intervening between external events and emotions or illness. What has become clear more recently is that these internal processes are central to both the experience of stress and its health consequences.

Stress as appraisal

In the early 1980s, Lazarus began developing of one of the most coherent and influential models of stress (see, for example, Lazarus and Folkman 1984). It described the cognitive precursors to the negative emotions associated with stress and the strategies we use to reduce them. According to Lazarus and Folkman, when faced with external demands, we engage in two types of appraisal. Primary appraisals consider the potential threat carried by the situation. If the situation is considered threatening, secondary appraisals consider how well we are able to cope with this threat. If we consider a situation to be potentially threatening and that we lack the resources to cope effectively with it, we will experience some degree of stress.

Our understanding of these appraisals and their attached emotions remains incomplete. Indeed, two of the leading researchers in this area have collaborated on studies while failing to agree on their exact nature. According to Smith (in Smith and Lazarus 1993), appraisals can be grouped into clusters linked together and sharing common themes. He identified two primary appraisal themes and four secondary ones. The components of primary appraisal are motivational relevance and motivational congruence. The first is an evaluation of the extent to which an event impinges on issues the person cares about, and reflects the extent to which it is personally relevant. Motivational congruence refers to the extent to which the event is consistent or inconsistent with the individual's desires or goals. The four components of secondary appraisal are accountability, problem-focused coping potential, emotion-focused coping

Table 2.2 Appraisals, core relational themes and their associated emotions

Emotion	Core relational theme	Important appraisal components
Anger	Other-blame	Personally relevant Motivationally incongruent Others' responsibility
Guilt	Self-blame	Personally relevant Motivationally incongruent Self-responsibility
Fear/anxiety	Danger/threat	Personally relevant Motivationally incongruent Unsure whether can cope emotionally Unsure whether can change the situation
Sadness	Irrevocable loss Helplessness about harm or loss	Personally relevant Motivationally incongruent Unsure whether can cope emotionally Do not expect situation to change

Source: Smith and Lazarus 1993

potential and future expectancy. Accountability determines who or what is responsible for the situation, and who will take the blame or credit for its outcome. Problem-focused coping appraisal considers the extent to which the situation is changeable and can be brought into line with the individual's desires. Emotion-focused coping potential reflects the extent to which the individual considers they can cope emotionally with the situation, through changes in interpretations about the situation ('Well, its not that disastrous . . .'), desires or other beliefs. Finally, future expectancy refers to the possibilities of the situation changing. Various combinations of these appraisals are linked to more generally descriptive elements known as core relational themes: other-blame, self-blame, danger/threat, and irrevocable loss or helplessness about harm or loss. Both appraisals and core-relational themes are associated with four emotions: anger, guilt, fear/anxiety and sadness, respectively (Table 2.2).

Lazarus (1991) identified a slightly different appraisal taxonomy. He considered there to be three types of primary appraisal: goal relevance, goal congruence (as in Smith) and type of ego involvement. He suggested that differing appraisals relevant to the latter will result in differing emotions: beliefs that one's self- and social esteem are at risk will result in anger; violation of one's moral structure will result in guilt; and anxiety will result from what Lazarus termed existential threat. Lazarus also identified three types of secondary appraisal: blame/credit, coping potential and future expectations.

Both Smith and Lazarus suggested that the appraisals made in response to everyday events may differ markedly among individuals. The appraisal

Table 2.3   Taxonomies of coping developed by various research groups

Lazarus and Folkman (1984)	Endler et al. (1998a)	Carver et al. (1989)
Confrontive coping	Task-oriented	Active coping
Distancing	Emotion-oriented	Planning
Self-control	Avoidance-oriented	Suppress competing activities
Seeking social support		Seek instrumental support
Accepting responsibility		Seek emotional support
Escape/avoidance		Positive reinterpretation
Planful problem solving		Restraint coping
Positive reappraisal		Acceptance
		Turn to religion
		Vent emotions
		Denial
		Behavioural disengagement
		Mental disengagement
		Alcohol/drug disengagement

of major negative events tends to be more closely aligned to common understandings of threat and, as a consequence, may be less idiosyncratic. Associations between previously encountered events and emotional responses may also be learned, and the emotional response to such events form a classically conditioned response. Appraisals may not always precede emotional responses.

Coping as a response to appraisal

According to Lazarus and Folkman (1984), the individual may engage in a number of coping strategies to reduce the adverse emotional states associated with appraisals of threat. These fall into two broad categories: problem-focused and emotion-focused. Problem-focused coping involves the individual in attempts to change the situation and thereby reduce its threat. Emotion-focused coping includes strategies aimed at reducing levels of distress while not actually changing the situation. A number of more specific coping strategies are subsumed within these categories, including avoiding thinking about the situation, planning how to cope with the problem and seeking social support (Table 2.3).

Various research groups have developed other taxonomies of coping strategies, some of which are reported in Table 2.3 (see also Chapter 12). No one strategy can be considered good or bad, and indeed many individuals, when faced with long-term stressors, may usefully engage in both emotion- and problem-focused coping strategies. Folkman *et al.* (1986) interviewed 85 married couples once a month for six months, asking each respondent to identify their most stressful encounter over the previous week and to note their appraisal, coping responses, and affect subsequent to the event. Appraisal factors accounted for 17 per cent of the variance in mood, and coping variables predicted a further 20 per cent. Use of both passive and active coping strategies, including seeking social support, confronting the problem and cognitive reappraisal, were associated with better psychological outcomes.

Stress as a lack of resources

In an interesting counterpoint to the idiographic model of Lazarus, Hobfoll's conservation of resources theory states that the level of stress that an individual experiences is a consequence of the extent to which their resources are lost, threatened with loss, or are invested without subsequent resource gain (see, for example, Hobfoll 1989). Central to his theory is the notion that resources are quantifiable and changes to them carry the same consequences for all, or almost all, individuals: they are not simply 'in the eye of the beholder'. Hobfoll further argued that resource loss is more problematic to the individual and therefore a more motivating mechanism than is resource gain. Where resources are lost, individuals are at increased vulnerability because they have both lost resources, itself stressful, and have fewer resources with which to cope with future demands. According to Hobfoll, regardless of any appraisals made, the lower one's resources, the more one experiences stress. Resources include internal factors, including knowledge and skills, and social and economic factors. He argued, for example, that the lack of resources associated with poverty is not a subjective stress, dependent upon an idiosyncratic appraisal process. Rather, it is a reality for those individuals that experience it, and can therefore be objectively measured. Support for this argument can be found in studies cited in Chapter 1, which show measurable health effects as a consequence of differing levels of resources such as social support, economic assets and so on. Hobfoll stated that coping resources may be deployed in a hierarchical manner: personal coping resources act as a first line of coping with controllable events, while social coping resources act as a buffer against stress resulting from uncontrollable events.

This return to a normothetic approach to stress is an interesting counterpoint to the idiographic approach of Lazarus and other coping theorists. It also gains some support from findings of a dissociation between the perception of stress and stress outcomes. In a study of stress and vulnerability to the common cold, for example, Cohen *et al.* (1993) found that measures of perceived stress were not predictive of susceptibility to a cold following viral challenge while the number of recent life events was. In contrast, perceived stress and negative affect were associated with rates of infection. Such findings suggest the possibility of differing pathways for the action of both perceived and environmental stress.

Psychophysiological substrates of stress

The autonomic nervous system

The control of bodily organs can be considered as having four layers of integration and control (Lovallo, 1997). At the bottom of this hierarchy is the intrinsic control that each organ has over its own function. The heart, for example, has an intrinsic rhythm of 110 beats per minute unless otherwise controlled by higher-level controls. However, this control is unresponsive to varying demands on the organ: the simple act of standing up would result in a failure of the heart to effectively pump blood to the upper body and brain unless external control was exerted. The next layer of control is provided by the autonomic nervous system, which has some reflexive degree of control over the organs it innervates. This, in turn, is controlled by the reticular system of the brainstem. These brainstem autonomic nuclei provide the first level of integrated control over the target organs. They are capable of adjusting central nervous system activity to meet rapid changes in external conditions and organizing coordinated activity across organ systems. However, these remain reflexive responses.

The hypothalamus provides the highest level of coordination of autonomic function. It receives blood-borne and nervous system inputs concerning the state of the body, including oxygenation and acidity of the blood, blood sugar and body temperature. In response to changes in these variables, it alters the activity of brainstem autonomic reflex centres. In addition, through activation of the pituitary gland it releases hormones which modulate metabolism, cardiovascular activity and renal function among others. Of central importance from a psychological perspective is that the hypothalamus also receives descending inputs from the cortex and limbic system. These higher functions express the result of behavioural and emotional demands.

Autonomic processes

The autonomic nervous system is divided into two opposing systems, each connected through synapses at the spinal column with the reticular system. The two systems arise from the medulla oblongata in the brain stem, and enervate and control the functioning of many of the internal organs, including the heart, arteries, skeletal muscles and colon. The sympathetic system is involved in arousal, whilst the parasympathetic system is involved in calming or reducing arousal. Because these systems are initially mediated by neurotransmitters, their activation is extremely fast but is not sustained. The neurotransmitter used to link neurones at the spinal synapses and to the brainstem is acetylcholine. Beyond this point, where the nerves innervate their target organs, activity within the sympathetic nervous system is mediated by norepinephrine and, to a lesser extent, epinephrine. The parasympathetic nervous system is mediated by acetylcholine and opposes activity, supporting feeding, energy storage and reproduction. The two systems tend to work antagonistically and the level of physical activation of the individual at any one time is a function of the relative dominance of each system.

Endocrine responses

A second system controlling bodily activity involves endocrine glands which control organs through the use of hormones. The adrenal glands are situated above the kidneys. They can be split functionally into two areas: the adrenal medulla, which is at their centre, and their surrounding cortex. Sympathetic stimulation of the adrenal medulla results in the release of the transmitter hormones norepinephrine and epinephrine, of which the most active is the norepinephrine. Beta-adrenoreceptors in the target organs are activated by this hormone and enhance and prolong the activation of the neurotransmitters, which act on alpha-adrenoreceptors. A second system, known as the pituitary–adrenocortical axis, is triggered by activation of the pituitary gland. This, in turn, is controlled by the hypothalamus. When stimulated by corticotrophin releasing factor (CRF) from the hypothalamus, the pituitary gland releases a number of hormones, including adrenocorticotrophic hormone (ACTH). In turn, ACTH stimulates the adrenal cortex to release hormones known as corticosteroids, the most influential of which is cortisol (Figure 2.1). These increase availability of energy stores of fats and carbohydrates, helping to maintain arousal. They also inhibit inflammation of damaged tissue. The pituitary gland can also release beta-endorphin, a powerful analgesic.

When the emotion of stress is experienced, concomitant physiological responses both activate the body and prepare to deal with physical damage. At its most dramatic, this response is known as the fight–flight response. At such times, sympathetic activity is clearly dominant, the heart beats more quickly and more powerfully, blood is shunted to the muscles and away from the gut (hence the experience of 'butterflies'), skeletal muscles tense in preparation for action, and so on. At the same time, steroids are released to increase energy and to inhibit inflammation should physical injury occur. This ancient response is clearly advantageous at times when the causes of stress are acute and life threatening: chronic activation in response to long-term stress may be less beneficial.

Higher-level control of the central nervous system

The central nervous system plays a controlling role in the body. At its most basic, it allows the body to respond to physical events such as being cold or simply moving from prone to standing position without problems.

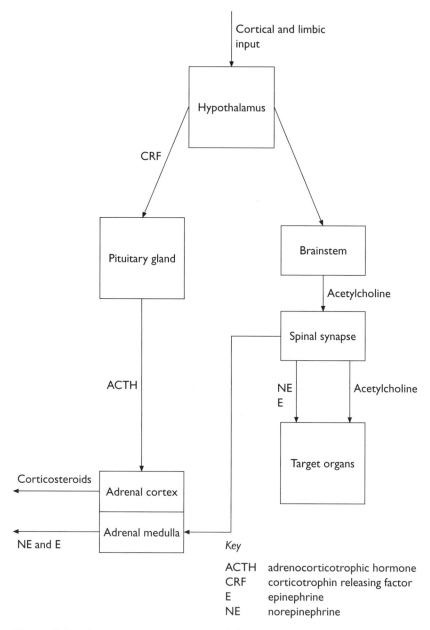

Cortical and limbic input

Hypothalamus

CRF

Pituitary gland

Brainstem

Acetylcholine

Spinal synapse

ACTH

NE
E

Acetylcholine

Target organs

Corticosteroids

Adrenal cortex

Adrenal medulla

NE and E

Key

ACTH	adrenocorticotrophic hormone
CRF	corticotrophin releasing factor
E	epinephrine
NE	norepinephrine

Figure 2.1   Schematic representation of the central nervous and hormonal response to stress

However, the central nervous system also responds to psychological factors, including feeling 'stressed' even in the absence of any physical changes or demands. Lovallo (1997) provided a five-stage model to explain these processes:

◆ Sensory intake and interpretation of the environment
◆ Generation of emotions based on the appraisal process
◆ Initiation of autonomic and endocrine responses
◆ Feedback to the cortex and limbic system
◆ Autonomic and endocrine outflow

Sensory information first involves cortical areas specializing in differing sensory types. This incoming information is passed through a series of sensory association areas, where stored information is linked with the present input. The endpoint of this process is the pre-frontal cortex where we attach meaning and significance to the incoming information: the neurological substrate of the primary appraisal process. Emotional links are added through connections with structures specializing in the forma-tion of emotional responses: in particular, the limbic system, including the amygdala and hippocampus. The limbic system is intimately linked with the hypothalamus and brainstem. Two subsystems operate at this level; one links the limbic system (and amygdala in particular) to the pontine reticular formation in the brainstem. Activation of this system results in the fight–flight response in behavioural emergencies. The second subsystem, known as the brainstem response subsystem, modulates more everyday levels of central nervous system activity. The second system, activated by the amygdala, is known as the hypothalamic area controlling emotional responses (HACER), which in turn influences pituitary output.

The immune system

The immune system protects the body against threats, collectively known as antigens, including viruses, bacteria, fungi, parasites and cancers. It has the capacity to recognize such threats, neutralize them, and to remember them in order to combat them more effectively in the future. It can be divided into three functional components: barriers to infection, including the skin, immune cells that identify and neutralize antigens, and the organs and tissues that produce the immune system cells.

Immune system cells are specialized white blood cells originating in the stem cells of the bone marrow (although T-cells – see below – mature in the thymus). They can be found in the circulation, the lymphatic system and spleen. There are two major classes of cells: phagocytes and lymphocytes. Phagocytes consist of macrophages, neutrophils and eosinophils; they destroy antigens by ingesting them. All three types of phagocyte migrate to sites of infection, attracted by chemical messengers produced in local tissues. Macrophages are particularly important as their action serves to trigger the second immune system, involving lymphocytes. Lymphocytes consist of various types of cells, including natural killer (NK) cells, T-cells and B-cells. NK cells slow the develop-ment of antigens, allowing other immune functions time to act. They are

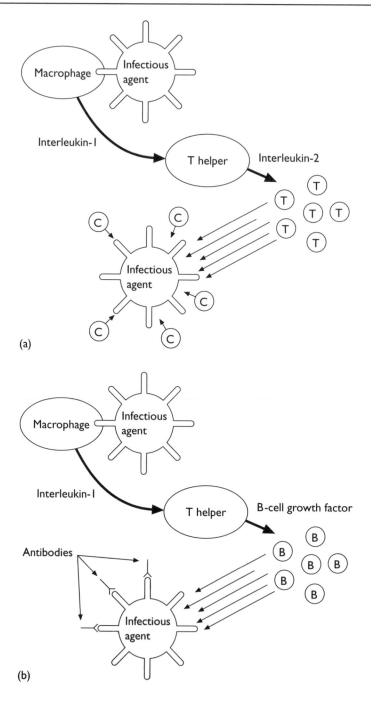

Figure 2.2   The immune system's response to challenge by antigens: (a) (b)

programmed specifically to recognize cancer and virally infected cells. T- and B-cells attack infectious agents in very different ways.

T-cell-mediated immunity is known as cell-mediated immunity. When an infectious agent invades the body, it is recognized by macrophages. They break down the antigen and attach the antigen particles to a protein, known as the major histocompatibility complex (MHC). They place this on their surface and 'present' it to T helper cells. In response, T helper cells begin to proliferate and stimulate the proliferation of cytotoxic T-cells which destroy the infectious agent. The information about the need to proliferate is transmitted through chemicals known as cytokines, of which interleukin is the most prevalent. Interleukin-1 mediates the link between macrophages and T helper cells; interleukin-2 interfaces between the T helper and cytotoxic T-cells (Figure 2.2a).

B-cell-mediated immunity is known as antibody-mediated immunity. The main task of B-cells is to differentiate and generate large proteins that will recognize and bind to some specific feature of the invading infectious agent, targeting it for destruction by a large group of circulating proteins known as Complement. In doing so, B-cells trap antigen on their surface, process the antigen and present fragments on their surface MHC to T helper cells. The T helper cells in turn stimulate two types of B-cell proliferation: plasma cells and B memory cells. Plasma cells secrete free antibodies that circulate for the duration of the disease. B memory cells live indefinitely following contact with a novel antigen and 'prepare' the body against future attack. The messengers carrying this information are interleukin-1, between macrophage and T helper cells, and B-cell growth factor between T helper cells and B-cells (Figure 2.2b).

It is noteworthy that the central organizing aspect of the immune response are the T helper cells (known also as CD4+ cells because of their chemical structure). It is their function that is disabled by the human immunodeficiency virus (HIV) with potentially disastrous results.

The central nervous system and immune interaction

The immune system is intimately linked to the central nervous system. The adrenal and sympathetic components of the stress response have pervasive influences on immune function. The thymus, spleen and lymph nodes all receive both sympathetic and parasympathetic innervation. Changes in these affect the tissues and alter the development and activity of lymphocytes including NK, T- and B-cells. Lymphocytes also have β-adrenergic and cortisol receptors and are affected by the hormones of both the adrenal cortex and medulla.

The impact of these neurotransmitters and hormones is complex. Epinephrine can stimulate the spleen into releasing lymphocytes into the bloodstream, increasing the response to infection. Beta-adrenergic activity can increase NK cell counts, while decreasing T-cell proliferation in response to acute experimental stress. Accordingly, the central nervous system has a mixed impact on immune function. Cortisol release has a more consistent immunological suppressing effect, including decreasing production of T helper cells, reducing cytokine production and decreasing macrophage cell ingestion. In general, while short-term acute stress may result in a variety of immunological changes but little that actually changes its effectiveness, even stress which lasts a only few days will result in down-regulation of the immune system.

Stress and immune function

Many studies now provide evidence of a relationship between immune function and stress. Cross-sectional studies have compared 'stressed' populations with non-stressed controls, and have shown impaired immune responses in groups as varied as bereaved individuals with high depression scores, carers of people with Alzheimer's disease, and people living near areas where natural disasters have occurred. Koh and Lee (1998) compared a group of clinically anxious individuals with a normal control group, and found the clinical group to have a reduced lymphocyte response. However, no relationship between the duration of illness or the degree of anxiety and immune function was found within this group.

Within-subject studies have measured changes in immune function over time in the same individuals. In one such study, Kiecolt-Glaser et al. (1984) followed a cohort of medical students, measuring immune function one month before and on the day of an important examination. In comparison to baseline measures, immune assays on the day of the examination revealed a reduction in NK cells and T-cells. Coping and appraisal may also influence immune function in response to life events: among recent divorcees, for example, those who initiated the divorce evidenced higher levels of immune function than those against whom such action was taken. Other studies have examined immune function in patient populations. In a prospective study of patients with operable breast cancer, for example, Tjemsland et al. (1997) collected psychological data one day before surgery and immunological data one day and seven days after surgery. Intrusive anxiety and anxious preoccupation were inversely correlated with the number of lymphocytes, B, T total and T4 lymphocytes, and depression with B and T4 lymphocytes.

These and many other studies have provided consistent evidence that stress and mood influence immune function. What the evidence has so far not shown is that the degree of immune downregulation is sufficient to affect the course of disease. Some suggestive evidence was provided by Kiecolt-Glaser et al. (1985). They found that immune function was depressed in a group of elderly carers of people with Alzheimer's disease and that, in comparison to a non-stressed group matched for age and gender, these people evidenced significantly slower wound-healing following a standardized medical procedure. The between-group differences were impressive, with carers' wounds taking an average of 49 days to heal, and those of the comparison group 39 days. More indirect evidence can be found in epidemiological studies that have measured the association between stress and disease.

Investigating the stress/disease relationship

The majority of studies exploring the relationship between stress and disease have adopted case-control or longitudinal methodologies. Some of the strengths and weaknesses of these approaches were considered in the previous chapter. One additional issue relevant to case-control studies exploring the relationship between stress and disease is that they are frequently conducted in populations who know their disease status. This knowledge may result in some of those who are ill attempting to find a reason for their poor health. As stress is commonly thought to be associated with disease, this search for meaning may lead to a biased recall of stressful events or to a retrospective labelling of events as stressful by those in the 'case' population, resulting in spurious between-group differences. For this reason, the results of studies where the individuals involved are unaware of their disease status should be accorded particular importance.

Three further methodological issues should be considered in interpreting the results of both types of study. The first relates to the definition of stress. Many studies have measured the frequency of life events prior to disease onset and have failed to consider the level of perceived stress associated with such events. This may attenuate the apparent strength of any relationship between the *experience* of stress and subsequent disease states. A second issue relates to the quantity and duration of stress that the individual experiences. We do not know how sustained or severe any stress needs to be in order to impact on the disease process. Accordingly, it is difficult to identify exactly what is and what is not a stressor in the context of such research. A final factor that has to be considered is that stress does not contribute to one disease process. Over fifty conditions are thought to be initiated or exacerbated by stress. This presents problems for theories linking stress and disease and for studies attempting to measure the association between stress and one disease endpoint.

This issue, and some of the other methodological weaknesses, can be addressed using a third approach that involves following a group of individuals with a known recurring disorder and measuring any relationship between stress and disease exacerbation over time. A similar gain may be had from measuring the relationship between stress and the progression of diseases such as cancer or CHD. A final method is to consider the impact of stress on the development of disease under highly controlled circumstances. This approach is exemplified by studies examining the impact of stress on wound-healing or susceptibility to the common cold.

As noted previously, over fifty diseases processes are thought to be influenced by stress. Any brief review has necessarily to be selective. Accordingly, the next section focuses on the relationship between stress and two of the most prevalent serious diseases: cancer and CHD. It then considers the evidence measuring the association between HIV progression and stress before considering the role of stress in two other common conditions: arthritis and irritable bowel syndrome. Finally, it considers some of the experimental work that has explored the relationship between stress and controlled exposure to known pathogens.

Cancer

Some studies exploring the stress/cancer relationship have employed novel methodologies. Hatch et al. (1991), for example, considered that the proximity of people's houses to a nuclear accident at Three Mile Island would act as a marker of the stress experienced during and following the incident. Accordingly, they attributed a significant, but modest, association between postaccident rates of cancer and site proximity to differential levels of stress. However, without actual measures of stress such a conclusion must remain speculative, with the findings potentially confounded by cell damage as a consequence of increased radiation exposure, increased utilization of services by these inhabitants, or more careful screening for health problems by local doctors.

Using a more traditional case-control methodology, Forsen (1991) found that women who knew that they had breast cancer reported higher levels of chronic stress prior to its onset than those in a matched control group without cancer. Geyer (1991) was able to avoid the problems associated with biased recall of stress as a consequence of knowledge of disease status by interviewing women attending a breast lump biopsy clinic prior to knowledge of their disease status. Women who were subsequently found to have a malignancy reported significantly greater numbers of chronic stressors than women whose lump was found to be benign. Unfortunately, although this study avoided the problems of biased recall, its results and those of a number of similar studies should be viewed with some caution, as the effects of other risk factors associated with both cancer and stress, such as smoking, were not partialled out in the analyses.

Longitudinal studies of healthy populations have found minimal relationships between stress and the initiation of cancer. One of the earliest, the Western Electric Study (WES: Persky et al. 1987), found that those who scored highly on a depression scale were twice as likely to develop cancer as those who did not. However, later consideration suggested that these findings might have occurred as result of high cancer rates among a stressed group of workers who also came into contact with highly carcinogenic materials. Subsequent large-scale studies failed to replicate the initial findings of the WES, although Everson *et al.* (1996) did find that moderate hopelessness was associated with incident cancer.

The failure to find a consistent association between stress and the onset of cancer may indicate that the two variables are not associated. It may also reflect the problems inherent in measuring an association between a transitory experience and a disease outcome measured up to 15 years later. For this reason, studies measuring the association between stress and the more immediate process of disease progression may be of more help in measuring any association between stress and cancer. In one such study, Ramirez *et al.* (1989) reported that women treated for breast cancer who later relapsed reported a nearly sixfold greater frequency of negative life events than those who continued in remission. Similarly, Forsen (1991) found that women who reported high levels of stressful life events prior to surgery for breast cancer were three and a half times more likely to experience a recurrence and nearly four and a half times more likely to die of cancer in the years following surgery than their less stressed counterparts.

Subsequent studies (for example Roberts *et al.* 1996) found no relationship between the occurrence of severe life events and risk of relapse. However, these relied on measurements of life events rather than participants' perceived stress. In contrast, Andrykowski *et al.* (1994) found an attitude towards cancer characterized by 'anxious preoccupation' and a poorer functional quality of life were each independently associated with poorer post bone marrow transplant survival.

A further strand of evidence of the stress/cancer relationship is found in the social support literature, summarized in Chapter 1. This suggests that the quality of social and marital support available to an individual is an important factor in the prognosis following a diagnosis of cancer. Finally, the evidence of treatment trials aimed at helping patients to cope effectively with stress (considered in Chapter 11) provides mixed evidence of the impact of stress and distress on cancer survival.

In summary, there is mixed evidence about the relationship between stress and both the initiation and progression of cancer. This lack of consistent findings led Spiegel and Kato (1996) to conclude that there probably is an association between stress and cancer, but that the methodologies used to explore this relationship have proven weak and have contributed noise rather than coherence to our understanding of this relationship.

Coronary heart disease

There is increasing evidence of a relationship between depression and the development of CHD. Vaillant (1998), for example, found that of 237 healthy men followed for a period of 55 years, 45 per cent of those who had experienced a depressive episode at or before their baseline measurement were dead at follow-up. This compared with 5 per cent of those who reported good mental health.

Psychological distress, and in particular depression, has significant prognostic significance following MI. Frasure-Smith et al. (1993), for example, found three robust predictors of mortality in the six months following hospitalization: degree of left ventricular damage, previous MI, and depression. Depression was the strongest predictor of reinfarction, with an adjusted hazard ratio of 4.29, contrasting with 3.52 for ventricular damage, and 3.2 for a history of MI. In a similar study, Allison et al. (1995) assessed post-MI patients using a psychiatric screening measure during the second week of cardiac rehabilitation and categorized those who scored above the 90th percentile for outpatient adults as 'distressed'. Over their follow-up period, these patients had significantly higher rates of cardiovascular rehospitalization and recurrent 'hard events', including reinfarction and cardiac arrest and resuscitation, than their less distressed counterparts. In a contrasting approach, Lim et al. (1998) operationalized poor psychological health in terms of low quality of life. Over an 18-month period, the reinfarction rates among patients who rated their quality of life as high was 9 per cent. This contrasted with mortality rates of 18 and 28 per cent among those with moderate and low classifications, respectively. In sum, however measured, depression appears to be a powerful risk factor for CHD.

Human immunodeficiency virus (HIV)

Tracking the effects of stress on HIV infection has proven problematic. Temoshok (1990) suggested that changes in the immune system's capacity to respond to psychosocial stress may differ according to both the degree of stress experienced and the stage of disease. In the early stages of infection to the time of early signs of HIV-related symptoms, stress may have only a modest impact on the immune system. As the disease progresses, the response may be a marked downregulation and more rapid disease progression. Certainly, there is no clear pattern of disease response to stress, although there is some evidence that stress impacts adversely on prognosis. Evans et al. (1997), for example, followed 93 HIV positive gay men without clinical symptoms at baseline for up to three and a half years. Their findings indicated that the more severe the life stress experienced, the greater the risk of early HIV disease progression. For every one severe stress per six-month study interval, the risk of early disease progression was doubled. In contrast, an earlier study that used a simple life events methodology, found that CD4+ counts and the progression of disease as measured by the development of fever or thrush did not co-vary with the number of life events experienced by a similar population (Kessler et al. 1991).

Gay men may experience social isolation and discrimination: many find this stressful. Studies by Cole *et al.* (1996) and others suggest it may also influence the progression of HIV infection. Analyses of data from a nine-year prospective study of 72 initially healthy HIV positive gay men indicated that rejection-sensitive individuals experienced a significant acceleration in times to a critically low CD4+ lymphocyte level, AIDS diagnosis and HIV-related mortality. Accelerated HIV progression was not observed in rejection-sensitive gay men who concealed their homosexual identity, suggesting that concealment may protect such individuals from negative health effects. However, social isolation may itself increase risk for disease progression (see Chapter 1).

Irritable bowel syndrome

A number of case-control studies have shown evidence of an association between stress and the onset of irritable bowel syndrome (IBS) symptoms. However, some of the most interesting data have come from more recent longitudinal studies measuring the co-variance between changes in stress and symptoms. Dancey *et al.* (1998) employed a within-person, lagged time-series approach to investigate the links between everyday stress and symptomatology in 31 patients with IBS. Half of those being monitored noted stress-related onset or exacerbation of symptoms. Symptom severity was most strongly related to the number of hassles in the two days preceding occurrence of IBS. In contrast to early models of IBS that considered it to be almost uniquely a consequence of stress, this evidence suggests that stress is implicated in its aetiology in some but by no means all those with the syndrome.

Rheumatoid arthritis

In one of the few studies to examine the relationship between stress and the onset of arthritis, Meyerowitz *et al.* (1968) studied eight sets of twins discordant for the disease. In a majority of cases, the arthritic twin experienced an increase in life stress prior to onset. More research has been conducted with individuals who already have arthritis, focusing on predictors of disease progression and periods of acute symptoms. These studies have typically found a relationship between stress and disease exacerbation. Zautra *et al.* (1997), for example, found disease activity to co-vary with the number of interpersonal stressors in the preceding week. Similarly, Urrows *et al.* (1994) found joint mobility and joint tenderness to co-vary with daily stress levels over a three-month assessment period.

Mood may affect the reporting of pain and symptoms. Accordingly, associations between physiological markers of disease provide important confirmatory evidence of any association between stress and arthritis.

Such evidence has been obtained. Stress has been shown to influence a number of biochemical markers of inflammation and immune factors involved in the arthritic process. Despite such findings, Crown *et al.* (1975) proposed that the importance of stress in the aetiology of rheumatoid arthritis might vary in different subtypes of patients. They suggested that patients with a low genetic predisposition to the disease might have a greater degree of stress preceding its onset, a more acute onset and a greater tendency for exacerbation as a consequence of stress than those with a higher genetic predisposition.

Controlled studies of disease

The most impressive studies of the influence of the stress on viral illnesses have involved challenging individuals with a known amount of a known virus strain and identifying factors that moderate the development of disease. Emotional distress and high levels of stressful life events have been found to increase risk of both the onset of infection and the expression of disease following controlled exposure to a cold virus (see, for example, Cohen *et al.* 1993). In a later study (Cohen *et al.* 1998), the same team attempted to delineate the characteristics of stressors that moderated disease outcomes. Their results indicated that volunteers inoculated with common cold viruses who had experienced stressful events of less than one month in duration were at no greater risk of developing colds than those with low stress levels. However, those who had experienced stress of a longer duration, primarily as a function of unemployment or family conflict, exhibited a substantially greater risk of developing disease. The same team also found that participants with low numbers of social ties were four times more likely to develop a cold following viral challenge than those with higher numbers of social ties.

From stress to disease: psychophysiological processes

Stress may influence the onset or course of a number of diseases. What is not clear is why different individuals develop differing diseases as a consequence of a similar psychological experience. The stress-diathesis model attempts to explain such individual differences. This states that stress places some degree of strain on the bodily systems. This may be mediated by the central nervous system, immune system, or both. However, whether and where this is translated into a disease process is a function of biological factors such as genetic phenotype or previous exposure to particular pathogens. These influence the sensitivity of differing bodily systems to these processes and lead to varying disease processes. The psychopathology of disease will differ markedly according to the disease endpoint.

Coronary heart disease

Both chronic and acute stress may impact on the physiological processes resulting in an MI. In the long term, episodes of high sympathetic arousal consequent to stress are associated with the release of fatty acids into the blood stream. If these are not completely utilized during the period of stress through, for example, high levels of physical activity, they are metabolized by the liver into cholesterol which may be laid down in the arteries to form atheroma. In addition, short-term increases in blood pressure at the time of sympathetic activation may damage the atheroma already within the arteries, leading to the initiation of repair processes, further exacerbating their development.

More acutely, a clot may be torn off a damaged artery wall, perhaps during an episode of increased blood pressure. If this reaches the arteries of the heart or brain and is too large to pass through an artery, it will occlude the artery and prevent blood flow beyond, resulting in an MI or a stroke. Catecholamines released during the stress process may also affect blood viscosity directly, making the platelets more likely to clot and increasing risk of an acute vascular event.

Irritable bowel syndrome

The most recent model of the aetiology of IBS has been developed by Nabiloff et al. (1998). It identified two key pathways though which psychological and physiological processes may come together to result in IBS. First, the gut may be more reactive to a variety of stimulants including stress. Such reactivity may result in pain and symptoms such as diarrhoea and constipation. In addition, some individuals may have a psychological set that is particularly vigilant to internal physical sensations. These people may be particularly aware of ordinary or reactive bowel processes and label them as painful and symptoms of illness. Research elsewhere (for example Pennebaker 1992) suggests that individuals with such a cognitive set are characterized by high levels of neuroticism. Accordingly, the link between stress and IBS symptoms may be a function both of stress being a trigger for some symptoms and an enduring negative appraisal style that may result in both high levels of stress and symptoms being reported.

HIV and cancer

Both HIV and cancer states involve impairments in the immune system. A number of mechanisms have been proposed to account for the long-term catastrophic decline in CD4+ cells in HIV positive individuals. The primary mechanism through which it may occur is consequent to the

HIV virus entering the CD4+ cells which, when they replicate, carry the virus to the new CD4+ cells. Proliferation of CD4+ cells in response to pathogens therefore results in an increase in HIV-infected cells. Activation of these cells in response to infection also leads to the death of the cell. Repetition of this process in response to repeated infection leads to a continuing decline in immune function. Stress may exacerbate this decline in CD4+ cells as a consequence of stress-related impairments in other parts of the immune system. These place additional demands on the T-cells at times of infection or other insults to the system, and result in increased CD4+ proliferation and, in turn, the activation of HIV. The mechanisms through which stress affects risk for cancer remain unclear. It appears to be mediated through a reduced response of NK cells to the development of tumours. However, whether this is a function of a reduction in the number of NK cells or a decrease in their killing ability is not clear.

Summary and conclusions

Models of stress have moved from focusing on environmental precursors or physiological processes of stress to models to focus much more closely its emotional *experience*. Such models suggest that 'stress is in the eye of the beholder', although Hobfoll's resource loss model of stress suggests that not all stresses are idiosyncratic to the individual. Stress, whether defined as environmental events or perceived stress, has been shown to impact on both autonomic and immune function, although whether the latter influences are sufficient to result in disease has yet to be established unequivocally. That said, there is clear evidence that stress does impact on health through a variety of pathways and mechanisms. Such results provide strong justification for the implementation of stress management procedures to help people both cope with disease and to alter its course.

Further reading

Lazarus, R.L. (1991) *Emotion and Adaptation*. New York: Oxford University Press.
Lovallo, W.R. (1997) *Stress and Health: Biological and Psychological Interactions*. Thousand Oaks: Sage.

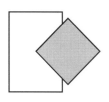

Part II
Understanding health-related behaviour

3 ▷ Health-related decision making

One of the key questions addressed by health psychologists is why individuals do, or do not, engage in a variety of **health-related behaviours**. The theories that address these questions are collectively known as social-cognition models. They each attempt to identify the cognitive processes underlying such decision making. Two distinct groups of models can be identified, each with different historical roots. Expectancy value models have their roots in learning, and then social learning theory, and assume that individuals work to maximize their gains and minimize their losses from the environment. Other models stem from research into attitudes conducted in the 1950s and onwards. All these models arise from a positivist framework and attempt to provide a theoretically driven and parsimonious model of health-related decision making. Studies are used to confirm or disconfirm pre-existing theories. In contrast, qualitative approaches use research to develop, rather than test, theoretical understandings of the processes underlying health-related behavioural decision making. Both approaches are discussed in this chapter.

The chapter reviews the following models:

- ◆ Expectancy value models
  - ◆ Social cognitive theory
  - ◆ Health belief model
  - ◆ Protection motivation theory
  - ◆ Health locus of control
- ◆ Attitudinal models
  - ◆ Theories of reasoned action and planned behaviour
- ◆ Stage theories
  - ◆ Health action process
  - ◆ Transtheoretical model
- ◆ Alternative approaches

Expectancy value models

Social cognitive theory

Originally termed social learning theory, Bandura's social cognitive theory (Bandura 1986) is an extension of Skinner's **operant conditioning** paradigm. Like Skinner, Bandura assumed that individuals work to maximize their gains from the environment. Unlike Skinner, he stated that this outcome is mediated by cognitive processes. According to social cognitive theory, individuals are motivated to gain the maximum reinforcement and minimum punishment from their environment. However, behaviours are not just governed by immediate behaviour/consequence contingencies: although short-term gains frequently do control behaviour more than long-term ones. Rather, the individual can defer immediate gratification and work towards long-term goals. In addition, individuals are capable of learning behaviour/outcome contingencies from the observation of others, and behave within a moral framework.

Behavioural choice is premised on two sets of expectancies. The first, action/outcome expectancies, reflect the degree to which an individual believes that an action will lead to a particular outcome. This outcome is then considered in terms of its value to the individual. The second set of expectancies, self-efficacy expectations, reflect the degree to which an individual believes him or herself capable of the behaviour being considered. According to social cognitive theory, the individual is most likely to engage in a behaviour if they believe it will achieve a desired outcome and that they are capable of successfully completing it. Efficacy beliefs operate at different levels. Generalized efficacy beliefs ('I can cope with most things life throws at me') may mediate a variety of behaviours, and are particularly relevant when the individual is faced with a novel behavioural decision. However, behaviour-specific efficacy beliefs are frequently more powerful determinants of behaviour than such generalized beliefs.

Both outcome and self-efficacy beliefs have been shown to be important predictors of a number of health-related behaviours including resisting peer pressure to use drugs, engaging in safer sex practices, weight loss and frequency of breast self-examination. A number of studies have measured the influence of these beliefs in patient populations. Bennett et al. (1999a), for example, found that self-efficacy and outcome expectations were strongly predictive of the frequency of aerobic exercise and alcohol and cigarette consumption following an MI. Only diet was not predicted by social cognitive variables. Again in the context of recovery from MI, Vidmar and Rubinson (1994) found a positive association between levels of exercise and self-efficacy beliefs concerning the ability both to exercise and to deal with any barriers to exercise. The latter was found to be the strongest predictor, accounting for 27 per cent of the variance in exercise behaviour. Dzewaltowski *et al.* (1990) similarly found adherence to a prescribed exercise regime to be correlated with perceived self-efficacy, outcome expectancies and dissatisfaction with previous levels of fitness. Individuals who were confident that they could adhere to a strenuous exercise programme and who placed a high value on gaining fitness exercised the most.

A final example of the role of social cognitive variables in relation to CHD-risk behaviours comes from work on smoking cessation. Godding and Glasgow (1985) reported that self-efficacy beliefs concerning the ability to resist smoking following cessation were strongly predictive of the numbers of cigarettes smoked, the amount of tobacco per cigarette and blood nicotine levels. Such is the influence of outcome and efficacy beliefs on behaviour, that Schwarzer (1992) suggested they form the primary determinants of many health-related behaviours.

A second component of social cognitive theory is the process of vicarious learning. According to Bandura, we can learn behavioural outcomes and establish efficacy expectancies without necessarily having direct experience of them ourselves. Observation of the outcomes of others' behaviour may in some cases prove a more powerful determinant of behaviour than personal experience. An important health-related behaviour that is frequently subject to this process is the uptake of cigarette smoking. Despite the immediate outcome of the first inhalation of a cigarette being highly aversive, many children continue to smoke because at the same time that they are suffering they observe in others that smoking can be a pleasurable and rewarding behaviour. They persevere in the expectation of future enjoyment. Such a process provides, at least in part, an explanation of why children who smoke are more likely to come from families or to have friends who smoke. The effectiveness of interventions based on vicarious learning principles is discussed in Chapters 8 and 9.

Health belief model

A second theory that assumes that we work to maximize our gains from the environment adopted a very different approach from social cognitive theory. The health belief model states that decisions whether or not to engage in health-related behaviours involve a form of cost/benefit analysis. Key elements to the decisional process are the health gains that will result from engaging in a particular behaviour and the costs (social, psychological, and so on) of doing so. These elements can be subdivided further to consideration of:

◆ the perceived susceptibility to illness;
◆ the severity of that illness;
◆ the health benefits of engaging in a behaviour;

♦ the various costs of carrying out the behaviour;
♦ cues to action, which prompt the decisional process.

Later versions of the model (Becker *et al.* 1977) added a fourth dimension, the individual's motivation or 'readiness to be concerned about health matters', although this has rarely been addressed by researchers when testing the model. According to the health belief model, engagement in health-protective behaviour is most likely if the risk of disease and its perceived severity are high, the behaviour is considered effective in reducing risk for disease, and the immediate costs of that behaviour are low.

Although this constellation of criteria may be most predictive of behaviour, research has concentrated on the relationship between single dimensions of the health belief model and behaviours as varied as engaging in exercise programmes, child vaccination, compliance with recommended medical regimes and attending preventive screening clinics. Johnson and Heller (1998), for example, found that cardiac patients who considered exercise to be beneficial to their health while in hospital were most likely to be following a recommended home exercise course six months later. Those who considered there to be many potential barriers to their engaging in the programme were less likely to be exercising at this time. Again in a population of cardiac patients, Koikkalainen *et al.* (1996) reported low levels of adherence to recommended dietary regimens. Over half the patients reported one or more barriers to these recommendations, the most frequent of which were associated with eating in company or in situations where too much food was available. Another common reason for non-compliance was that many healthy foods were not thought to taste particularly pleasant.

Interesting cross-generational differences were found in the cost/benefit analyses relating to gay men's sexual behaviour by Bakker *et al.* (1997). They found that for younger men, strength of intention to use a condom was positively related to the number of persons known to them who had AIDS and to the perceived benefits of HIV preventive behaviour. The former was not predictive of behavioural interventions among older men. These differences may reflect differing experiences of both the impact and treatment of AIDS and HIV infection since its entry into the population in the 1970s. In general, frequency of condom use among younger people appears to be low, perhaps because a majority of young persons do not see themselves as being at risk of HIV infection or have feelings of invulnerability towards the disease.

Despite these findings, the utility of the health belief model has been questioned. Taking a positive perspective, a review of nearly fifty studies conducted by Janz and Becker (1984) reported that measures of susceptibility were significantly associated with health behaviours in 82 per cent of studies, with measures of perceived severity in 65 per cent, with benefits in 81 per cent, and with costs in 100 per cent. Less positive were the findings of Harrison *et al.* (1992) following a series of analyses measuring the average correlations between health belief model dimensions and behaviour. These were only modest: 0.15 for susceptibility, 0.08 for severity, 0.13 for benefits and −0.21 for barriers. Individual components of the health belief model accounted for an average of between 0.5 and 4 per cent of the variance in behaviour across studies. However, Harrison *et al.* reported highly variable results from different studies, suggesting that for some behaviours the predictive utility of the model may be stronger than their overall results would suggest.

A number of theoretical criticisms have also been made of the model. First, it takes no account of environmental or social factors that may influence decision making. Second, it assumes that the primary motivation to engage in health-related behaviours is one of health gain. However, such an outcome is long term and probabilistic. Social cognitive theory suggests that shorter-term contingencies are likely to be more influential than the promise of potential long-term gains. These theoretical predictions have been sustained in relation to a number of health-related behaviours: weight control and aesthetic outcomes are more influential rewards of healthy eating than potential health gains: enjoyment appears to be the primary determinant of engaging in exercise.

A third criticism of the health belief model stems from its failure to clarify the links between the various factors or to consider the relative importance of each factor in any decision-making process. In response to such criticism, Stretcher and Rosenstock (1997) suggested that rather than 'throw' health belief variables into a multivariate analysis and find out which are the stronger individual predictors of behaviour, a number of algorithms should be followed, including: a heightened state of severity is required before perceived susceptibility becomes a powerful predictor of behaviour; perceived benefits and barriers will be stronger predictors of behavioural change when perceived threat is high than when it is low; the factors will be stronger predictors of intentions than behaviour (see below); and, cues to action will have their greatest influence on behaviour in conditions where the perceived health threat is high. These new hypotheses now need empirical testing.

Protection motivation theory

Protection motivation theory (Rogers 1983) combines elements of the health belief model and social cognitive theory in a description of how fear-arousing health communications are processed and acted upon. The model focuses on two broad categories of response: threat appraisal and coping appraisal. The outcome of this appraisal process is an intention to behave in either an adaptive or a maladaptive manner, the strength of which reflects the degree of motivation to protect one's health. This intention, in turn, predicts behaviour (Figure 3.1).

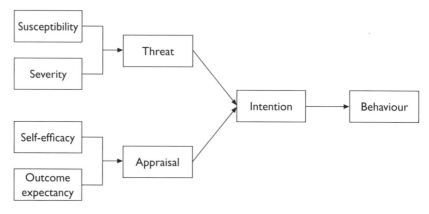

Figure 3.1   Protection motivation theory

As in the health belief model, threat appraisal is a function of both the perceived susceptibility to illness and its severity. Consideration is also given to the benefits of maintaining maladaptive behaviours. Coping appraisal is a function of both outcome and self-efficacy beliefs. Accordingly, an individual is most likely to change their behaviour in response to a fear-arousing health message if they believe they are susceptible to disease, that the disease will have severe consequences, they perceive a link between protective behaviours and reduced risk for disease, and consider themselves capable of engaging in those behaviours. Although similar to the health belief model, there are some important differences between the two theories. The health belief model is a theory of health-behaviour decision making; protection motivation theory is a model of responses to fear-arousing communications. In addition, the consideration of both outcome and self-efficacy expectancies is more explicit in protection motivation theory than in the health belief model.

A number of studies evaluating the model have adopted an experimental methodology, measuring behavioural responses to a variety of experimental manipulations of vulnerability and efficacy expectations. In one such study, Boer and Seydel (1996) measured the impact of a leaflet accompanying an invitation to attend a mass screening clinic for breast cancer. The leaflet emphasized the high vulnerability of older women to breast cancer and the efficacy of mammographic screening as a means of cancer control. It also attempted to induce feelings of high self-efficacy by explaining that a mammographic examination was an easy procedure and involved only minimal discomfort. Women who rated themselves as most vulnerable to breast cancer and who had high self-efficacy were most likely to attend screening. Similarly, Sturges and Rogers (1996) found that adolescents and young adults responded to threat appeals with increased intentions not to smoke cigarettes only if they believed they could successfully quit smoking; if they believed they could not do so, higher levels of the threat resulted in decreased intentions to refrain from tobacco use. Other research focusing specifically on the influence of outcome and efficacy expectations provides evidence of the strengths of at least one aspect of the model.

Health locus of control

Health locus of control refers to the degree of control an individual believes they have over their health. Following the work of Rotter (1966), who focused on generalized control beliefs, Wallston et al. (1978) identified three statistically independent dimensions of perceived control over health: internal, chance, and powerful others. Individuals who score highly on the internal dimension consider their health as largely within their own control. Conversely, those who score highly on the chance dimension consider their health to be relatively independent of their behaviour. Finally, those who score highly on the 'powerful other' dimension consider their health to be controlled by others, operationalized as doctors in Wallston et al.'s measure of perceived control.

The historical roots of locus of control theory lie in social learning theory, and like Bandura, Wallston argued that individuals are motivated to engage in behaviours that lead to valued outcomes. Accordingly, health locus of control should predict behaviour most strongly in those who place a high value on their health. The strongest prediction of the model is that those who value their health and who have high internality scores are more likely to engage in health-protective behaviours than those who have low internality beliefs. Those who value their health and have high powerful-others scores are most likely to seek and adhere to medical treatments should they fall ill. Predicting engagement in more routine health-behaviours is more difficult. High powerful-others scores may indicate a receptivity to health messages endorsed by medical authorities and be associated with active participation in health-protective behaviours. Conversely, they may suggest a strong belief in the ability of the medical system to cure any illness and predict, as a consequence, low uptake of health-promoting behaviours. Regardless of their value for health, those with a high belief in chance factors are least likely to engage in health-protective behaviours of any type.

Surprisingly few studies have considered the relationship between locus of control and value for health. Of those studies that have, some, but not all, have found stronger relationships between internality and behaviour among individuals with a high value for health than among those with a lower score (see Wallston and Smith 1994). However, it is possible that differences in value for health may not be a critical issue: finding people who do not value their health may actually prove quite difficult.

In perhaps the largest study population on which the model has been tested, Norman and colleagues (1998) reported data from a representative British population sample of over 13,000 people and found locus of control and value for health dimensions to predict up to 5 per cent of the variance in measures of exercise, smoking, diet, alcohol consumption and a composite lifestyle measure. Research outcomes in smaller studies have been mixed. Slenker *et al.* (1985) found joggers to have higher internal health locus of control scores than non-joggers. Conversely, Calnan (1989) found no relationship between exercise and internal health locus of control scores. Kelley *et al.* (1990) found gay men who reported having unprotected anal intercourse were less likely to have internal AIDS-related locus of control beliefs and more likely to believe that the likelihood of HIV infection was attributable to chance factors than those who did not do so. The same research group later found no relationship between internal beliefs and the use of condoms in a sample of African-American adolescents.

Health locus of control is perhaps a better predictor of discrete, one-off behaviours in response to challenges to health than more routine health-related behaviours (Wallston and Smith 1994). However, similarly mixed findings in other health domains have led Wallston to draw a number of pessimistic conclusions about the ability of the health locus of control construct alone to predict preventive health behaviour. Indeed, by the early 1990s, Wallston accepted that efficacy is a more powerful predictor of behaviour than control (see, for example Wallston 1991). Since then, he has argued that the primary determinant of behaviour is a generalized self-efficacy belief. This is a more global, overarching construct than the domain or behaviour-specific efficacy described by Bandura. Wallston stated that, where health is a valued outcome, locus of control is a moderator variable that interacts with self-efficacy to predict behaviour. Individuals are most likely to engage in health protective behaviours if they believe both that they can engage successfully in the required behaviour and that their health is under their own control. In this, locus of control seems analogous to a health-specific outcome expectation.

Attitudinal models

Despite early optimism, research into the relationship between attitudes and behaviour increasingly revealed a lack of association between the two variables (see Eagly and Chaiken 1993). Attitudinal research has therefore focused on variables that combine with attitudes to predict behaviour.

Theory of reasoned action

The theory of reasoned action (Ajzen and Fishbein 1980) identified a number of factors that, in combination with attitudes, are thought to predict behaviour. The model states that the proximal determinant of behaviour is a behavioural intention. This represents the person's motivation or conscious plan to carry out the behaviour. Intentions are derived from two parallel processes: the relevant attitudes of the individual and those thought to be held by others, known as subjective or behavioural norms (Figure 3.2).

Attitudes have two components: beliefs about a behaviour, usually expressed as its perceived consequences, and a value placed on each behavioural outcome ('Exercise makes me slim: I value being slim.'). A number of, possibly contradictory, beliefs and related values may be held about a particular behaviour. However, the sum total of these belief/value pairings provides a measure of the strength of attitude towards a particular behaviour. Subjective norms also comprise two elements. The first is the strength of belief about whether salient others would wish the individual to engage in a behaviour. These beliefs interact with the individual's motivation to comply with these wishes ('My girlfriend would like me to exercise. I want to do as she wishes.'). Consideration may be given to a number of salient others' perceived wishes, with the final strength of normative beliefs represented by the sum of these belief/value pairings. Attitudes and subjective norms are derived at some stage in a behavioural sequence, and once formed are not necessarily reviewed at every behavioural opportunity.

Many studies of the theory of reasoned action measure attitudes and social norms relating to one behaviour. However, Ajzen and Fishbein (1980) recommended that where various behavioural choices exist, measures should be taken in relation to each of the possible behaviours. One may, for example, find that smokers express negative attitudes towards smoking, but hold even more negative attitudes towards not smoking. Studies that have adopted this methodology have been in the minority, and the gain in predictive strength of the model has not always been great, particularly where the decision has been of a dichotomous nature. However, where a variety of behavioural choices are possible, such as the choice of contraceptive pill, this procedure adds significantly to model's explanatory power (Davidson and Morrison 1983).

Evaluations of the theory have shown attitudes and social norms to be strongly predictive of intentions. Meta-analyses have variously reported the mean correlation of attitudes and social norms with intentions to be about 0.67 (see Conner and Sparks 1996). The relationship between intentions and behaviour is of a somewhat lower magnitude, with mean correlations varying between 0.53 and 0.62. However, the strength of this relationship varies considerably across studies, with correlations between intentions and measures of behaviour varying between 0.01 and 0.94.

While the theory of reasoned action has proved an effective predictor of behaviour, it has a number of limitations. First, it is in essence linear: attitudes and social norms influence intentions, which in turn influence behaviour. No attention is given to the potentially transactional relationship between these variables: behaviour may influence attitudes or change

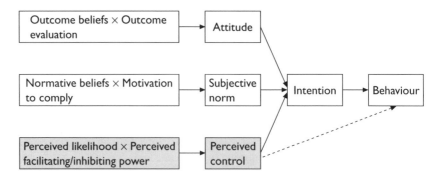

Figure 3.2   The theories of reasoned action and planned behaviour: note that the shaded elements comprise the theory of planned behaviour component

awareness of social norms, which can feed back to change future intentions and behaviour. In addition, by confining the model to an explanation of volitional behaviour, it cannot explain behaviour that occurs with little or no intervening thought, that which is habitual and may occur independently of attitudes (Triandis 1977), or behaviour over which the individual has little or no control.

Theory of planned behaviour

In response to the weakness just described, Ajzen extended the model, adding a third factor measuring perceived behavioural control: the individual's estimation of how easy or difficult it would be to perform a particular behaviour (see Figure 3.2). It is similar to, but not synonymous with, self-efficacy as it relates to both one's own abilities and the impact of other, external, variables. This extended model is known as the theory of planned behaviour (for example Ajzen, 1985).

In a review of the relevant evidence, Ajzen (1991) reported the mean correlation between measures of perceived behavioural control and intentions to be 0.71. In general, the theory of planned behaviour is a better predictor of both intentions and behaviour than the theory of reasoned action (see, for example, Hausenblas *et al.* 1997; Sheeran and Orbell 1998), although in a majority of studies behavioural intentions account for more of the variance in behaviour than perceived behavioural control. Nevertheless, Eagly and Chaiken (1993) point out that a direct causal association between perceived behavioural control and behaviour may be questioned: one does not necessarily engage in a behaviour just because one is capable of doing so. Instead, they suggest that the ability to engage in a behaviour when combined with the desire to do so will predict action: that is, an interaction between attitudes and behavioural control may be predictive of behaviour, and perhaps more so than a direct effect of either variable.

Explaining the intention–behaviour gap

Intentions do not always predict behaviour. Indeed, such is the disparity between stated intentions and any subsequent enaction of those intentions that this phenomenon has been named the intention–behaviour gap. Considerable effort is now being directed at increasing our understanding of the processes that mediate between intentions and behaviour. However, before considering some of the proposed mediators, it is worth reflecting that the failure to find a consistently strong association between intentions and behaviour may not reflect so much a 'gap' as a failure to address the intention–behaviour link appropriately. An intention is typically stated in terms of one behaviour ('I intend to use a condom with a new sexual partner . . .') and little consideration is given to other, potentially relevant, intentions. However, the intention measured may well compete with or even contradict other, perhaps more important intentions held by the individual. One may intend to use a condom during intercourse with a new partner; one also may intend not to lose face through potentially embarrassing negotiations. If the latter intention is more important than using a condom, the intention to use a condom may never be implemented. Accordingly, intentions may be stronger predictors of behaviour than is sometimes apparent: we may simply be measuring the wrong intentions and the wrong behaviour.

More theoretical models have also been applied to this problem. Gollwitzer (1993), for example, suggested that the intention to act is followed by the development of plans, known as implementation intentions, which specify where and when the intention will be enacted. The more considered these implementation intentions are, the more likely they are to be acted upon. A failure to consider implementation plans increases the risk of intended behaviour not being enacted. In a test of this hypothesis, Orbell *et al.* (1997) asked a group of women to complete measures of attitudes, social norms and intentions to breast self-examine. Half their sample was then asked to consider where and when they would perform their examination. Despite equivalent strengths of intentions, those in this group were twice as likely to report performing breast self-examination than those in the group that simply reported their behavioural intentions. In a later study, the same research group found a modest but reliable gain in the taking of vitamin C pills following the development of implementation intentions.

Stage theories of behavioural change

Health action process

The theories so far described implicitly assume that behavioural decisions are made in an 'all or none' fashion, with consideration being given to each relevant element at the same time. A number of theorists have argued

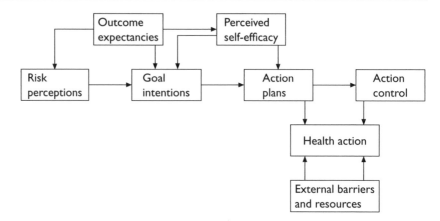

Figure 3.3   The health action process

that decision making may involve a more temporally dynamic process, with consideration of different elements influencing the decision-making process at different times. The health action process (Schwarzer 1992) has adopted elements of the social cognition models so far described, and identified a temporal pattern in which they are considered (see Figure 3.3). It states that the adoption of health-related behaviours involves two stages: a motivational and volitional stage. The latter is further subdivided into planning, action and maintenance phases.

The motivational stage is triggered by the perception of a threat to health. However, unlike some expectancy value models, Schwarzer argued that only a minimum level of threat or concern is required to initiate consideration of change. More important in the motivational stage are the relevant action/outcome expectancies and self-efficacy judgements. Consideration of action/outcome expectancies temporally precedes self-efficacy judgements, with the outcome of such deliberations being an intention to adopt a precaution measure or to change risk behaviours in favour of other behaviours.

Once an intention is determined, the individual moves to the action phase. This involves consideration of how an intentional goal may be achieved. A global intention (for example, to get fit) can be specified in a set of subordinate intentions and action plans that contain proximal goals and algorithms for action sequences (lose two pounds in weight, start jogging twice a week). The more plans and contingencies that are considered, the more likely is behavioural change. Self-efficacy judgements determine the amount of effort and perseverance invested in a new behaviour once initiated. The context in which change is attempted will also influence its outcome. Behaviours that are supported by the social and structural environment are more likely to be maintained than those that are not.

The importance of outcome and efficacy judgements in determining behavioural change has been established earlier in the chapter. Work by

Gollwitzer (1993) and others has confirmed the role of implementation intentions and planning. The unique element of the theory, which suggests a temporal structure to decision making has a strong logic, but requires further empirical support.

A transtheoretical model of behaviour change

The transtheoretical model of behavioural change of Prochaska and DiClemente (1986) attempted to provide a general model of the process of behaviour change. It postulated five stages through which the individual passes sequentially in the process of self-determined behavioural change:

* Pre-contemplation: not considering change
* Contemplation: considering change
* Preparation: ready to change
* Action: attempting change
* Maintenance or relapse: change maintained (or not) for six months

Prochaska and DiClemente do not claim to have developed a theoretical model of change: the factors that trigger or facilitate shifts between stages are deliberately not specified, and are left to be determined by other theories.

A more theoretical model has been described by Heckhausen (1991), who identified four stages of change: pre-decisional, post-decisional, actional and evaluative. Heckhausen suggested that the content of cognitions differs between each stage. In the pre-decisional phase, cognitions concerning the desirability and feasibility of a new behaviour predominate and may result in an intention to change. The decisional phase begins with consideration of plans for behavioural change and ends with the successful initiation of the new behaviour. In the final, evaluative phase, the individual is thought to compare achieved outcomes with initial goals in order to regulate and maintain behaviour.

The stage model has received some support. DiClemente *et al.* (1991) categorized smokers taking part in a self-help smoking cessation programme into one of three groups: pre-contemplators, contemplators and 'prepared for action'. Those in the preparation stage at baseline were most likely to attempt to quit, and be abstinent at one- and six-month follow-up. However, later studies have failed to support the notion of a sequential process of change or that individuals can be identified as being within one particular 'stage' at any one time. Budd and Rollnick (1996), for example, found that a readiness to change questionnaire was only able to categorize 40 per cent of heavy drinkers into a single stage and that factors based on items corresponding to the transtheoretical model were highly interdependent and lacked discriminant validity. Their analysis indicated that one underlying factor provided a better description of their data, suggesting that readiness to change amongst heavy drinkers corresponds more closely to a continuum than a series of states.

Data such as these have led critics of stage theories (see, for example, Sutton 1996) to suggest that a stage model of change is not theoretically tenable. Instead, they argue for a 'states of change' model that could be provided by other social cognition models such as the theory of planned behaviour. Here, the strength of intention to change behaviour would be analogous to the 'stage' of the individual, with changes in the strength of intentions not being premised on shifts from one discrete cognitive 'state' to another, but representing linear changes in relevant attitudes, social norms and perceived behavioural control.

Social cognition models: some dilemmas and questions

The theories outlined provide a parsimonious description of at least some of the processes involved in health-related decision making. Their development has answered many questions about how we make health-related decisions. However, many more issues need to be addressed before we have a full understanding of how and why we make health-related behavioural choices.

The central assumption of all the models so far reviewed is that decisions are the outcome of a formal, rational decision-making process. Such deliberation need not take place at the time the behaviour is enacted, and may have occurred sometime previously. Strong evidence of this routinization of behaviour can be found in a study of working-class households reported by Cullen (1979). Their respondents considered 90 per cent of their waking day to involve no real choices but, instead, an adaptation to a relatively stable long-term environment. An unresolved question is how such behavioural decisions become routinized and 'thoughtless', and when and how they become subject to change and reconsideration.

A further assumption of social cognition models is that attitudes, social norms, and so on, are relatively stable and 'fixed' over time: otherwise they would have no predictive utility. Ingham and van Zessen (1997) gathered qualitative data that contradicted such an assumption. They noted, for example, how one participant in their study reported strong intentions to use a condom but at the last minute changed his mind as he reappraised the cost and benefits of their use. A further issue relates to the timing of, and reason for, the 'rational decision-making' processes. Ingham and van Zessen (1997) found that over one-third of a sample of young people reported that they frequently considered the risks associated with unsafe sex: but did so only *after* the event. Such consideration appeared not so much a rational assessment of potential danger, but a way of coping with, and perhaps rationalizing away, any perceived risk.

Further evidence suggesting that reported attitudes and beliefs may form a *post hoc* explanation of behaviour was reported by Bennett and Clatworthy (1999). They found measures of attitudes, perceived social norms and behavioural control to discriminate between women who did and did not continue smoking while pregnant. Women who continued smoking were less likely to endorse statements about the potential harmful effects of smoking on their developing child. However, more predictive than these cognitive factors were levels of nicotine dependence. In addition, most of those who denied that smoking impacted adversely on the health of their baby and continued to smoke had nevertheless cut their level of smoking down to an average of 12 cigarettes per day. Together, these data suggest that at least some women did believe that smoking may damage their child, had tried to cut down or quit smoking, but were unable to do so as a consequence of their addiction to nicotine. Their denial of the harmful effects of smoking may well have been a defensive *post hoc* attempt to reduce the dissonance associated with smoking at the same time as holding negative attitudes towards smoking.

A final assumption of many of the models reviewed is that decisions are governed by a desire to preserve health. However, behaviour may be guided by other rationales. Jacobson (1981), for example, found that many working-class women smokers made a 'rational' decision to use smoking as a means of controlling the stresses of coping with adverse social and material circumstances, in the full knowledge of its long-term health-damaging effects. Social rationales may also influence behaviour. Sobo (1993), for example, was able to identify a number of HIV positive women who did not use a condom with their regular partner or husband, but did so with more casual sexual partners. Their rationale for this behaviour was that it implied commitment to a long-term relationship, and a desire to become as intimately involved as possible only within that relationship. Their risky behaviour was viewed as strengthening the relationship between them and their partner.

Alternative approaches to the study of behavioural decision-making

These various theoretical and practical concerns have led a number of researchers to argue that we should engage in other methods and draw upon other theories to help increase our understanding of why people behave the way they do. Ingham and van Zessen (1997) noted that the complexity of behaviour and the process of making behavioural choices contradicts the very rationale of social cognitive models: to explain behavioural choices in as parsimonious a way as possible. They suggest that we should explore the complexity of behaviour rather than attempt to artificially simplify it. Qualitative methods provide one means of doing so.

The term 'qualitative methods' encompasses a variety of approaches, including symbolic interactionist, social constructionist, interpretivist, and so on. Each brings its own methodology and strategies, most of which fall outside the scope of the present volume. Instead, the chapter focuses on the qualitative method used most often in health psychology: grounded theory (Strauss and Corbin 1990).

Grounded theory

Grounded theory is the methodology adopted by symbolic interactionists (Mead 1934). This framework suggests that our behaviour and under-standings of the world are shaped by our interactions with others. We develop shared understandings of the world, which change over time, and provide a rationale for our behavioural decisions. A simple example of this process can be found in studies of drinking alcohol in groups and 'round buying' by young men. This behaviour is promoted by a shared feeling of belonging to a group, demonstrating independence and equality of individuals within a group, and enabling mutual exchange. Similar meanings can be attached to the use of condoms with non-regular partners and not using condoms with regular partners by some HIV positive women. Here, the use of a condom implies a casual, non-committed relationship, while not using it enhances feelings of intimacy and commitment (see, for example, Sobo 1993 above).

Grounded theory permits the exploration of these shared meanings and understandings of the world. It accepts that any theory is not absolute or static, but stems from a shared negotiated process between the observer and the observed. The positivist approach of theory-testing is rejected. Instead, theory is developed in an iterative process from information given by the population under study. The researcher develops new ques-tions and hypotheses to address as information is gathered, and the search for new information stops only when no new information is obtained from the questions asked. Theory-testing in this framework is one of constant comparison of data with an emerging conceptual framework or theory. This method provides a rich understanding of the reasons for behavioural choices, not confined to predetermined categories or theories. Some examples of qualitative research are provided below. Note that the issue is now one of explaining a particular behaviour rather than developing a theory that is applicable to a number of behaviours.

Explanations of dietary choices

Dietary choice is frequently not premised on issues of health. Indeed, while many people accept the potential impact of diet on health in general, they discount its personal impact, considering chance or other ungovern-able factors as the ultimate determinants of health. More important may be social and cultural factors. Backett (1990), for example, found that much of the food eaten within families results from a negotiation between family members. The women in her sample did most of the cooking, yet many followed the dietary choices of their partners. Compromises were also determined by what children wished to eat, with meals including both food that the children liked, but which had poor nutritional value, and food that was healthy. Parents may even eat food quite different from their preferred choice in order to provide healthy role models for their children.

Douglas and Nicod (1974) provided an anthropological interpretation of food choice, divorcing it from any nutritional or health aspects and emphasizing the shared meaning of the ways in which food was prepared and eaten. In particular, they found that working-class meals were highly structured events and the choice of food determined by family history and tradition: the 'Sunday roast' perhaps forming the epitome of such ritual. According to Douglas and Nicod, such rituals have social and cultural meanings beyond that of the nutritional elements of food and may prove resistant to change premised entirely on health issues.

The differences between middle- and working-class women's understandings of food and health were explored by Calnan (1990). He found that differing elements of food were important to each of these groups. Middle-class women placed a strong emphasis on the need for a balanced diet, with everything in moderation. In contrast, working-class women were more concerned with making a meal substantial and filling. This may reflect differences in the function of food. Middle-class respondents were concerned about long-term health and appearance. For the working-class respondents, food choice was focused on providing sufficient energy to permit the accomplishment of work or other shorter-term tasks. Commonalities between the two groups were a focus on the need for fresh food that was free from additives and considered healthier than its processed equivalent. However, these beliefs impacted more on middle-class women's food choices than those of working-class women. In addition, although both groups saw high sugar and high fat foodstuffs as unhealthy, the working-class women purchased significantly more of these foodstuffs than did the middle-class women. Calnan concluded that the food choices of the working-class women did not appear to be driven by issues of nutrition or health; rather, they were based on availability, the choices of other family members, and how 'filling' they were.

Lupton and Chapman (1995) explored through a series of discussion groups how women dealt with, often contradictory, media stories concerning diet and dietary choices. Members of each group were given real, but conflicting, newspaper clippings on diet, cholesterol and heart disease. Participants were asked to say what they thought of these disparate views and how they knew what was the 'right' thing to eat. Finally, they were asked whom they could trust to give appropriate advice on health matters. Most participants were aware of the orthodox accounts of the relationship between diet and CHD: most also considered that good health was obtained through conscious planning and eating healthy foodstuffs. In addition, many considered that this involved controlling their own desires to eat the more pleasurable but unhealthy foods. Participants noted the pleasure of indulging oneself in eating, but also expressed moral beliefs about the need to 'work' at being healthy and the 'guilt' of eating the 'wrong types of food'. Medical advice was treated with some caution, and the adage 'everything in moderation' was applied regardless of official advice.

Summary and conclusions

This chapter has described a number of models used to explain health-related behaviour change, most of which fit within the rubric of social cognition models. These models attempt to identify common psychological constructs that underlie all such decision making. Their goal is one of parsimony: to provide a general model of health-related decision making that utilizes a minimum of extraneous explanatory variables. In this paradigm, the key variables appear to be those relating to personal control (and in particular self-efficacy), the costs and benefits of a particular behavioural choice, and the personal and perceived attitudes of others towards a particular behaviour. The models are better at predicting behavioural intentions than behaviour, although as the latter becomes the focus of more research our understanding of the processes mediating the intention–behaviour gap is likely to increase.

The goals of parsimony and generalizability, however, are achieved at the cost of a detailed understanding of the processes underlying particular behavioural choices. This level of understanding is better provided by qualitative methods. In addition, such methodologies permit the initial exploration of factors governing behaviour that may be subjected to later positivist, theory-testing methods.

Further reading

Conner, M. and Norman, P. (eds) (1996) *Predicting Health Behaviour: Research and Practice with Social Cognition Models*. Buckingham: Open University Press.

Murray, M. and Chamberlain, K. (eds) (1999) *Qualitative Health Psychology: Theories and Methods*. London: Sage.

Health- and illness-related cognitions

Our understanding of both adults' and children's perceptions of illness has been drawn from a number of research traditions. Theories relating to children have to accommodate changes in understandings over time, and take into account developmental processes. Accordingly, some theorists have argued that children's understandings of illness mirror more general cognitive changes over time. These theories have adopted the 'stage' model of Piaget. Others have argued that children's developing understandings of illness are more idiosyncratic and reflect their encounters with disease and illness. Among adults, various research approaches have been used to study concepts of health and illness, including ethnographic, symbolic interactionist, and more cognitive methodologies. In addition, recent research has focused on the cognitive processes underlying the strategies we use to cope with both acute and chronic illness. Each of these issues is considered in the chapter. In addition, the role of cognitions in mediating the experience of pain is considered. When Melzack and Wall first developed their integrated model of pain, it encountered considerable resistance from those who continued to argue for a purely physiological model of the perception of pain. Now, however, the evidence that cognitions play an important role in the pain experience is overwhelming. Some of the relevant literature is reviewed.

This chapter considers:

◆ Children's understandings of health and illness

◆ Adults' understandings of health and illness

◆ Coping with illness

◆ A cognitive model of pain

Children's understandings of health and illness

Two major theoretical stances have been adopted in the study of children's understandings of health and illness. One important research approach is rooted in the work of Piaget. Those who have adopted this approach (for example, Bibace and Walsh 1980) suggest that children's understandings of health and illness follow an invariant developmental sequence, mirroring more general and equally sequential cognitive changes. More environmentalist explanations (for example, Eiser 1989) suggest they are driven by children's experiences of health and illness.

Stage theory

According to Bibace and colleagues, the first stage of understanding illness, corresponding to the Piagetian phase of pre-operational thinking, occurs between the ages of 5 and 7 years. (The age ranges identified for each type of thinking are very general as there is considerable variation at what age children achieve each stage of illness representation.) The first stage is dominated by thoughts of magic or punishment. Illness is seen as a result of magic, witchcraft, or as a punishment for not obeying parental instructions: a phenomenon known as imminent justice. During this time, there is also the emergence of an understanding that illnesses can be contagious, though the child may over-extend this principle to assume that *all* illnesses are contagious. The child explains illness solely in terms of any phenomenon that they have associated with it without clear differentiation between cause and effect.

The next stage of beliefs corresponds to the concrete-operational stage. During this stage, typically between the ages of 8 and 10 years, the child begins to consider the mechanisms of disease. He or she can describe the experience of symptoms and explain their cause in terms of external agents or events, through contamination, and that they involve the body as a whole: 'You catch a cold by going out in the wet weather . . . It stays in your body . . . and goes up into your chest.' They understand a germ theory of disease causation and begin to realize that not all diseases are contagious. They acknowledge a limited number of causal agents in precipitating illness. They are also beginning to identify the processes through which illness affects the individual, focusing on explanations describing how mechanical actions lead to changes in specific internal body parts: 'You catch a cold from germs getting into your lungs and clogging them up. You sneeze to get the germs out.'

By the age of 11 years, the child develops an abstract understanding of disease and realizes that illness can result from the failure of a specific body part. By this time, they have a sophisticated understanding of the physiological processes underlying the disease: 'A cold involves symptoms such as . . .'; 'You catch the germs that are all around us. Coughing and running nose are the side-effects of the body's fighting them off. It makes mucus to carry away dead germs.' Around the age of 14 years, some children begin to recognize that disease may be a consequence of psychological stress.

While the theory is attractive in that it presents a parsimonious explanation of children's developing concepts of illness, the specifics of this stage approach and the methodology used to develop it have been strongly criticised. Bird and Podmore (1990), for example, noted that there were several aspects of Bibace and Walsh's work that questioned the validity of its findings. Perhaps the most important methodological shortcoming was their failure to code children's responses using a Piagetian-levels coding scheme, as many of the children's answers to their questions were too short to allow such analysis. Further challenges to their theory are provided by a number of studies that have failed to support a Piagetian approach. Dimigen and Ferguson (1993), for example, failed to find a strong relationship between Piagetian stages and children's understandings of the nature of cancer.

While Bibace found evidence of age sequential processing in children's understanding of AIDS, work by Aggleton and colleagues revealed adolescents to have relatively unsophisticated understandings of HIV transmission, although the research was done in the early days of public awareness of AIDS. Warwick *et al.* (1988) identified three models of causation in this group: miasmatic ('there's a lot of it about . . .'; 'It's everywhere. You get it from the environment you live in, the people you mix with'): serependitious ('whether you fall prey to infection depends on chance or luck'): and endogenous ('like cancer, it's in everyone from the start, just waiting to be brought out').

Magical thinking, too, is not confined to young children: many adults believe at some level that an illness they are experiencing is because they are a 'bad person'. Even Bibace found that college students evidenced an extreme range of illness conceptions, from the lowest magical levels to the mature psychophysiological stage, across a variety of illnesses. Such evidence presents significant problems to a stage theory of illness cognitions and has led a number of researchers to suggest that children's understandings of illness are better explained by accumulated increases in knowledge than by a qualitative shift from one cognitive stage to another (see, for example, Eiser 1989).

An alternative explanation for the phenomena described by Bibace and colleagues can be found in the work of Carey (1985). Carey acknowledged that children develop their behaviour and beliefs much as the Piagetian-based theory. However, she argued that beliefs change according to different principles. She suggested that from about 4 years of age children attempt to explain the function of the body in terms of wants and beliefs. Explanations of events are initially based on a 'naive psychology' of behaviour that shifts towards explanations based on a 'naive biology' as the child grows older. Accordingly, explanations of eating as a behavioural phenomenon ('You eat because your mum tells you it's ready') move to more biological explanations ('You eat because you need the food to keep your body healthy'). Thus explanations of health change too. Initial explanations in terms of behaviour or human action ('You get ill because you have done something wrong') change to more biological explanations ('You become ill because of germs').

The critical difference between Carey's and Bibace's explanations for the same phenomena is that Carey does not propose that a child's understandings of illness are constrained at a structural level (the Piagetian explanation). Rather, the beliefs are logical within the child's theory of intuitive knowledge of the world, which changes and develops as a function of their increasing understanding of human behaviour and biology.

Representations of illness and health

The theories addressed so far have focused on children's theories of illness causation. Moving beyond this focus, Goldman *et al.* (1991) sought to identify additional dimensions along which young children's conceptions of illness might be organized. To explore this issue, they interviewed a group of children aged between 4 and 6 years about their understandings of common illness. From their interviews, they identified five core characteristics of illnesses, which differed according to the illness being described. Children considered illnesses in terms of their causation, identity, consequences, probable duration and whether they were curable. These dimensions map strongly onto adult understandings of illness discussed in more detail later in this chapter. Less research has focused on children's understandings of health. In one such study, Normandeau *et al.* (1998) examined conceptions of health held by boys and girls of differing ages, socio-economic groups, and from urban and rural areas of France. Their findings indicated that children's conceptions of health were multidimensional, rooted in their daily experiences, and organized around three main dimensions: functionality, adherence to good 'health habits', and mental health. Again, these are very similar to adults' representations of health discussed later in the chapter.

Adults' representations of health and disease

Social representations of health

One of the first investigators to apply a social representation framework to the study of health was Herzlich (1973). She conducted detailed unstructured interviews with 80 French adults concerning their views of health and illness. She found that health was often taken for granted and only considered when contrasted with disease. Nevertheless, she was able to construct some elements of representations of health held by her study population. These focused on health as a state of equilibrium of various aspects of the individual, including physical and psychological well-being, evenness of temper, absence of fatigue, freedom of movement, effectiveness of action and good relations with other people.

Other ways of categorizing Herzlich's data categorize health as 'being', 'having' and 'doing'. 'Health as being' refers to the absence of illness: one is healthy if one is not ill. In contrast, 'health as having' considers health to be a positive asset, a reserve upon which one can draw at times of illness. These reserves allow an individual who is temporarily ill to be still regarded as 'healthy' as they have a reserve of health. 'Health as doing' represents functional fitness: the ability to carry out activities and duties. These categories have been replicated in subsequent studies, including one with working-class Scottish respondents.

Within this general framework, definitions of 'good health' differ across age and gender. Blaxter (1990) found that young men focused on health as being strong, active and fit. In contrast, while young women also placed an emphasis on fitness as a component of health, they saw health as more rooted in the social world. Liveliness and alertness, exemplified by not staying in bed and having good relationships with family and friends were considered indicators of good health. For men and women approaching middle age, concepts of health became more complex and diffuse, emphasizing a more rounded state encompassing both mental and physical well-being. This included such things as being happy, relaxed and living life to the full. The idea of vitality remained, but for older men this was expressed in terms of enthusiasm for paid work and for women in their ability to tackle housework. The importance of the social aspects of health was maintained in women, who continued to define health in terms of social fulfilment, including their attitude towards and their ability to get on with others.

Herzlich found that her study population represented illness along two dimensions: organic and behavioural or psychosocial. She also found that only when the organic components impinge on the individual's life will symptoms be considered as an illness: for most people the major criterion for illness is an enforced inability to engage in everyday activities. Individuals respond to health threats in a way consistent with three conceptions of illness: illness as destructive, as a liberator and as an occupation. Those who think of their illness as destructive consider it to be a threat to their social being as it excludes them from a social involvement from which they gain their self-esteem. In order to maintain their self-esteem they deny their illness and continue their involvement in society. Those who see their illness as a liberator consider it a reason to bow out from excessive demands being made of them: they become 'ill'. Those who see their illness as an occupation struggle against it. In its more active form, this involves the individual in attempts to participate in their own treatment. Their goal is to be a good patient and to do whatever is necessary to gain a cure.

On a micro-level of analysis, a number of studies have focused on understandings of particular illnesses. In some cases, these are dramatic. Cancer and AIDS, for example, are closely associated with death. Cancer is often described as an 'eating away disease': something separate from the individual, which has a life of its own. The language we use may also lead to inappropriate social constructions of disease. Using the example of hypertension, Blumhagen (1980) noted that its name provides a powerful suggestion that hyperactivity and tension are key symptoms and causes of the disorder. This, in turn, suggests that stress is the cause, and stress management a potential way of curing or controlling the disorder.

Cognitive representations of disease

A more formal cognitive methodology has been used by Leventhal and colleagues to determine how individuals represent and cope with the threat of disease (see, for example, Nerenz and Leventhal 1983). Leventhal's self-regulation model is similar to the more general coping models discussed in Chapter 2 in that it assumes that the individual faced with a health problem will be motivated to reduce any consequent emotional distress and return to a state of equilibrium by engaging in a variety of coping strategies. In contrast to more general models, it focuses uniquely on how the individual represents and responds to the threat carried by illness.

The model identified a number of stages following divergent, but interacting, pathways. The first stage, termed representation, concerns the reception and interpretation of information in order to develop an understanding of the health threat. It is based on information gleaned from a variety of sources, including the signs and symptoms of illness, and information from doctors and others in the individual's social sphere concerning the illness's diagnosis and nature.

Leventhal initially identified four dimensions along which individuals represent the nature of their illness: its identity, consequences, causes and time-line. Understandings of illness identity can involve both abstract labels, typically the name of the disease, and signs and symptoms such as bleeding or pain. The consequences may be physical, social, economic and emotional. Causes may be both internal, including genetic factors, and external environmental causes, such as work, stress or dietary factors. Finally, the time-line focuses on the chronicity of the illness or illness threat. Illnesses may be considered as a single acute episode, a cyclic process with recurrences, or chronic, where the disease is expected to be ongoing for some considerable duration. Nerenz and Leventhal (1983) suggested that most illness episodes are initially represented as acute, although representations may change over the course of the illness, moving through intermediate and then chronic representations if appropriate. Leventhal and colleagues found, for example, that 29 per cent of women with metastatic breast cancer considered their illness to be acute and curable during the early cycles of chemotherapy. Six months later, only 11 per cent held this view. Representations may differ markedly from traditional medical conceptions of disease. Many chronic asthmatics consider their asthma to be an acute illness: presumably they do not think of themselves as ill or asthmatic while they are symptom-free.

Other researchers have identified similar factor structures in representations of illness. Turk *et al.* (1986) identified four dimensions: its seriousness, personal responsibility for cause and cure, controllability, and changeability. Turk suggested that these represent a more personal, emotional, appraisal of the illness than the dimensions identified by Leventhal. Lau and Hartman (1983) identified a further factor: that of curability or controllability. They also suggested that the time-line factor was the weakest component of the model. Despite these differences, there is an increasing consensus that five dimensions form the basis of our understandings of a wide range of diseases, from the common cold to chronic to severe conditions including CHD and cancer. They are:

◆ disease identity;
◆ its consequences;
◆ its causes;
◆ its timeline;
◆ its curability or controllability.

Nerenz and Leventhal (1983) warned that despite a generic underlying structure, illness representations are not always well integrated and not necessarily complete. Only some dimensions may be present. Heijmans and deRidder (1998), for example, were able to discriminate between the illness representations of patients with chronic fatigue syndrome and Addison's disease. In patients with chronic fatigue syndrome, a four-factor solution was identified with manageability, seriousness, personal responsibility and external cause as the factors. In patients with Addison's disease a four-factor solution was also identified but here the factors were seriousness, cause, chronicity and controllability. Even when an individual has included all the dimensions in their illness representation, the dimensions need not be consistent: the time-line may disagree with a disease identity, for example, and both may be at odds with the perceived cause.

Attributions of stress as causal appear to be almost ubiquitous throughout a variety of diseases and conditions, including epilepsy, breast cancer and rheumatoid arthritis. Fielding (1987), for example, asked patients to identify factors that contributed to their MI. The most common explanations were stress, worry and tension. Other more medically validated explanations such as smoking or high cholesterol were much less endorsed. These attributions may be a defensive attribution reducing personal blame and attributing the incident to short-term, changeable external factors. However, they hold for other diseases. Taylor *et al.* (1984) asked women with breast cancer whether they had 'some sort of theory about how they got cancer'. Ninety-five per cent of the women were able to provide some theory of causation. These fell into six main categories: stress, endorsed by 41 per cent of the women; a specific carcinogen, 32 per cent; heredity, 26 per cent; diet, 17 per cent; and blow to the breast, 17 per cent. Fifty-six per cent of respondents felt that they had some degree of control over their illness; 68 per cent thought that someone else had control over their cancer.

Disease prototypes

The Leventhal model suggests a number of ways in which we move from the perception of a set of symptoms to labelling them as disease: we utilize information provided by doctors and other relevant sources. A further process by which we label clusters of symptoms as diseases is by comparing them with prototypes or schemata of disease (Bishop 1987). Disease prototypes are not clearly defined categories; rather, they are fuzzy sets, and individuals appear to match their symptoms to the prototypes on the basis of family resemblance rather than exact matches. The more symptoms a person has that correspond to a disease prototype the more likely they are to interpret these symptoms as an indication of that disease. Disease prototypes mirror illness representations, with the dimensions of identity and cause being the most important in defining illness. Bishop also identified a number of dimensions into which physical symptoms are categorized in such prototypes. The first dimension reflects the degree to which symptoms are considered contagious or virally caused. The second dimension involves the location of the symptoms. The third considers possible psychological causation, while the final one involves consideration of the extent to which the symptoms may cause disruption of activity.

Individual differences in representations of disease

At any given time, between 70 and 90 per cent of the population have a medical condition that is diagnosable and potentially treatable. The vast majority do not seek any form of treatment. Even among people who report feeling ill, only 40 per cent seek medical aid. The relationship between the development of symptoms and the interpretation of such symptoms as warranting seeking medical treatment is only modest. However, there are significant and enduring differences in the attention that people pay to internal events, and their likelihood of defining these as symptoms of disease (Pennebaker 1992). Trait neuroticism or negative affect increases the risk of an individual both being aware of symptoms and labelling them as symptoms. Bennett *et al.* (1996), for example, examined the differences between two groups of individuals who presented in a hospital casualty department complaining of chest pain, subsequently diagnosed as being an MI or non-cardiac chest pain. The latter group had higher neuroticism and symptom awareness scores than the former, whose scores did not differ from those of a matched general population group.

Transient factors, such as mood and social context, can also play a critical role in these processes. Depressed patients are likely to exhibit biased processing of negative illness-related information. The salience of symptoms within the individual's environment may also moderate their reporting of such symptoms: a majority of medical students report having at least one of the diseases they are studying in the course of their training period. The influence of contextual factors on the experience and reporting of pain provides further evidence of how affect and context can influence individuals' awareness of physical sensations (see below).

Stress may also play a moderating role in the awareness and interpretation of symptoms. Cameron *et al.* (1995) found that in a sample of 45–90 year olds, frequency of care-seeking was high when an ambiguous symptom such as headache or fatigue occurred in the presence of chronic life stress. When both stressor and symptom were new, the frequency of care-seeking was low. A strong temporal association between the onset of stress and symptoms signified that the symptoms were stress-related and most people did not seek medical help. Where the ambiguous symptoms occurred against a background of chronic stress, this interpretation was considered less likely and the patients were more likely to seek medical help.

The outcomes of appraisals

Illness representations may predict mood, behavioural responses to illness and, where behaviour will influence the disease process, disease outcome. They may be more strongly associated with levels of disability than with the coping strategies used by patients to manage their condition (Heijmans 1998). In addition, representations have been found to explain more of the variance in reported pain and disability levels than medically confirmed measures of disease activity, such as degenerative changes on X-rays and so on.

Illness representations may impact directly on mood. Heijmans (1998), for example, reported that patients with chronic fatigue syndrome who believed their illness to be serious, that they had little or no control over it, and saw little possibility of a cure, reported greater mental health problems and less vitality than those with the opposite constellation of beliefs. A similar finding was reported in patients who had multiple sclerosis (Schiaffino *et al.* 1998). In contrast, external attributions of disease causality have been associated with less distress and depression than attributions of a psychosocial or behavioural origin among individuals with lung cancer.

Illness representations may interact with disease variables to influence mood. Schiaffino found that patients with progressive rheumatoid arthritis who saw their condition as potentially curable or who saw themselves as responsible for their deterioration reported significant increases in depression over time. If patients expected the consequences of their condition to be serious, and they were, they were highly likely to be depressed. Disconfirmation of their fear resulted in low levels of depression. When the arthritis was initially viewed as only moderately serious, illness progression was associated with particularly high levels of depression. Internal control beliefs may result in less disability but carry the cost of lower mood. Schiaffino and Revenson (1992) found that when beliefs about rheumatoid arthritis controllability were high, attributions for the cause of a symptom flare that were internal, global and stable were linked to greater depression scores but less disability than the opposite constellation of beliefs.

One of the earliest studies to examine the effects of illness representations on behaviour found that patients undergoing cardiac surgery who considered themselves as having a long-term illness appeared depressed and were unlikely to engage in a rehabilitation programme. Those who considered themselves 'at risk' were more likely to engage in rehabilitation and health-promoting practices. Meyer *et al.* (1985) identified patients' representations of high blood pressure and their influence on adherence to antihypertensive medication. Contrary to medical opinion, patients claimed to be able to identify a number of symptoms of hypertension, including warmth, dizziness and flushing. The longer that individuals had been identified as hypertensive, the more likely they were to monitor and label such experiences as symptoms. One-quarter of those interviewed considered their condition to be acute, and one-third considered it to be cyclic. Those most likely to adhere to the recommended treatment were newly diagnosed patients who considered their condition to be a chronic one. Perhaps surprisingly, long-standing patients who considered their condition to be chronic were less likely to adhere to their medication regimen: perhaps because of a fear of long-term medication use (see below). Patients who experienced what they considered to be a reduction in symptoms were most likely to drop out of treatment, believing themselves to be cured.

In a further study of cardiac patients, Petrie *et al.* (1996) found that patients' attendance at a cardiac rehabilitation course was significantly related to a strong belief during admission that their condition could be cured or controlled. They also found that return to work within six weeks was predicted by the perception that the illness would last a short time and have only minimal negative consequences. Patients' beliefs that their heart disease would have serious consequences was significantly related to later disability in work, around the house, in their recreational activities and social interactions. Finally, a strong illness identity was significantly related to greater sexual dysfunction at both three- and six-month follow-up. Illness representations may even impact on the outcome of disease. Affleck *et al.* (1987) found the attributions of cardiac patients seven weeks following their MI were predictive of their health outcomes eight years later. Those who attributed the MI to stress were more likely to have a further MI than those who did not: perhaps because their external attribution did not prompt them to take action to reduce their future risk of reinfarction.

Treatment beliefs

People seem to hold stable beliefs about medicines, and the majority have a negative orientation towards them. Echabe *et al.* (1992), for example, found 70 per cent of a representative sample of nearly 1000 participants to hold an 'against medicine' orientation. Only 12 per cent expressed a strong positive orientation towards medicines, the rest having some degree of ambivalence.

A critical determinant of adherence to a medication regimen is its perceived effectiveness. This may be particularly pertinent where the consequences of a failure to take medication are not immediately apparent: for example, in the cases of antiretroviral medication to prevent HIV progression, antihypertensive medication, and even antibiotics once the obvious signs of illness have gone. Beliefs about effectiveness can be confounded by beliefs about side-effects, with patients engaging in a cost/benefit analysis when making choices about medication usage (Horne 1997). Such analyses may be quite sophisticated and take into account a number of beliefs about medication. More effective medications, for example, implicitly have more side-effects. This may make high levels of side-effects acceptable, even on occasion desirable. Leventhal *et al.* (1986) found that some women receiving chemotherapy for breast cancer found the absence of side-effects distressing as it implied that the treatment regimen was not sufficiently powerful. However, those taking longer-term medications may be less willing to accept side-effects. Siegel *et al.* (1999) found that HIV positive men and women withheld taking their antiretroviral medication if they considered it to make them sicker or to have greater risks than benefits. A further reason for not taking their medication was the belief that the medication was not having any effect. This is a particularly concerning finding, as many medications do not make identifiable changes to symptoms, yet are essential to the effective treatment of a variety of conditions.

Other frequently held beliefs reflect an expectation of diminishing effectiveness over time. Donovan and Blake (1992), for example, found many rheumatology patients to be concerned that their pain medication would become less effective over time. A similar concern was found in a

sample of HIV positive men in the context of their antiretroviral medication. Many people believe that continual taking of tablets is in itself
harmful. Morgan and Watkins (1988), for example, found that a number
of patients receiving antihypertensive medication stopped taking it for
periods of up to a few months at a time in order to give their body a
break from medication.

Coping with illness

A central tenet to the Leventhal model is that illness representations
are representations of threat, and both influence mood and motivate
behaviour intended to reduce the threat potential carried by the disease.
Leventhal *et al.* (1997) state that the experience of illness sets off two
parallel response processes (see Figure 4.1). One set of procedures involves
responding to cognitive representations of disease threat, and processing
and coping with fear or other emotional reactions to illness. The second
procedures involve coping with the implications of the disease itself.

Both sets of processing involve developing strategies to reduce distress
or enhance disease control. The system is recursive, so the effectiveness of
each procedure is monitored, allowing for changing strategies over time
should this be necessary. The two systems work in parallel and interact
in complex ways, and any coping strategy used may impact on either or
both of these systems. Leventhal *et al.* (1997) provided the example of
taking aspirin for a headache to indicate the complex cognitive work

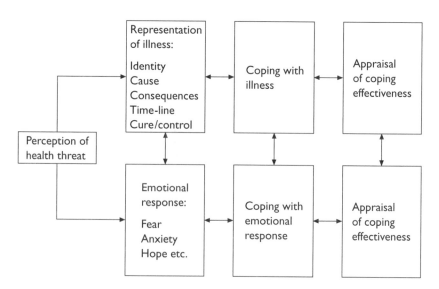

Figure 4.1   Leventhal's model of representation and coping with illness

involved in even such a simple action. Taking an aspirin to relieve a stress-induced headache leads to an expectation of symptom relief within a given timeframe. By removing the symptom and the emotional distress associated with it, the need to call on others for assistance is obviated and the initial hypothesis, that it is stress-related headache, is confirmed. If, however, the response is ineffective, works too slowly or for too brief a time, it may suggest alternative representations of the problem, such as a migraine or stroke. These potential alternatives will stimulate additional searching for symptoms, such as impaired vision, and may suggest the need for further action, including taking stronger painkillers or visiting the doctor. It may also increase the threat value carried by the symptoms and increase anxiety levels.

Most researchers have not explored the complexities of a recursive system and have focused instead on the relationship between coping strategies and a single outcome at one point in time. Dunkel-Schetter *et al.* (1992) found that 55 per cent of male and female patients with cancer reported having no primary coping strategy. Of those reported, all involved emotion-focused strategies: 42 per cent used distancing, 22 per cent used 'positive focus', 19 per cent used social support, and 17 per cent used cognitive escape/avoidance. In a more fine-grain analysis of patients with cancer, Heim *et al.* (1987) found that the nature of the threat carried by cancer and the coping strategies used to deal with it differed according to the stage of the cancer, with greater use of active coping strategies, including problem solving or positive reappraisal, occurring in the earlier stages of the disease and more avoidant strategies as the disease advances. In a very different population, Brown *et al.* (1995) found that adolescents who were HIV infected as a consequence of blood transfusion became upset or angry when they encountered reminders of their HIV status. In response to this, their most frequently used strategies were resignation, self-calming and distraction. The least frequently used strategies were self-blame, engaging in risky behaviours, and drug or alcohol use. The most effective strategies were cognitive restructuring, seeking social support, and physical activity; least effective were passive strategies such as wishful thinking and blaming others.

Both problem- and emotion-focused coping strategies can be effective in reducing distress. In addition, different coping strategies may help individuals to cope with different aspects of disease, and may work in apparently contradictory ways. It has been estimated that up to 80 per cent of the coping efforts used by people with diabetes involve active coping strategies. However, this may be at the cost of mental well-being. Sinzato *et al.* (1985) found that individuals with diabetes who used passive or avoidant coping strategies reported lower levels of depression and anxiety than those who used active coping strategies, but evidenced less disease control. Avoiding the distress of demanding adaptive tasks may help to maintain emotional equilibrium, but at the cost of future disease complications. Maes and Schlosser (1987) illustrated some of the problems associated with the use of apparently appropriate coping strategies at inappropriate times. They found that asthmatics who maintained a restrictive lifestyle as a consequence of focusing on their illness, but who reacted emotionally during an asthma attack fared less well than those with the opposite constellation of coping strategies.

The threat value of illness is governed by the illness representations that the individual holds. Maes *et al.* (1996) identified a number of illnesses as carrying high threat levels, which require complex revision of the self and its relation to the social context, and may require substantial emotion-focused coping efforts. These include metastatic cancer and AIDS. Lesser health threats, which have less impact and may benefit from the use of more active coping strategies, include asthma and diabetes. Maes and colleagues argued for the development of a model which directly ties individual coping attempts to the illness representations that the individuals hold. The beginnings of this specific link can be found in work which has shown beliefs about the lack of controllability of an illness to be related to avoidant, emotion-focused coping, about changeability to be related to problem-oriented forms of coping, and ambiguity of outcome to passive forms of emotion-focused coping (see Maes *et al.* 1996).

Inter-relationship of illness cognitions and other schemata

Illness schemata do not arise *de novo*. Their nature is influenced by other, pre-existing schemata, and their emotional and behavioural consequences are governed by interactions with these schemata, which may come from a variety of domains. Interactions with beliefs about treatment have already been noted. Beliefs about the competence or trustworthiness of doctors may influence willingness to accept a diagnosis and the model of illness presented by the diagnosing physician. Health locus of control beliefs and beliefs about one's competence to cope, or value as a person may also powerfully mediate reaction to illness. Moorey and Greer (1989) noted that the belief 'I am defective' in response to a diagnosis of cancer typically led to a passive acceptance of illness and a failure to engage in appropriate health-related behaviour. Beliefs about the social context that the individual inhabits, including the acceptability or otherwise of illness and illness-behaviours, may strongly influence the reporting of illness and the coping behaviours adopted. A full understanding of reactions to illness needs to incorporate an assessment of these other, potentially interacting belief systems as well as the appraisals of illness identified by Leventhal.

A cognitive model of pain

Perhaps the most thorough consideration of the inter-relationship between cognitive and physiological processes has been developed in the 'gate

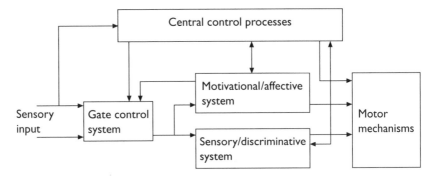

Figure 4.2   Melzack and Wall's gate theory of pain perception

control' theory of pain developed by Melzack and Wall (1965). This model described the integration of peripheral stimuli with cortical variables such as mood or anxiety in the perception of pain. It suggested that pain is neither entirely somatic nor entirely psychogenic: instead, both factors have either potentiating or moderating effects on pain perception.

Gate control theory suggests that the experience of pain is an ongoing sequence of activities, largely reflexive in nature but modifiable even in the earliest stages by a variety of excitatory and inhibitory influences. The model is based on the following propositions (see also Figure 4.2):

- The transmission of nerve impulses from afferent fibres to spinal cord transmission cells is modulated by a spinal gating system in the dorsal horn.
- The spinal gating mechanism is influenced by the relative amount of activity in large-diameter and small-diameter fibres: activity in the large fibres tends to inhibit transmission (close the gate) while small-fibre activity tends to facilitate transmission.
- The spinal gating mechanism is also influenced by nerve impulses that *descend* from the brain (the psychological input).
- A specialized system of large-diameter fibres (the central control trigger) activates selective cognitive processes that then influence, through descending fibres, the modulating properties of the spinal gating mechanism.
- When the output of the spinal cord transmission cells exceeds a critical level, the action system is activated. This triggers those neural areas that underlie the somatic experiences and behaviour associated with pain.

The model as stated had problems in accommodating the pain experienced by paraplegics and patients with phantom limb pain in areas of the body below the level of a spinal lesion. This has led Melzack to develop a more complex model of pain and pain generation known as the neuromatrix (see Melzack 1996).

The next section focuses on some of the cognitive factors that have been shown to influence the experience of pain. Melzack's theory does not specify the exact nature of these cognitions; however, a number of differing categories of cognitions have been shown to influence such experiences.

Beliefs about the nature and causes of pain appear to influence both the experience of pain and pain-related behaviour. Patients with cancer frequently increase the number of complaints of pain they make once they know their diagnosis. Here, the diagnosis of cancer may legitimize complaints of pain and result in those previously withheld being expressed. More central cognitive factors may be involved in the higher pain severity ratings made by patients who attributed changes in pain to disease progression when compared with those who assigned more benign interpretations to such changes (Spiegel and Bloom 1983). Cassell (1982) cited a clear case of the power of attributions in determining pain experience, with the case history of a patient whose pain could be easily controlled with codeine when he attributed it to sciatica, but required significantly greater amounts of opioids to achieve the same degree of relief when he attributed it to metastatic cancer.

Many patients establish strong pain schemata that they are unwilling to test and which remain unchallenged and very difficult to modify. Council et al. (1988), for example, found that 83 per cent of patients with low back pain reported that they were unable to complete a movement sequence including leg lifts and lateral bends because of anticipated pain: only 5 per cent were unable to complete the activities because of lack of ability. A large proportion of chronic pain patients believe that they have only limited control over their pain. Such negative, maladaptive appraisals about their situation and their personal efficacy may reinforce the experience of demoralization, inactivity and overreaction to nocireceptive simulation. Newton and Barbaree (1987) used a thought-sampling procedure to evaluate the nature of patients' cognitions during and immediately following headache both prior to and following treatment. Prior to treatment, patients typically engaged in a series of negative self-statements, often referring to their control over the pain: 'It's getting worse. There's nothing I can do.' Complaints about more intense pain were associated with a higher frequency of such statements. Those patients who gained most from the intervention also evidenced the greatest changes in their cognitive dialogue. More general cognitive errors are also apparent in patients who report significant chronic pain. Lefebvre (1981) found that lower back pain patients were more likely to make a number of 'cognitive errors' in response to a variety of stressors unrelated to pain. These included catastrophizing (assuming the outcome of events will be particularly negative), overgeneralization (assuming the outcome of one event necessarily applies to other future events), and personalization (interpreting negative events as reflecting personal meaning or responsibility).

Summary and conclusions

We each carry a cognitive representation of our own and others' health. This representation carries a strong psychosocial component: health permits us to engage in both physical and social activities. Cognitions have also proven to be a powerful determinant of both our emotional and behavioural responses to illness. The beliefs we have about illness and their associated emotions may, in some cases, prove to be more powerful determinants of the outcomes of disease than the underlying physiological processes. Such findings emphasize the need for those involved in the care of patients to have an understanding of the psychological processes influencing patient behaviour and provides a strong justification for the interventions aimed at changing health-related cognitions discussed later in this book.

Further reading

Petrie, K. and Weinman, J.A. (1997) *Perceptions of Health and Illness*. Chur: Harwood.

Zeidner, M. and Endler, N.S. (1996) *Handbook of Coping. Theory, Research, Applications*. New York: Wiley.

Part III
Applied health psychology

5 ◆ Hospital issues

Health psychology is intimately associated with the provision of health care and has developed an understanding of many of the elements that impinge on the individual as they become ill and enter the health care system. It has also developed an understanding of how these processes may, on occasion, be manipulated to maximize the well-being and appropriate care of patients, which is the focus of the next chapter. This chapter examines the understanding we have of some of these factors.

The chapter addresses:

◆ The experience of hospitalization

◆ Coping with a diagnosis and mortality

◆ Patient and staff interactions

◆ Adherence

◆ Medical decision making

◆ Stress and the hospital system

The experience of hospitalization

Entry into hospital is generally considered a stressful experience, initiated by the onset of symptoms not treatable at home or by the need for specialist investigations or treatments. It carries with it not only the potential threat to health, but also uncertainty over treatments and their associated pain and discomfort, being away from home, loss of control over everyday functions and privacy, and increased dependency on others. Reactions to hospitalization are complex. Engaging in the hospital system is a process of socialization: one adopts the role of the patient. Patients are expected to be co-operative, pleasant and quiet. They turn much of the responsibility for their day-to-day behaviour over to others, and are expected to follow the instructions of others. They believe, probably quite correctly, that physicians expect co-operation, trust and confidence, while nurses expect them to be undemanding, respectful and considerate. A key goal of many patients is to conform to these expectations and to 'behave properly'. About 25 per cent of patients fall into the 'good patient' category. These people have simple medical problems, are uncomplaining, and take up little staff time. 'Average patients' are much like good patients, although they express some minor complaints that could usually be handled routinely. 'Bad patients' fall into two categories: those who were seriously ill and complain, and those who were not seriously ill but complain anyway. The latter can provoke high levels of irritation and even anger among staff.

Staff-defined good and bad behaviour has significant implications for the care given to patients. Negative labels may result in condescension towards or avoidance of particular patients. Less benign reactions may involve inappropriate medication or even inappropriate discharge from hospital. However, both 'good' and 'bad' behaviour may hide adverse psychological reactions to the health care environment. Good or passive behaviour, defined in terms of compliant passivity, may reflect some degree of learned helplessness and depression. Associated with this may be an impaired inability to concentrate on and retain new information, and a failure to provide relevant health information. This may hinder rehabilitation or increase the risk of medical complications. Bad behaviour, defined by repeated information-seeking and complaints to staff, may reflect high levels of anxiety or concern about diagnosis or treatment. Paradoxically, both types of behaviour may serve to reduce appropriate staff contact and lead to continuing problems.

Hospitalization of children

For children, there are many fears and concerns associated with hospitalization. Some, such as fear of stressful medical procedures or pain, are similar to those of adults. However, children may also experience a number of other fears as a consequence of previous separation experiences and their lack of understanding of hospitals.

A variety of factors may influence the experiences of children in hospital. These include contextual factors, such as the type of ward, its architecture and facilities for parental contact, the child's previous experience or knowledge of hospitalization, and child and parent factors. Previous hospitalizations may have negative effects, especially if the child has experienced painful or distressing procedures. For children with chronic diseases, continued contact with their parents seems critical to a good psychological outcome. However, high levels of supportive nursing care and continuity of care may, to some extent, offset lack of parental contact in some cases. Schmidt (1997) reported a study conducted by Sail (1988) that analysed the emotional reactions of children aged between $1\frac{1}{2}$ and $4\frac{1}{2}$ years receiving elective surgery with and without rooming-in. Rooming-in only benefited children under the age of 3 years.

One admission into hospital, even for a period of up to a month, appears to confer no substantial risk for long-term emotional or behavioural problems at home or school. However, repeat admissions may be accompanied by some form of emotional or behavioural disturbance, although this typically reduces in severity the more remote the period of time spent in hospital.

Coping with a diagnosis

Coping with a medical diagnosis is akin to dealing with any other threat. Accordingly, a variety of psychological processes are likely to be initiated. That is, the individual appraises the potential threat carried by a diagnosis, responds emotionally and develops coping strategies to reduce the perceived threat. Moos and Schaefer (1984) suggested that the threat conferred by a diagnosis of serious illness is characterized by a number of factors, including a threat to identity in which the individual may move from a capable, autonomous agent to that of patient, dependent on others. It may threaten future plans and carries the threat of removal from one's own home and social support network. It may also carry the future threat of pain and unknown medical procedures. Threat is likely to be highest where the future is unknown, the individual has little knowledge of the illness, and the onset of illness is rapid. These uncertainties can make it difficult for the individual to cope effectively with the threat of illness.

Following the appraisal of threat, the individual engages in coping strategies to minimize any emotional discomfort. Moos and Schaefer suggested a number of goals that patients set themselves to achieve at this stage:

◆ coping with pain and other symptoms;
◆ coping with the hospital environment and treatment procedures;
◆ developing effective relationships with those involved in providing care;
◆ preserving an emotional balance;
◆ preserving self-image, competence and mastery;
◆ maintaining relationships with family and friends;
◆ preparing for an uncertain future.

Moos and Schaefer suggested a different, albeit similar, categorization of coping strategies to those of Lazarus and others. These were appraisal-focused, problem-focused and emotion-focused coping. Appraisal-focused coping involves the individual in attempts to break down the situation into manageable components, redefining it in a way that makes it more manageable, and in denial or avoidance. Problem-focused coping includes seeking information and support, and using the information to maximize the chances of achieving the goals set. Finally, emotion-focused coping involves maintaining hope, emotional discharge and acceptance. If successful, these coping strategies will lead to healthy adaptation and improvements in affect and effective coping behaviours. Failure to achieve any identified goal is likely to result in a deterioration of mood and reduced coping efforts. Just as there are prototypes of illness, there appears also to be prototypes of what constitutes coping well with disease, with maintaining autonomy and acceptance being the most important factors (DeRidder *et al.* 1997). Ill people may measure their coping not just in terms of how well they reduce the distress associated with illness but also by comparing their strategies with prototypes of how they consider the particular stresses they face should be dealt with.

A number of authors have suggested that there are few differences between the levels of distress experienced by patients diagnosed with diseases as disparate as cancer, rheumatoid arthritis, hypertension or diabetes. However, differences certainly appear in the reaction to various types of cancer. Patients with breast and gynaecological cancers, for example, appear less depressed or anxious than women with other forms of cancer, including those of the lung, gut or head and neck. Similarly, cancer patients with more extensive disease report greater mood disturbance than those with more limited disease. Whether such differences reflect different responses to illness, its treatment or both is unclear. Findings from Fallowfield *et al.* (1986) illustrate the complexity of such responses. They found that women who underwent mastectomy following a diagnosis of breast cancer reported lower levels of depression and anxiety than those who had a lumpectomy. This finding may not be immediately explicable: one may hypothesize that women who had the more mutilating treatment would experience the highest levels of depression. However, a possible explanation for such findings is that women who 'only' had a lumpectomy worried more about the possibility of recurrence than those who had more radical surgery.

Psychological factors may be more important in determining mood than the actual disease process. Those who consider their illness to be severe (regardless of its 'true' extent), who have a general pessimism about life, or are low on measures of hardiness are more likely to become depressed than others. Similarly, the frequency of negative intrusive thoughts appears to be more predictive of low mood in young women with breast cancer than time following diagnosis and the type of treatment received (Bloom *et al.* 1998). Perceptions of control over a potential breast cancer may also moderate the impact of breast symptoms on reports of breast cancer worry.

Psychological problems are not necessarily restricted to the patient.

One survey of cancer patients found that half their sample was clinically depressed, as were one-third of their spouses and one-quarter of their children, suggesting that psychological distress reverberates substantially throughout the nuclear family. High levels of psychological morbidity have also been reported in the spouses of people who have had an MI. These may be highest where the patient has denied their infarction. In such cases, partners may feel high levels of anxiety when their spouse engages in levels of physical exertion that they feel are inappropriate but which they are unable to control. In addition, many wives appear to inhibit angry or sexual feelings, and become overprotective of their husbands.

Mood and other psychological factors may contribute to long-term reactions to illness. Depression in hospital ten days after discharge following an MI has been associated with the number of cardiac symptoms reported at six-month follow-up, independently of any cardiological evidence of symptomatology. In addition, several studies have reported a negative association between levels of depression and return to work following MI. Myrtek et al. (1997), for example, compared men who returned to work with a matched sample of those who did not in a survey of cardiac patients one, three and five years post-infarction. No substantial differences were observed on any medical variables, but they did differ on a number of psychological and social factors. Retired patients were characterized by lower work satisfaction, complaints of being more handicapped by the disease, higher 'propensity for pension', more frequent complaints concerning their general state of health, and lower education levels. In terms of risk behaviours following an MI, depressed patients have been found to have lower rates of exercise, to smoke more and to adhere less to recommended treatment regimens than those who are not depressed. Finally, depression has been linked to high use of health care resources, including attendance at general practitioners' surgeries and readmission to hospital.

Coping with mortality

Some individuals will inevitably die of their illness. Most wish to know about their fate, but many doctors question the value of giving such information. The rule of thirds is often said to apply to such situations. Two-thirds of patients wish to know their prognosis and two-thirds of doctors do not wish to tell them. While this is a little trite, it accords with the available data. These data reflect, and also contribute to, some of the many problems faced by patients, their relatives and by the staff caring for the individual who is known to be dying. While it is potentially distressing for a doctor to tell a patient that they are dying, many patients are likely to acknowledge that they are dying without this formal process of information provision, but fail to discuss this with doctors and even their relatives. Not infrequently, relatives, but not the patient, are told of the likely prognosis, placing them in a distressing and ethically problematic situation. Hinton (1999) reported relevant data from a British hospice. The survey indicated that throughout the eight weeks prior to death, less than half of the patients surveyed were fully aware of their impending death. The percentage of relatives to be so aware rose from 53 to 81 per cent over this time.

Illnesses such as cancer and HIV tend to progress in stages. At each setback the patient is faced with another cluster of losses. Initially, the loss of security of body parts affected by the disease form the focus of the loss and can result in intense feelings of yearning for those parts. In the later stages of disease, increasing illness may cause loss of mobility, occupation and an increasing range of physical functions. In the last phase the patient faces the prospect of losing life itself and all the attachments that go with it.

Once told of their prognosis, the majority of people experience severe grief that may reduce even within the space of an hour or so. A minority will react with a more profound and prolonged depression, which may require some form of treatment. Kubler-Ross (1969) identified a more complex reactive process through which an individual passes. Initially, they experience shock and numbness. This is followed by a stage of denial and feelings of isolation. The individual may become angry or blaming, or bargain for goals that they wish to achieve before dying. Eventually, the person comes to some acceptance of their impending death. The popular understanding of Kubler-Ross's theory is that these proceed in an invariant and inevitable forward direction: although not all steps may be achieved before death. However, she did not regard these as discrete stages and observed that individuals can move backwards and forwards between each reaction, sometimes extremely quickly. Other models have also been proposed, including two key stages: fear of death, followed by depression concerning loss of life. Hinton's (1999) data suggested an overall move towards acceptance of death, although by the time of death only half the patients and two-thirds of the relatives who took part in the study were fully accepting of death. In addition, 18 per cent of patients and 24 per cent of relatives showed fluctuating or falling acceptance as death approached. Patients were more anxious if death seemed 'probable' rather than 'certain'.

Kubler-Ross identified a number of strategies that people use to cope with the knowledge of their impending death, including the emotion-focused coping strategies of denial and regression. Summing up the current understanding, the individual is likely to experience some or all of the above reactions. How well and by what strategies they cope will reflect how they coped with other stresses they experienced during life. Many may benefit from the use of more active coping strategies, including completing significant life tasks and ensuring the future for remaining family members.

Patient and hospital staff interactions

Professional/patient communications

Gaining information to make a diagnosis and giving information to facilitate patient understanding of the problem they are facing are central elements of the process of care. It should therefore be of some concern that these transactions are frequently less than optimal. Chaitchik *et al.* (1992), for example, found that following a consultation with their doctor, a significant percentage of oncology patients stated that they had gained hardly any new information concerning their illness and their overall state, and there remained information they still wanted to know. One-quarter of the participants reported reductions in anxiety about their condition, but this was replaced by anger about their treatment. Unfortunately, these findings are far from unique. Furthermore, they may have powerful implications for the well-being of patients. In a follow-up of 600 newly diagnosed cancer patients, Parle *et al.* (1996) found that one of the strongest predictors of later anxiety and depression was the number and severity of patients' unresolved concerns.

Despite such communication failures, between half and three-quarters of patients who want more information during a medical consultation do not ask for it. Possibly as a consequence of such a failure, between 7 and 53 per cent of people report not having fully understood the information they were given, or wanting more (see Ley 1997). The reasons for this failure are idiosyncratic to individual consultations but may be consequent to both health professional and patient behaviour. Some people may not prepare questions to ask the doctor or may not be able to develop and articulate them during the consultation. They may not ask questions because it is only later that they realize they need more information. Health professionals may actively inhibit questions by the use of closed questions and other non-verbal cues. This may be facilitated by some patients' reluctance to ask questions of a busy doctor: a frequent claim in hospital wards. In the hospital setting, poor communication may be exacerbated by a lack of clarity about who has permission to tell patients what information. Encouraging questioning can significantly influence the number of questions asked during an interview and adherence to any behavioural recommendations made (see Chapter 6). Of course, some people may not want information from the consultation: those who typically engage in emotion-focused or avoidant coping may prefer consultations where little information is provided.

Not only the content but also the way that content is framed can be a critical element of doctor/patient communication. When asked whether they would consider surgery under various probabilities of success for their hypothetical lung cancer, students, patients and even surgeons were more likely to choose surgery when the same outcome was presented in terms of the probability of surviving rather than dying (McNeil *et al.* 1982). The advice that doctors give to patients may also be influenced by a similar framing effect. Marteau (1989) found that medical students were more likely to recommend surgery to hypothetical patients if the information they had been given about the outcome of surgery had been framed in terms of survival rather than more negatively.

Health professionals differ in their beliefs and attitudes towards treatment and the patients they care for. Such biases may influence their relationship with patients and even the treatment choices they engage in. Some of these may be overt, namely some doctors' refusals to treat continuing smokers for smoking-related diseases. Others are more covert and may not even be the result of a conscious bias. Nurses offer pain medication less often to men than to women and are more likely to refuse men's requests for analgesia during the postoperative period than those of women. Similarly, physicians are more likely to recommend taking part in a cardiac rehabilitation programme to men than women.

Patients frequently place considerable emphasis on pain and on symptoms that interfere with their everyday activities: practitioners are more concerned with the severity and treatment of an underlying illness. As a consequence, patients may misunderstand the doctor's emphasis on factors they consider to be incidental, and pay little attention when vital information is being communicated. Alternatively, they may dismiss the practitioner's advice because they think they have made an incorrect diagnosis. Patients may also give practitioners faulty cues about their true concerns. A significant percentage of patients have concerns that they are suffering from serious diseases. Anticipating the worst, they present the symptom that is most worrying to them as something of minimal concern and frequently towards the end of the consultation.

In an attempt to develop evidence-based guidelines for the content of consultations in which information is given about a diagnosis and its treatment, Beeney *et al.* (1996) asked a large sample of diabetic patients about their concerns and information preferences at the time of their diagnosis. Sixty per cent of patients found the process of being told their diagnosis to be distressing and nearly 25 per cent wished for more emotional support at the time. Their conclusions were that clinicians giving a diagnosis of diabetes should be aware of patient variability in needs for emotional support and information preferences. They should ask patients about their preferences and offer choices if available, and should maximize patient involvement in discussions about treatments.

Memory for consultations

Memory for information given in medical consultations is not good. Ley (1997) summarized the findings of a number of studies conducted with patients and analogue subjects, reporting the average percentages of information recalled to vary between 47 and 54 per cent among hospital populations, rising to 65 per cent in general practice patients. The lowest rate of information recalled was just 7 per cent. Montgomery *et al.* (1999) provided relevant data from a different context. They interviewed 100 patients undergoing radiotherapy at a British regional oncology centre. Twenty-two could not remember signing a consent form for treatment: they were later verified as having done so. Of those who did recall completing the form, one-quarter could not remember being told of the side-effects of radiotherapy, and only half of those who did remembered the most frequent side-effect (tiredness).

Factors influencing memory are a function of both the individual receiving the information and the way in which information is given. One important factor is that patients may simply not understand the information given. There is frequently a mismatch between the language used by health professionals and that understandable to the patient. The potential enormity of this gap is perhaps best illustrated by many patients' ignorance of basic medical and anatomical knowledge. The percentages of patients understanding the meaning of arthritis, jaundice, palpitation and bronchitis have been found to be 85, 77, 52 and 80 per cent, respectively. Even in a well educated sample of students, half did not understand the meaning of anti-emetic, dilated, and haemorrhoids. The content of leaflets and booklets also frequently fails to increase understanding, as numerous studies have shown. Ley (1997) suggested that about one-quarter of published medical leaflets would be understood by only 20–30 per cent of the adult population.

Patients' memory of information given in the consultation is best when the information given fits with their preconceived ideas of the nature of the problem and the treatment required. The likelihood of errors is exacerbated when the patients' views are not explored. The manner in which information is given is a further mediator of the amount of information remembered. There are clear primacy and recency effects: information given first and last is remembered best. Statements that are considered important are better remembered. In addition, the more information that is given, the less that is likely to be retained. Ley (1997) identified a linear relationship between the amount of information given and the percentage recalled. Seventy-five per cent of information given in four statements is likely to be retained; only 50 per cent of information given in ten statements will be. Methods by which understanding and recall can be increased are discussed in Chapter 6.

Staff's ratings of patient mood

Ward staff are not good at assessing or monitoring the mood of patients on the ward. In an empirical test of this assertion, Lampic *et al.* (1996) asked nurses who had cared for particular patients for three days to rate the patients' anxiety levels. At the same time, the patients completed the same instrument. Their results showed very little agreement between the two measures, with the nurses tending to overestimate patient anxiety levels. The authors speculated that discrepancies between the two sets of measures may be explained by the 'requirement of mourning' hypothesis, which suggests that staff's estimation of patient anxiety was strongly associated with the nurses' estimation of their own hypothetical anxiety if they were to be in the patient's situation. Some evidence suggests that a better guide to patients' levels of distress may be the ratings of their fellow patients.

Adherence

Adherence to treatment

Adherence to any form of intervention involving some degree of behavioural choice is likely to be less than maximal. Only about 60 per cent of patients are likely to comply fully with medication regimens (see Ley 1997): adherence with complex or demanding interventions is likely to be even lower (see, for example, changes following screening advice discussed in Chapter 7). Even small increases in demands and complexity can impact adversely on adherence to medication regimens. Non-adherence rates as a function of patient error alone is about 15 per cent when one tablet is prescribed, 25 per cent when two or three are prescribed, rising to 35 per cent if five or more are prescribed. Even where the implications of non-adherence to medical regimens are serious, non-adherence rates can be high: 90 per cent of participants in an early AZT trial for the treatment of HIV, for example, dropped out voluntarily. The main reasons for this dropout were the complexity of the drug regimen and the need to make multiple clinic visits (Chesney and Folkman 1994). Even when AZT was a well established HIV treatment, about one-quarter of those prescribed it failed to follow the treatment regimen fully, with even higher non-adherence rates among the less well educated or minority groups. Malow et al. (1998), for example, found only 17 per cent of a sample of African-American, inner city and drug-abusing men to be fully adherent to combination antiretroviral therapies.

Non-adherence to required medication has a number of important sequelae.[1] The US Department of Health and Human Services estimated that non-adherence to medication may lead to between 10 and 20 per cent of patients requiring an otherwise unnecessary further prescription, and between 5 and 10 per cent requiring a further visit to the doctor or one or two days off work. A small but nevertheless significant number of people (between 0.25 and 1 per cent of patients) will require hospitalization as a consequence of not adhering to recommended medical treatments.

Explanations for this degree of non-adherence lie both within the characteristics of the intervention and with the individuals themselves. While some people carry an 'against medication' bias (see Chapter 4), adherence to treatment regimens appears to be the outcome of a more subtle interplay between the individual and the demands and characteristics of the required behaviour. The same individual may be non-adherent with one element of a treatment regimen while adhering fully with others: levels of adherence to dietary and fluid restrictions, for example, may vary markedly among individuals receiving renal dialysis.

Ley (1988) suggested that adherence is a function of three treatment factors: patients' understanding of the treatment regimen, their memory of the information provided, and their satisfaction with the consultation in which the information was given. Some of the implications of this model are discussed in Chapter 6. Other factors include the complexity of the treatment, patients' beliefs about the treatment and how they should cope with it, and the coping strategies they adopt to cope with their illness (see Chapter 4). Many cancer patients fail to take their analgesia for cancer-related pain not as a consequence of forgetfulness, but in the belief that pain should be tolerated, concerns about side-effects, and 'fear and disdain' of dependence, addiction and tolerance (see also Chapter 4).

Further moderating factors are the costs and benefits associated with adherence. Some interventions may be so distressing that many patients feel unable to comply with the demands being made upon them. Adherence to antiretroviral drugs may be powerfully influenced by the severity of their side-effects, as may be adherence to other highly demanding regimens such as chemotherapy. More subtle may be the less dramatic costs associated with drugs such as antihypertensive medication that can cause a variety of side-effects, none of which may be particularly problematic, but in the context of no obvious gains from treatment may be greater than is acceptable (Horne 1997).

Not surprisingly, just as levels of adherence to medication are low, so too are adherence rates with treatment programmes requiring patients to engage in new or time-consuming behaviours. Knowledge about disease is not, in itself, an important predictor of adherence. Katz *et al.* (1998), for example, found a significant inverse relationship between knowledge of disease and dietary compliance in a group of dialysis patients. However, a number of non-treatment factors are likely to impact on adherence. Some, such as illness representations and patient coping strategies, are discussed in Chapter 4. Patient outcome expectations and their perceived ability to achieve change, and the relative costs and benefits of engaging in a particular behavioural programme also form powerful determinants of levels of engagement: these issues are discussed in Chapter 3. Two further factors appear particularly relevant: affect and family support.

Affect may powerfully influence adherence. It is estimated, for example, that 50 per cent of cardiac patients in exercise programmes drop out within the first six months of treatment, and that one of the key predictors of dropout is emotional distress. Similarly, lower levels of adherence to recommended medical regimens have been found among depressed post-MI patients than among their non-depressed counterparts. In a different patient group, Friedman *et al.* (1998) found not only a high prevalence of psychiatric disorders among diabetic outpatients, but that the presence of these disorders was associated with impaired glycaemic control, frequent consultations, and poor compliance with a dietary regimen.

Family dynamics may also influence adherence to medical regimens. Parental involvement in blood glucose monitoring is significantly related to adherence to this regimen among adolescent patients. More complex dynamics may also affect compliance. TubianaRufi *et al.* (1998) found that children whose families were characterized as rigidly disengaged had a greater number of hypoglycaemic episodes and six times as many episodes of ketoacidosis than the other diabetic children. Similar family dynamics have been associated with adherence to medication and dietary adherence in paediatric kidney transplant patients. The role of the family in influencing outcome and adherence is not limited to young people. The uptake of preventive behaviours such as appropriate levels of exercise or dietary fat intake in cardiac patients is also governed, at least in part, by other family members.

Some of the factors influencing adherence to treatment regimens are summarised in Table 5.1.

Adherence among health professionals

It is not only patients who do not adhere to required behaviours. Health care workers can also be non-adherent to recommended practice. Most practitioners fail to follow recommended or required actions at some time or other. Between 12 and 76 per cent of medical practitioners, depending on the sample, fail to prescribe antibiotics appropriately, while only about 50 per cent provide the required information about their use (Ley 1988). Health professionals have also been found regularly to fail to adhere to behaviours as disparate as the provision of cancer screening tests, completing treatment, arranging necessary follow-up appointments and providing enough information about treatments.

Health care workers may also be non-adherent to behaviours relevant to their own safety. Elford and Cockcroft (1991) found that most of the medical students in their sample and about half the medical staff did not comply with hospital precautions against the transmission of HIV. Some of this non-compliance may simply result from lack of knowledge. It may also be a consequence of individuals' beliefs about the costs and benefits of engaging in the recommended behaviours. Valanis *et al.* (1991) found that few workers used protective garments when handling chemotherapy drugs, despite this being hospital policy, because they did not

Table 5.1 Some of the critical determinants of adherence to treatment recommendations[*]

Provider/patient interaction	Patient characteristics	Treatment factors
Explanation of required behaviours	Understanding of the treatment regimen	Demands on time and resources
Use of appropriate language	Beliefs about treatment	Costs and benefits of treatment
Breaking down explanation into manageable units	Coping characteristics	Treatment complexity
Use of memory aids	Memory of required behaviours	Treatment duration
Empathy achieved	Illness representations	Degree of behavioural change required
Patient satisfaction	Outcome and efficacy beliefs	
Degree of patient involvement in decision making	Mood	
	Family context	
	Previous behaviour	

* See also Chapter 6

believe that this carried any personal risk. Subjective norms and the hierarchical power structure of the health care system may also powerfully constrain behaviour either towards or against compliance with hospital rules. Nurses, for example, may defer to doctors' decisions even though they may result in non-compliance with legal or hospital requirements.

Medical decision making

Studies reviewed by Schwartz and Griffin (1986) revealed that doctors show substantial disagreement over the interpretation of single tests such as X-rays and electrocardiograms as well as more complex processes such as diagnosing depression. They will sometimes disagree with their own judgements. One study that asked pathologists to examine the same tissue sample on two occasions, for example, found that dichotomous decisions (malignant or benign) differed across 28 per cent of judgements. A classic study highlighting the problems of diagnosis and medical decision making was reported by Bakwin (1945). In it, a panel of three physicians screened 389 schoolboys, of whom 45 per cent were recommended for tonsillectomy. A second panel of doctors screened the remaining 215 boys and recommended a further 46 per cent of them have surgery. A third panel assessed the survivors of this group, and recommended that a further 44 per cent should also have their tonsils removed. The criteria for tonsillectomy have in the past been unclear, and the study was conducted some time ago. One can only hope clinical judgements have improved since this time.

Medical decision making is a special case of more general decision making, and prone to the same errors. One decision-making model (Tversky and Kahneman 1981) suggests that because human information capacity is limited, people under uncertainty do not use systematic strategies. Instead, their judgements are based on a series of heuristics (or 'rules of thumb'). These heuristics may be erroneous or biased by a variety of factors. In a landmark study, Meehl (1954) compared the accuracy of intuitive, heuristically driven medical diagnostic judgements with those made by a statistical formula designed to maximize the statistical relationship between potential predictor variables and the disease under investigation. The statistical algorithm proved more accurate. In all the many studies conducted since this time, the statistical model has proven the more effective, with the intuitive judgements at best equalling but never bettering the statistical algorithm. Such findings have caused considerable chagrin within the medical community.

The heuristic processes leading to a diagnosis may be biased by a variety of factors including emotionally salient events, such as the recent death of a patient with one of the possible diagnoses, the frequency with which doctors have encountered particular clusters of symptoms, and knowledge of a diagnosis made by colleagues. In addition, a doctor may consider the potential 'pay-off' of various diagnoses, and this may determine the final diagnosis they assign. That is, at times of uncertainty they will assign the diagnosis that provides the maximum pay-off. They may, for example, diagnose appendicitis in cases of childhood abdominal pain as the benefits of treating this problem through appendicectomy are considered to outweigh the costs of an unnecessary operation.

An additional factor that may influence decision making is the mood of the doctor making the diagnosis. Isen *et al.* (1991) attempted to study the impact of mood on the process of making a diagnosis. They manipulated the mood of medical students by telling some that they had performed in the top 3 per cent of all graduate students on an anagram task. All students were then given a task that involved asking which of a series of hypothetical patients was suffering from lung cancer. Participants who were in the positive affect group took less time to reach a decision and were less focused on the central task of diagnosis. Whether this manipulation actually translates to the ward situation is questionable. However, it is not unreasonable to suppose that mood does influence medical decision making. Although not directly measuring diagnostic errors, there is some evidence that doctors who report high levels of emotional distress report more medical errors than their less stressed colleagues (Houston and Allt 1997).

Stress and the hospital system

There is substantial evidence that health care workers experience significant stress as a consequence of the work they do and the settings they do it in. In a large UK survey, Borrill *et al.* (1996), for example, studied over 11,000 members of staff in 19 NHS Trusts around the country and found that 27 per cent of employees reported significant levels of psychological disturbance. This compared with an 18 per cent prevalence among the wider national workforce. Levels of stress differed marginally across the professions, with 33 per cent of managers, 29 per cent of nurses, and 28 per cent of doctors reporting significant levels of distress. Rates of depression in doctors appear to be highest in the years immediately following qualification, and to fall over time.

Moos and Schaeffer (1997) identified the links between the hospital working environment, personal stress and the quality of patient care. They suggested that two sets of factors contribute to work-related stress among health care workers: the nature of the health care system in general and the individual's situation within it. Depending on the coping resources that the individual brings to bear on these factors, they will experience more or less stress, and the quality of care that they provide will vary accordingly.

Table 5.2 Factors contributing to stress among hospital workers

Individual characteristics	Job demands	Institutional characteristics
Coping strategies	Job autonomy permitted	Management style
Personal competence	Patient group	Degree of personal support
Job involvement	Workload	available
	Physical setting	Teamwork
	Work/home interface	Shift structure
	Relationships with team	Quality of communication
	members	Value given to workers
	Time pressure	Level of supervision and support
	'Difficult' patients	Interdisciplinary cooperation
	Job flexibility	Degree of autonomy permitted
		Extent of available training
		Performance monitoring

Moos suggested that the work climate can be organized into three dimensions: relationships, tasks and system maintenance. Relationship factors include the extent to which employees and supervisors are involved and supportive of one another. Issues here include the quality of communication within the organization, teamwork, and relationships with co-workers. Bennett *et al.* (2000) found this to be the most important moderator of work-related stress in a sample of British nurses. Tasks refer to the goal and task aspects of the work setting, and include factors such as autonomy, task orientation and work pressure. Task stressors are a function of the demands that the job places on individuals and how well trained they are to deal with them. System maintenance refers to the amount of structure, clarity, and openness to change that exists within the organization. Table 5.2 summarizes the factors contributing to stress among hospital workers.

Compared to employees in non-health-related settings, American health care employees often report less job involvement and less co-worker cohesion and supervisor support. In addition, health care settings are seen as lacking in autonomy, less physically comfortable, and placing more emphasis on work demands and managerial control than non-health-care settings. Each of these factors is independently associated with staff stress. Whether some or all of these transpose to other health care settings is unclear. Most ring true from a British perspective. However, the development of ward teams and primary nurses who provide full nursing care to specified patients appears an important factor in increasing job satisfaction and reducing levels of work stress among nurses.

Few surveys show that factors associated with health care *per se* are considered particularly stressful by health care workers. The most frequently cited sources of stress among nurses, for example, are organizational factors such as a perception of being unvalued, poor communication, inadequate support, time pressure while at work, and overspill between work and home. For doctors, key stressors include relationships with senior doctors, making mistakes, and the stress placed on personal relationships by the time spent away from home. Few studies have found health care workers to report stress as a consequence of working with severely ill or dying patients. However, Firth-Cozens and Morrison (1989) questioned whether this consistent finding reflected the reality of health care workers' experience. They noted that if doctors complete formal questionnaires they typically do not rate dealing with dying patients as particularly stressful. However, more informal methods reveal this to be a major stressor. It is possible that the questionnaire method, typically used to assess stress in health care workers, is insufficiently sensitive to explore the complex issues surrounding the death of a patient, including concerns over choices of treatment, the rapidity of making a correct diagnosis, or even the quality of life of the patient had they lived. Exploration of such issues may require the use of qualitative methods rather than the blunter measures used in quantitative surveys.

Of interest is that within any health care system there are clear variations in organizational structure and climate and that these are associated with differences in staff morale and stress. A report by the Nuffield Trust (Williams *et al.* 1998), for example, reported average levels of stress in the health service to be similar to those found by Borrill and colleagues (1996). However, they differed across health care providers of different sizes and management styles. Those with the lowest levels of stress were relatively small, reported greater interdisciplinary co-operation, better communication, and placed a stronger emphasis on allowing staff control and flexibility over their work, training and performance monitoring than those with relatively high levels of stress. These data suggest that while some degree of stress may be inevitable within the health service workforce, the structure and ethos of the organization can influence its prevalence.

One of the seemingly intrinsic stressors within the hospital environment is the long hours worked by junior doctors. These do not seem to reduce despite recent legislation regulating doctors' working hours. However, while long hours may contribute to poor social conditions and reduced job satisfaction, evidence that they impair medical decision making is surprisingly sparse. Most studies of this phenomenon have asked doctors to undertake a variety of cognitive tasks following both a good night's sleep and a night when they have been deprived of sleep. Few have found evidence of any significant decrement in performance. The overall conclusion of such studies is that tasks involving sustained concentration are not affected by sleep deprivation, while decrements occur in monotonous, undemanding tasks.

These findings are thought to support the argument that long working hours do not impact on doctors' performance. However, the relevant studies have typically focused on somewhat artificial tasks and have not followed doctors in the context of their everyday work. The impact of sleep deprivation on medical care may be more subtle. Most doctors' tasks are routine in nature and even according to this model are prone to increased errors following periods of sleep deprivation. In addition, a number of studies have shown sleep deprivation to decrease arousal, increase fatigue, depression, tension and confusion. Such changes may contribute to decrements in communication between doctor and patient or other health professionals and further hamper effective care-giving. They are also independently associated with the frequency of errors made by hospital doctors (Houston and Allt 1997).

A second inevitable factor associated with providing 24-hour care is that of shift-work. Particularly problematic is the experience of constantly changing hours of sleep and work. Although a permanent shift from working day to night duties may eventually result in a substantial, though not perfect, degree of alteration of biological functioning, even this may take several weeks to achieve. Accordingly, shift-work may impair sleep and performance on a variety of intellectual tasks, including those involving memory. Ostberg (1973) attempted to find whether there were individual differences in people's ability to adapt to continual changing shifts. He found that the 'evening type' of person was most able to adapt to such changes.

Brewin and Firth-Cozens (1997) provide an interesting postscript to discussion of environmental and structural factors in the stress of health professionals. They noted a psychoanalytical model that suggests that many health care workers take up this career path because of early life experiences, including having poorly functioning parents and being, as a child, unable to make this better. This, they suggested, may lead to feelings of guilt and lead the adult to attempt to rectify these early experiences by choosing a helping profession where they feel it is possible to make up for the past. An almost inevitable failure to do so increases their sense of failure and guilt and leads to depression and stress. In a test of this hypothesis, they found that doctors who scored highly on measures of self-criticism (central to this process), who perceived their father to be strict, powerful and hard to please, or who lost their mother when young were more likely to become depressed than those without this constellation of predisposing factors. These factors overwhelmed the effects of more proximal stressors such as hours worked, bed responsibility and so on. However, these may represent general measures of vulnerability to any environmental stressors and not be peculiar to those who choose a medical career. Brown and Harris (1978), for example, identified a number of factors that rendered some working-class women vulnerable to depression. The key factors they identified were similar to those of Brewin and Firth-Cozens, and included a lack of supportive relationships, and the loss of a mother due either to death or to separation before the age of 11 years.

Summary and conclusions

Hospitalization is as much a social as a medical experience, as are many of the processes involved in planning and providing care. As such, the processes of providing case are prone to a wide range of influences, including the social context in it takes place and conscious and unconscious biases on the part of both patients and health care providers. These may impact on the diagnostic process, the nature and quality of interactions between health-care workers and patients, and patients' and health-care workers' behaviour. The influence of these biasing processes makes them both issues worthy of academic study as well as potential intervention points. How, and with what effect such interventions have been conducted are discussed further in the next chapter.

Further reading

Edelmann, R. (2000) *Psychosocial Aspects of the Health Care Process*. Harlow: Pearson.
Myers, L. and Midence, K. (1998) *Adherence in Medical Conditions*. Chur: Harwood.

6 ▷ Working in the hospital system

In Europe, the emergence of the profession of health psychology has been relatively recent and against a background of established professional groups who have laid claim to certain territories. Health psychologists have had, therefore, to develop a role that allows their theoretical knowledge to be used in applied settings within these constraints.
The reality of this process has meant that, so far, the majority of health psychologists have worked in research settings. Those who have also had a clinical training, and who could therefore be truly called clinical health psychologists, have had a wider choice of roles, and most have focused on the provision of psychological care to patients with physical health problems. Perhaps more than in any other specialism of clinical psychology, many practitioners have also developed substantial research roles. However, health and clinical health psychologists may also work at many other levels within the health care system.

In her presidential address to the American Psychological Association Division 38, Cynthia Belar applied the following definition to clinical health psychology:

> A clinical health psychologist applies, in professional practice, the
> specific educational, scientific, and professional contributions of the
> discipline of psychology to the promotion and maintenance of health;
> the prevention, treatment, and rehabilitation of illness, injury, and
> disability; the identification of etiologic and diagnostic correlates
> of health, illness, and related dysfunction; and the analysis and
> improvement of the health care system and health policy formation.
> (Belar 1997: 411)

The British Division of Health Psychology has identified three training elements for the professional role of the health psychologist that map onto Belar's somewhat wider definition: teaching, research and consultancy. Translation of these definitions into the practice of health psychology suggests that health psychologists may work at a number of levels within the health care system and beyond to improve the effectiveness of care as well as working therapeutically with patients. Examples of such practice include:

- working as an educator or consultant;
- conducting projects to evaluate specific aspects of care, or acting as consultant to others doing so;
- working on clinical audit;
- developing policy and giving advice on stress management at an individual and systemic level.

This chapter focuses on some of the interventions that have been shown to impact on patient and health outcomes, tying into some of the issues raised in Chapter 5, before addressing how health psychologists may influence the use and impact of these interventions through education or consultancy. As most health psychologists work in health care settings, this chapter considers in particular the influence of psychological interventions within the health care system.

The chapter addresses the following issues:

- Preparation for surgery and stressful medical procedures
- Increasing adherence
- Working with the dying
- Working as a health psychologist

Patient-based interventions

Preparation for surgery and stressful medical procedures

Before surgery, all patients are required by law to sign an informed consent form stating that the nature of their surgery has been explained to them and that they consent to its proceeding. Such a procedure should safeguard against uninformed patients and inappropriate surgery.

Unfortunately, this may not always be the case. There is substantial evidence that many patients do not understand the nature of the surgery they are about to undergo. A British study in the late 1980s, for example, found that among 100 patients who had given informed consent prior to surgery, 27 were unaware of which organ was involved in their surgery and 44 did not understand the basic procedural elements of their surgery. Such lack of understanding may contribute to the anxiety of an already stressful situation and impact adversely on recovery from surgery on outcomes as varied as recovery time, use of painkillers, time to mobilization, and wound-healing. Such outcomes are disappointing, particularly in view of the wealth of information concerning the benefits of appropriate preparation for surgery.

Several strategies may be used to prepare patients to cope with the stresses associated with surgery. The simplest strategy is one of giving appropriate information. This may be divided into a number of elements. Procedural information involves telling patients about the events that will occur: medication injection, anaesthesia, waking in the recovery room, and so on. Sensory information involves telling them what they will feel before and after surgery. They may be told, for example, that it is normal to feel some degree of pain in the days following surgery in order to allay any anxiety about the occurrence of unexpected pain. More complex interventions involve teaching patients a variety of coping strategies, including relaxation and cognitive restructuring (see Chapter 8).

In a series of meta-analyses, Johnston and Vogele (1993) found significant treatment effects for all these approaches on measures of mood, pain, distress about pain, and behavioural and physiological indices of recovery including getting out bed, comfort following operations, and heart rate. The impact of the various interventions varied across studies and patient populations, and there seems to be no clear optimal intervention. Nevertheless, comparisons between the various approaches may provide some indications of the intervention of choice. Marshall *et al.* (1986), for example, compared the effectiveness of structured or unstructured information about normal postoperative recovery with patients about to undergo cardiac surgery. Following surgery, both groups had higher total knowledge scores than before. Levels of engagement in most health behaviours were also comparable between groups. However, those patients who received the structured teaching adhered more closely to their postoperative treatment programme than those who received the unstructured intervention. In a comparison of cognitive and education-based interventions, Ridgeway and Mathews (1982) randomly assigned patients having a hysterectomy to one of three conditions: a placebo condition involving the provision of general information about the ward; procedural and sensation information; or training in cognitive restructuring methods. Three days after their operation, patient groups did not differ in self-report pain, nausea or sleep duration. However, patients who received the cognitive intervention took fewer oral analgesics and received fewer injections for pain while in hospital, and experienced fewer days of pain following discharge than those in either of the other two groups.

Interventions benefit from being matched to the characteristics of the patient. In a meta-analysis permitting such factors to be examined, Hathaway (1986) found that patients with low anxiety levels evidenced the greatest benefit when procedural information was used in the intervention. In contrast, patients with high anxiety scores responded best to relatively unstructured interventions that combined discussion of feelings with practice of coping strategies. Wilson (1981) further considered the influence of patients' coping style. Patients were separated into one of four groups according to patient characteristics of high and low fear and coping styles described as 'denying' or 'aggressive'. Treatments were routine care, sensation and procedural information, relaxation, and a combination of information and relaxation training. All the patients in the treatment groups had significantly shorter stays in hospital than the control patients. However, those classified as 'low fear' tended to be discharged sooner if they were in a group that included relaxation training. Relaxation did not help 'high fear' patients: perhaps because they were unable to practise and implement the procedure effectively in the short time available. Patients rated as highly aggressive benefited most from information on measures of recovery and pain medication. Low aggression patients in the information condition actually increased their use of pain medication and decreased their in-hospital recovery scores.

In a later study of emotional reactions to endoscopy, the same team studied the interaction between coping styles, information provision, and instruction in relaxation techniques (Wilson *et al.* 1982). Patients in the information condition listened to an audio-taped message describing the process of endoscopy and the sensations typically experienced. The relaxation group listened to an introduction to relaxation followed by a 20-minute practice session. Patients who had an avoidant coping style benefited most from relaxation, while those with a more active coping style benefited most from sensory information. In contrast to their previous findings, and reflecting the idiosyncratic responses to such interventions, relaxation was the most effective intervention for those patients who were particularly anxious prior to the endoscopy.

Preparation of children

A number of studies have examined the effects of preparing children or their parents for highly aversive procedures. Most have involved minor procedures and have shown preparation to be of some benefit. In an evaluation of the effects of preparation for the more serious process of cardiac catheterization, Campbell *et al.* (1992) compared three methods of preparing mothers of pre-school-age children: education and hospital orientation, **stress management training**, and brief supportive psychotherapy. Both mothers who received stress management training and their children evidenced significantly more adaptive behaviours at key stress points in the procedure than those in the other conditions. In addition, the children adapted more positively at home following catheterization. Mothers in the education group also benefited. They reported significantly less anxiety and tension and greater competence in caring for their children than those in the other conditions.

In an unusual comparison between medical and psychological methods of coping with child distress, Jay *et al.* (1995) compared the efficacy of cognitive-behavioural therapy and general anaesthesia in alleviating the distress of 3–12 year old cancer patients undergoing bone marrow aspirations. Children who received the psychological treatment showed the most distress during the first minute lying down on the treatment table. However, parents' ratings indicated that they benefited more than those in the anaesthesia group in the longer term, as they evidenced less distress in the day following the procedure. No differences were found in children's and parents' preference for cognitive behavioural or anaesthetic interventions.

Managing acute pain within the hospital setting

Acute pain, whether as a result of injury or operative procedures, can be reduced through the use of psychological procedures, some of which have been discussed earlier in this chapter. Minimizing the use of analgesia can be facilitated by increasing patients' perceptions of control over their pain and reducing pain-related anxiety. This may be achieved by the provision of procedural and sensory preparation, prompt reactions to requests for pain medication, or the use of patient controlled anaesthesia (PCA). The latter allows the patient to directly titrate the amount of analgesia they receive. It can involve various routes of drug administration, doses and times between doses. The most commonly used drugs are potent analgesics, including morphine or its derivatives. The prescriber can choose the drug and dosage to be used, and can impose a 'lockout interval' to prevent overadministration by the patient. Nevertheless, giving patients control over the timing of their analgesia reduces many of the anxieties associated with lack of control. It should not be surprising, therefore, that PCA results in better pain control and less use of analgesia than more conventional approaches. Patients consider the major benefit of PCA to be the avoidance of the difficulties of disclosing pain or securing pain relief within the usual nurse/patient relationship: they may report dissatisfaction with PCA if it simply replaces good patient care and reduces contact with nurses.

An alternative approach that has proven of benefit is the use of hypnosis. Faymonville *et al.* (1997), for example, compared the effects of hypnosis against a minimal treatment control group in patients undergoing plastic surgery. Hypnosis focused on reducing discomfort during the operative procedures during which patients were sedated but not unconscious. Patients in the hypnosis condition gained significantly in comparison with those in the control condition on measures of peri- and postoperative anxiety and pain, despite using less analgesia during the procedure. Hypnosis has also been found to be more effective than cognitive behavioural procedures with paediatric cancer patients undergoing bone marrow aspirations. Liossi and Hatira (1999) found that patients receiving each of these interventions fared better on measures of pain and anxiety during and after aspiration than those in a normal treatment control group. However, nurse ratings indicated that children in the hypnosis condition evidenced less anxiety and behavioural distress than those in the cognitive behavioural intervention group. Hypnosis has also proven a highly effective intervention in patients suffering pain as a consequence of burns, particularly during the extremely painful process of changing their dressings.

Increasing adherence

Consultation factors

One of the most significant contributions to our understanding of factors that influence adherence to medical regimens is provided by the work of Ley (see, for example, Ley 1988), who identified three strategies for increasing adherence to recommended treatments:

- increasing understanding of the condition and its treatment;
- increasing memory for information given;
- maximizing satisfaction with the process of treatment.

Increasing understanding

A number of strategies have been used to encourage patient involvement in consultations, in an attempt to increase understanding and memory for information given them. Roter (1977), for example, examined the impact of a health educator identifying the questions that a group of poorly educated women wished to ask the doctor and writing them on a piece of paper to be taken into the consultation. A second group of women who acted as a control group took in a similar piece of paper on which was written the telephone numbers of various clinics. Women in the experimental group asked more direct questions and were more likely to attend subsequent appointments than those in the control group. However, they did find the session quite stressful. Such anxieties, and the time and costs involved, may preclude this type of intervention becoming routine. Nevertheless, these and other data suggest that if patients are encouraged to voice their opinion or given explicit instructions to ask clarifying questions, modest gains in satisfaction and adherence may be achieved. Unsurprisingly, perhaps, the best levels of understanding and adherence have been found where there was no conflict between the patient's and doctor's view of the problem and where patients were prescribed the medication they requested.

Increasing memory

Ley (1988) identified a number of strategies by which information can be presented in order to maximize its chances of being remembered. Information is best provided in a structured form: 'I am going to tell you about three things . . . a, b, and c', and using language and terms that the patient can understand. The most important information should be given early so as to maximize primacy effects, and its importance should be emphasized. Further strategies include repetition and the use of specific rather than general statements. Additional reminders such as telephone calls or letters may also be useful triggers to action.

If asked, over three-quarters of patients state they would like some form of permanent information about their condition and its treatment: preferably concise, clear and illustrated with graphics if appropriate. If provided, about 70 per cent of patients report using such materials. Written or other permanent sources of information have significant benefits: the most obvious being that they provide an opportunity for the clinician to provide carefully thought through information, presented in a way designed to be maximally effective. From the patient's perspective, they provide a record that can be consulted when necessary to remind them of salient information. Critical to the effectiveness of such interventions is that they are understandable by the patient. Unfortunately, this criterion is not always met: Ley (1997) suggested that about one-quarter of published medical leaflets would be understood by only 20–30 per cent of the adult population.

Appropriately presented information can have a positive impact on both the doctor/patient relationship and adherence to recommended treatment regimens. Tang and Newcomb (1998), for example, reported that receiving health-related information from their doctors favourably affected the participants' trust in and relationship with their physicians. In addition, when given printouts with graphic trends depicting their responses to therapy, participants reported that they were more motivated to adhere to a treatment plan and were more satisfied with their care. Information need not necessarily be pre-prepared. Tattersall *et al.* (1994) compared the impact of an audiotape of a consultation with that of individualized summary letters sent to patients after their first consultation with a medical oncologist. Patients listened to the tape an average of 2.3 times and read the letter 2.8 times over the following month, and 90 per cent shared the contents of the tape or letter with a friend, relative or doctor. Both methods impacted equally on measures of recall, anxiety or depression. However, the audiotape proved the more popular method: when asked to rank six communication options, 46 per cent of patients gave the highest rank to the tape and 21 per cent to the letter.

Maximizing patient satisfaction

One of the most consistent influences on patient satisfaction is that doctors are seen to be communicating appropriate information. Accordingly, the strategies so far considered should in themselves foster high levels of patient satisfaction. A number of other factors have also been found to influence satisfaction, including the duration of the consultations (longer is better), continuity in the doctor/patient relationship, and accessibility and availability of doctors.

To summarize the issues raised here and in Chapter 5, Ley (1997) identified a number of key elements in the process of maximizing adherence to medical regimens:

◆ Make the treatment as simple and short in duration as possible.
◆ Identify the patient's representations of their illness and its treatment. Identify misconceptions and try to resolve them. Use an alternative treatment if possible and necessary.
◆ Tailor the regimen to fit in with the patient's pattern of behaviour.
◆ Ensure that the patient is satisfied with the amount of information given.
◆ Make sure that the patient fully understands when and how to take their medication.
◆ Ensure that the patient understands the rationale of the treatment regimen.
◆ Where possible, provide written back-up information.
◆ At follow-up, check on adherence and factors that may have affected it.
◆ Provide feedback about progress, perhaps through self-monitoring.

Beyond the consultation

The procedures suggested by Ley are not the only ways to maximize adherence: effective treatment of depression, environmental cues, engaging other family members, as well as use of reminders and the provision of appropriate pill containers may promote adherence to medication in appropriate populations. The skills of taking medication unobtrusively may help those with complex and demanding drug schedules, such as HIV positive individuals who do not want others to know they are taking medication, to adhere to medication regimens.

Many of the strategies to increase adherence to behavioural regimens are implicitly based on the social cognition models discussed in Chapter 3. Many programmes focus on reducing the costs of engaging in the required behaviour or on maximizing the gains to be had from doing so. Marcus *et al.* (1992), for example, randomized over 2000 women with abnormal cervical cytology into one of three follow-up groups: a personalized follow-up letter and pamphlet, a slide-tape programme on pap smears, or transportation incentives (bus passes/parking permits). For the sample as a whole, all the interventions had a significant positive impact on screening follow-up. However, transportation incentives emerged as the most effective intervention among socio-economically disadvantaged women.

Incentive-based programmes have proven effective both within the worksite (see Chapter 7) and beyond. **Token economies** may also be useful to increase adherence in children. Building in social support has been shown to increase adherence (see also Chapter 7), although such a finding is not universal and the costs and benefits of such a process need to be fully considered. Many exercise programmes, for example, have found the provision of social support to encourage attendance at planned episodes of exercise. However, Perri et al. (1997) found adherence to a twelve-month group-based exercise and weight loss programme for obese women to be lower than that of a home-based programme. These particular women clearly preferred exercising on their own rather than in the company of others. Additional strategies that have been shown to be effective in increasing adherence include the establishment of behavioural contracts or providing written commitment to a treatment programme or package and feedback on performance or gains made as a function of adherence to a programme. Finally, many of the interventions discussed in Chapter 8, including cognitive behavioural and self-management interventions will also impact on adherence rates.

Should we be increasing adherence?

The preceding discussion has implicitly accepted that increasing adherence is 'a good thing', acted upon by those in the health care system. An alternative perspective is that, except in the cases where non-adherence is a function of misunderstandings or failures of memory, non-adherence represents an active choice. Accordingly, while the previously considered interventions may influence adherence in some people, others may still choose not to follow medical instructions. From a purely medical perspective, such choices may be inappropriate and unsatisfactory. Nevertheless, they have to be respected.

One way of avoiding deliberate non-adherence is to ensure that the patient be prescribed treatment, be it behavioural or pharmacological, that they are actively motivated to engage in. To achieve this, it may be necessary to change the nature of the consultation from one in which the doctor adopts the 'expert' role and dictates treatment options to a more collaborative process in which the patient is helped to make informed choices about the treatment they receive. In this patient-centred approach, the final treatment decision made, where possible, is one that is satisfactory to both patient and doctor. Elwyn *et al.* (1999) provided a template for this process:

- Explore ideas, fears and expectations of the problem and possible treatments.
- Identify how much information the patient would prefer and provide tailor-made information.
- Check the patient's understanding of ideas, fears and expectations of possible options.
- Assess patient's decision-making role preference.
- Make, discuss or defer decisions.
- Arrange follow-up.

Such a process acknowledges the need for the doctor to understand the patients' illness representations, their varying levels of motivation to make choices relevant to its treatment, and to work *with* the patient as far as is wanted and possible. This model is increasingly seen as applicable by British doctors. However, one of the few formal assessment of the merits of this approach suggested that many patients struggle to adapt to this shift of power. Savage and Armstrong (1990) randomly assigned patients attending a family doctor service into one of two conditions. In the first, patients took part in a traditional doctor-led consultation. In the second they engaged in a more sharing consultative process. All patients reported high levels of satisfaction with the doctor's understanding of their problem, the explanation given, and being 'helped'. However, both immediately after the consultation and one week later, the doctor-led style was preferred. This relatively new consulting style may not match with all patients' expectations, and both doctors and their patients may need to make and adjust to such changes over time.

Despite such a cautionary note, some gains in patient understanding following similar interventions have been noted. In addition, there is some evidence that **client-centred consultations** can result in improved levels of adherence to agreed treatment plans. Greenfield *et al.* (1988), for example, found that a 20-minute consultation with their doctor during which diabetic patients were prompted to engage in an active dialogue about their condition resulted in improved blood sugar control and decreased functional limitations in comparison with patients passively provided with information. However, patients may make decisions that are not in keeping with recommended clinical practice. Kinmonth *et al.* (1998) compared a patient-centred approach to the care of patients with newly diagnosed non-insulin-dependent diabetes in a primary care setting with standard care. Compared with patients in the usual care group, those in the intervention group reported better communication with the doctors, greater treatment satisfaction and greater well-being. However, their body mass index was significantly higher as were their triglyceride levels. Differences in lifestyle and glycaemic control were not significant.

Working with the dying

Breaking bad news

There comes a time when terminally ill patients and their relatives need to be told of their prognosis. Many health care workers find it extremely difficult to discuss such issues with patients. Not infrequently, relatives, but not the patient, are told of the likely prognosis, placing them in a distressing and ethically problematic situation. Information may be withheld for a variety of reasons. Many professionals consider their patients to be vulnerable and likely to be emotionally damaged by information about their health status. Many doctors feel personally unsupported and wish to avoid the emotional burden of dealing with patient's distress. In addition, few health professionals have any formal training in strategies that would help them to break bad news in a way that fosters psychological adaptation. Nevertheless, good practice states that the patient should be given the opportunity to be informed of, and discuss, their condition.

A key aspect of giving bad news is to provide information appropriate to the individual's knowledge and needs at the time of the interview. From this perspective, breaking bad news is a specific example of good patient-centred communication (see Chapter 8). The first step is to explore what the patient already knows. If they are already aware of the severity of their condition (up to 80 per cent are), this may lead the health professional to confirm the patient's perceptions ('Yes. I'm afraid you are right. We are not going to be able to cure it.').

Breaking bad news to patients who have little or no awareness of the seriousness of their condition is more difficult. It is important to avoid giving potentially distressing information abruptly, as this may push the patient into denial or cause unwarranted emotional distress. Accordingly, the health care worker should become involved in a series of subtle responses to patient behaviour as the interview proceeds. Bad news should be given in a gradual manner, which permits the patient to learn slowly of their condition and control the speed with which information is given. This can be achieved through the use of a series of euphemisms. These may begin with a warning shot ('I am afraid it is more serious than we originally thought'), followed by a pause to allow the patient to indicate whether they wish to explore the implications of this statement or move to another topic. Although patients should be given the opportunity to discuss their condition, they should never be forced to confront it if they indicate they do not wish to do so.

Once information has been provided, it is crucial that patients are given support in assimilating and dealing with it. Initially, it is important to acknowledge the distress they will almost inevitably express: 'I can see what I have told you has been very upsetting. . . .' This should be followed by exploration of their personal reasons for this upset. This may be facilitated by a simple question: 'I can think of lots of reasons why you may be upset. But, could you cope with telling me what is making you so upset now?' If the patient does not wish to do so, their wishes should be respected. If they wish to talk, time should be taken to listen. Once the patient's concerns have been elicited, they can be addressed by the health care worker. In an initial interview, it may be useful to ask the patient to identify the two or three major concerns they have and try to deal with them. Others may have to be dealt with on subsequent occasions.

Allowing the expression of negative emotions is an important element of this type of interview (see Chapter 8). However, it is important that if the patient appears to be too distressed they are given the opportunity to end the interview. Hogbin and Fallowfield (1989) reported a novel method of helping people to cope after these initial meetings. They gave audiotape recordings of their 'bad news' consultations to 46 patients, 35 of whom has breast cancer. These tapes contained explicit statements of the diagnosis and descriptions of the tests and treatment available. Participants found them very helpful in coming to terms with their illness. They helped them to recall forgotten information, made them more confident, and helped them to break the bad news to their family and friends.

As noted previously, patient's mood and ability to cope with information may differ over time. In addition, their memory for information given at times of high emotion may be poor and selective. Good practice should mean that whether or not patients are informed of their condition, they are given the opportunity to talk about issues relevant to them on other occasions. Such conversations need not necessarily be with the health care worker who initiated the process. However, if they are with other people, it is important that those involved are aware of what each patient has been told. Given the emotional demands on the health care professional involved in the process of giving bad news, it is also important that the professional has access to a support network should they need it.

Helping the dying

Working with the dying does not only involve issues to do with psychological preparation for death. An important element of such care involves monitoring and treating the physical symptoms that such people may experience. People with cancer may experience pain, breathing difficulties, sleeplessness, loss of bowel and bladder control, and loss of appetite. Some of these may be helped by psychological means: others may be helped by pharmacological treatments. Pain control, for example, may require an appropriate pharmacological regimen in combination with some form of psychological intervention.

A number of interventions have been conducted with individuals who have a terminal illness. Some, such as group support interventions, are considered in Chapter 11. The gains made by those attending such groups include their regaining a sense of control over their lives, helping them live their lives 'to the full', and being able to express their needs and fears openly. Group interventions may be more effective than one-to-one work because group members can share common problems and solutions to them. In addition, group interventions provide an opportunity for individuals to give to one another at a time when they may feel isolated from those not sharing their situation. Communication with a therapist or group members may be particularly important to the dying, as other people who are more emotionally close to them may begin to withdraw at this time as a consequence of preparatory grieving (see below).

Some people may neither want nor have access to group interventions, and may benefit from individual work. Approaches to working with the dying vary. Humanistic approaches emphasize the need to address issues initiated by the patient. The list of such issues may be long and includes: expressing hope and despair about what is happening, wanting to live and die, being angry about the situation, revolting against it and submitting to it, worries of rejection, fear of loss of bodily or self-control, and fear of pain. Behavioural approaches used with the dying typically adopt a goal-setting approach. These consider the individual's problems, strengths, abilities and available resources in some detail. Problems and potential solutions can be identified and prioritized, and behavioural goals can be set. These may address 'unfinished business', as well as more future- or present-oriented concerns. Patients may, for example, work on strategies to help them continue with tasks that give them self-esteem or to finish tasks that are important for them to complete. Goals may be set and achieved in conjunction with other family members. Advocates of this behavioural approach generally maintain an eclectic approach to therapy and state that the therapeutic principles underpinning more humanistic approaches should also be adopted within a behavioural framework.

It is frequently not only the dying person who is experiencing distress close to the time of their death. Relatives and friends may experience a similar reaction to the patient. This process, known as anticipatory grieving, may involve denial, anger and depression. Allowing such people to talk issues through, much as could be done with the person who is dying, may help them to cope with the situation. This period may also be used to allow the dying person and their relatives to reminisce about all the good things they have done together, to mourn experiences that were less successful, and to express their disappointment about events that will never now occur. There may be unfinished business to complete, a chance to express their feelings about each other and to make their goodbyes. Some families may benefit from help in managing these processes.

Working as a health psychologist

The research so far reviewed considered how some variables of interest to health psychology can impact on the quality of care of patients in the health care system. Ironically, perhaps, except under unusual circumstances most will be implemented by other health professionals such as nurses and doctors. This section considers work that health psychologists may become actively involved in within the health care system, focusing on the three elements of the British Division of Health Psychology's emerging definition of the role of the professional health psychologist: teaching, research and consultancy work.

Teaching

Health psychologists have a substantial formal and informal teaching role. Indeed, this and research constitute the basis of much of the work currently conducted by health psychologists. Clearly, a practitioner should be able to teach on any area of health psychology with adequate preparation. However, most research examining the effectiveness of teaching psychology in the context of health care has focused on the teaching of communication skills. It is on this literature that the next section focuses.

The Royal College of General Practitioners has adopted a six-stage problem-solving model of consultation: problem(s) stated, examined and defined, solution generated, examined and selected. These processes should be conducted jointly by doctor and patient. The skills required of the doctor are those of helping the patient to identify and articulate their problems and concerns: defining and agreeing problems with the patient, giving information and dealing with worries and concerns, generating, exploring and agreeing possible solutions, and committing patients to implement those that are agreed. Such a process demands high levels of communication skills. It is therefore highly appropriate that training in communication skills is now a central element to doctor training at both undergraduate and postgraduate levels.

At undergraduate level, students are provided with an overview of the skills of active listening, including the importance of developing good rapport, the use of open-ended questions early in the consultation, appropriate eye-contact and other facilitatory strategies (see Chapter 8). Courses typically involve active learning, using role-play with simulated patients, as well as real patient interviews. Feedback is used to identify problem areas and directions for improvement, and is now increasingly provided by videotape. In addition, students are taught the skills needed to deal with distressed patients and relatives and to break bad news. There is now consistent evidence that such training can considerably enhance communication skills. Maguire *et al.* (1986), for example, compared the effectiveness of this type of training with a more traditional teaching package, primarily involving didactic provision of information. Immediately following the intervention, and at five-year follow-up, participants in the active learning programme evidenced greater proficiency in the use of skills and strategies including open questions, clarification of patients' statements, and verbal and visual encouragement, than those in the traditional learning group. Gains have also be found following communication skills training in groups as varied as trained doctors, psychiatrists and medical interns.

Context-specific skills may also be taught and implemented. Cornuz *et al.* (1997), for example, found that hospital interns who had attended training in smoking cessation counselling were significantly more likely to discuss smoking cessation with their patients than before their training. In addition, the patients who saw these doctors after their training were more likely to attempt to quit than the equivalent group seen before this time. The likelihood of sustained cessation was, however, not increased.

Research

A central role for health psychologists within the university and health care systems is that of developing high quality research programmes. Increasingly, health psychologists are contributing to multidisciplinary research teams as well as conducting more specialist research. The nature of such research needs little introduction; indeed, without it this book could not have been written. However, most clinical and health psychology practitioners will not become involved in high-level research. Nevertheless, research remains an important element of the work of both professional groups, even if this is limited to monitoring individual performance. Another area that the research skills of psychologists may contribute to is that of clinical audit: ensuring that medical and other therapeutic services are monitored and meet required standards.

Clinical audit

The British National Health Service employs nearly 1500 individuals as audit advisors. Their role involves educating and training clinical staff to evaluate the quality of care provided by a particular service, including design, data analysis and the use of results to guide practice. Only a small percentage of this group are psychologists. However, the core research skills involved match onto those of psychologists, and there has been a call for them to become involved in audit teams or to provide training and advice through consultancy to audit groups.

Attempting to improve the quality of care, either by the establishment of clinical audit or by publishing outcome data, can be extremely threatening to the staff involved. National legislation relating to audit and other health care innovations is frequently being imposed on unwilling individuals and systems. As a consequence, even where innovations in health care are formally implemented, in practice they are not always adopted fully into health care procedures. Mansfield (1995), for example, reported findings from a survey of British hospital doctors that indicated that while most respondents welcomed clinical guidelines, only a minority of doctors were actually using them.

Introduction of innovations should therefore involve substantial planning if they are not to be rejected by those involved. Psychologists' expertise in facilitating systemic transitions may usefully inform such developments, although any intervention need not be complex. Hearnshaw *et al.* (1994) involved all members of a health care team in devising and undertaking audits that made sense to them in terms of the way they worked. The resultant sense of ownership was considered crucial to completing the audits and implementing subsequent changes to the system of care. Innovations are most easily effected when staff feel secure, skilled and not overloaded by unreasonable pressures. Unfortunately, many innovations are introduced at times when professionals feel under pressure, unskilled and fearful of the implications of change: a set of circumstances likely to result in resistance to change. Psychologists may usefully identify how an organization can implement changes in a way that minimizes additional stress and is seen as fitting the values and needs of the professionals involved. Strategies here may include consultations with staff to identify their views, discussion groups, developing mutually agreed change, or providing appropriate training before the implementation of an innovation. These issues move the role of psychologist from that of researcher to one involved in complex interventions to change whole organizations. Further consideration of this role is given below.

Consultancy

Working with others either formally or informally provides an opportunity to provide advice, skills or information: all of which may be considered a process of consultancy. However, health psychologists are likely to become increasingly involved in developing a more formal consultancy role, on either a short- or a long-term basis, with health care providers. This section considers three examples of such consultancy work.

Facilitating staff changes

The previous section has already considered some of the problems in initiating change among staff. Enabling such change may require input from someone outside the system. Tadmor (1988) provided an example of such an intervention in relation to one group of hospital nurses' preparation of patients for caesarean section. Practice prior to Tadmor's intervention involved withholding information about the procedure until as late as possible, as it was thought its early introduction would evoke unnecessary anxiety. However, preliminary research indicated that this procedure actually increased unrealistic fears and slowed postoperative recovery. To bring about change, Tadmor ran a series of workshops and provided on-the-job training that emphasized the need to provide early information. This she was so successful in doing that not only did the health workers provide information relevant to caesarean sections earlier, they also established a support group for women who had undergone this procedure. A further positive outcome to the intervention was that these activities resulted in an increased level of emotional attachment between mother and infant.

A similar intervention involving group work was reported by a team working in Indonesia. The goal of their intervention was to reduce the overuse of injections by primary care physicians, who gave up to 70 per cent of patients an injection following each medical consultation. The team ran a series of groups involving both clinicians and patients with the intention of testing prescribers' assumptions about patient beliefs, imparting scientific information about injection efficacy, and establishing peer norms about correct behaviour. Following these discussion groups, injection rates fell from 70 per cent to 42 per cent: an effect not found in a control group. There was also a significant reduction in the average number of drugs per prescription, indicating that injections were not substituted with other drugs.

Reducing stress in a hospital workforce

A variety of factors have led health employers to pay increasing attention to the impact of organizational stress on their employees. High levels of stress are associated with high levels of sickness, poor recruitment and retention of staff, and poor performance while in work. As the available workforce has dwindled, these issues have become of increasing concern to human resources departments trying to maintain an adequate and capable workforce throughout the health care system.

In response to these concerns, a number of health providers have engaged clinical or health psychologists on a consultancy basis to develop initiatives aimed at reducing work-related stress. This section describes some of the work conducted in a British hospital over a period of one year as part of this consultancy role. As with Maes *et al.* (1998: see Chapter 7), a systemic approach was adopted. This may have included some of the possible organization-directed strategies to reduce stress identified by Elkin and Rosch (1990):

- redesign the work environment;
- establish flexible work schedules;
- encourage participative management;
- include the employee in career development;
- analyse work roles and establish goals;
- provide social support and feedback;
- build cohesive teams;
- establish fair employment policies.

However, rather than implement such strategies regardless of the particular needs of the organization, the decision was taken to run a series of focus groups to identify key sources of staff stress within the organization, and staffs' views on how these could be remedied. These groups proved an extremely useful method of gaining an understanding of factors in the work environment contributing to work stress and low morale. Among nurses, for example, the main stressors included high job demands, lack of recognition from senior management, lack of support in decision making and management role, and work spillover. A report based on the findings of these groups was taken to the Trust Board who tasked a working party to develop a series of targets for policy and institutional change. These were agreed and a number of changes instituted, including a review of ward dependency ratings, the establishment of a peer supervision system, developing strategies for improved communication with line managers, and the long-term provision of information technology more appropriate to the ward needs. A formal survey using psychometric measures of work stress, morale and mood was conducted on a representative sample of staff before these changes were instituted. A repeat of the survey six months subsequently was used to determine whether the changes impacted substantially on stress and morale levels within the organization.

At the same time as these changes were beginning to be implemented, the health psychologist contributed to a further development intended to reduce nurse stress within the workforce. This involved a year-long training course on leadership skills for ward managers. The psychologist not only contributed to a workshop on methods of reducing stress on the wards, but also developed the instrument used to evaluate the effectiveness of the teaching and workshop programme. Finally, the psychologist provided an *ad hoc* consultancy service, through which managers and senior staff could request advice on managing or reducing stress in particular 'hot spots' around the hospital. This proved a popular and useful consultancy and dealt with issues as wide-ranging as developing a response to help staff to cope with a major public enquiry, ward morale following prolonged abuse from the mother of a dead child, and helping clerical staff to moderate and cope with anger and abuse from the public in high stress situations.

Using patient feedback to improve services

An example of a health psychologist leading a project in which patients' views of a service were taken into account in the ongoing development of that service was provided by Hill (1999). The Patient Care Development Programme involved a three-phase process. In the first, the project was discussed with senior professionals across different specialisms within the hospital. Speciality-based project groups, which took ownership of the project, were established, with the psychologist facilitating their development rather than leading them directly. Phase 2 involved the project teams meeting and identifying the areas of care that formed the core part of their service and on which they would focus their efforts. Phase 3 involved gathering data from patients about the quality of service provided. Interviews were conducted with patients in their homes by the specialist department staff and focused on the patients' experiences of care. In phase 4, the findings of these interviews were fed back to the project team. Issues identified were considered in the light of the views of others involved in the provision of services and decisions were made about the priorities to be taken for development and change. Finally, an implementation programme was written by each project team to plan the practical process of change. This process was conducted within four specialist areas within the hospital, surgery, medicine, women and children's services, and support services, and in over 30 patient groups, including patients receiving treatment for cancer of the bladder, cataracts, MI, special care babies, and fractured neck of femur.

The process of patient review was intended to be ongoing and to form a continuing process of feedback, response and further feedback. The initial report, however, focused on changes made following the first set of patient surveys and the institutional response to them. Changes to the system were significant and fully relevant to patient care, and included the development of new patient information leaflets and care summary sheets, improved communication with patients on waiting lists, and increased involvement of patients in their discharge care planning. A further initiative involved patients being given follow-up appointments while attending outpatient clinics, instead of notification being sent in the post at a later date.

Summary and conclusions

Health psychology research has led to a significant understanding of the processes of care that impact on patient well-being. It also suggests a number of intervention points that may impact on both the quality of care given to patients and elements of the health care system that impact on those who work within it. Some of these interventions will be informed by, rather than conducted by, health psychologists. However, an increasing number of interventions will actually be conducted by health psychologists. It is for the emerging profession of health psychology to determine what these interventions will be and the shape of the emerging profession of health psychology.

Further reading

Myers, L. and Midence, K. (1998) *Adherence in Medical Conditions*. Chur: Harwood.

Edelmann, R. (2000) *Psychosocial Aspects of the Health Care Process*. Harlow: Pearson.

Health promotion

The goal of health promotion is to maximize health within the population at large. It achieves this through a variety of means, including economic, social and psychological and works at a number of levels including the individual, community and societal. Chapter 11 addresses some of the literature relevant to individual interventions, focusing on screening as an agent of behavioural change. Elsewhere in the book, issues related to individual health education are also addressed. This chapter widens the focus and considers how health psychology may inform interventions targeting whole populations. In doing so, it suggests that the traditional focus of health promotion programmes is becoming increasingly difficult to justify and that health promotion may usefully adopt a new focus, targeting new factors that influence health and actively involving communities in health promotion rather than simply acting upon them.
   This chapter focuses on:

♦ The contribution that psychology has made to the development of health promotion programmes
♦ The need to identify new targets for health promotion
♦ Future strategies for health promotion

Applying psychological theory to health promotion

Health education and health promotion are often considered to be synonymous. They are not. Health education is a planned activity with the specific intention of increasing knowledge or skills to promote healthy behaviour. Health promotion is a wider concept, encompassing education but also including the creation of environments supportive of health and health-enhancing behaviours, developing appropriate public health policy, increasing individuals' personal resources and strengthening community action (see, for example, World Health Organization 1991).

In order to achieve these goals, the World Health Organization (WHO) stated that health promotion should work with individuals and communities to maximize health potential. An important element of its philosophy is that public policy should, as a priority, create environments that foster good health. It stated that health gains can be made by political and economic policy as well as through individual behavioural change. This emphasis on public health may suggest that psychology has little to contribute to health promotion. Such a conclusion would be unwarranted. Psychological theory has contributed strongly, both explicitly and implicitly, to the theoretical rationale of a number of key community initiatives and will continue to do so.

Social cognitive theory

Social cognitive theory has guided the development of a number of sophisticated health promotion and health education programmes. It has provided a theoretical underpinning for a variety of media-based interventions aimed at individuals, some of which are described in Chapter 11. It has also informed those aimed at the wider community. The 'Pssst . . . the really useful guide to alcohol' television series broadcast throughout the UK, for example, encouraged young people to drink within 'sensible' limits. It provided age- and gender-appropriate models of consumption, and followed the fortunes of its presenter as he cut down his drinking over the course of the series. In addition, skills such as planning to cut down consumption and resisting pressure to drink were modelled within a humorous framework intended to be attractive and relevant to its target audience. A limited analysis of its impact (Bennett *et al.* 1991) suggested that it resulted in short-term changes in knowledge and attitudes towards alcohol consumption.

Social cognitive theory has also been used to guide more wide-ranging intervention programmes. One of the first, the Stanford Three Towns Project, included a media-based intervention lasting over a year aimed at changing CHD-risk behaviours in three communities around Stanford, USA (Farquhar *et al.* 1977). Based explicitly on social cognitive theory, the media programme involved a series of stages: agenda-setting, the provision of information, modelling change and skills for change, and finally 'cues to action'. In the case of smoking, for example, the media first provided information on the risks of smoking and the benefits of cessation. This was followed by information on how to stop smoking and was augmented by televised smoking cessation groups that provided models of behavioural change, intended to increase relevant skills and self-efficacy judgements in smokers. A similar strategy was used with other risk behaviours. A number of high-risk individuals also took part, with their partners, in a behavioural skills learning programme of change. They were asked to disseminate knowledge and skills to their friends and colleagues, acting as models of behavioural change to the wider public. The impact of this intervention in considered later in the chapter.

Attitude theory

Attitudinal models, including the theory of planned behaviour, have further contributed to the development of health education programmes. One model of attitude change that has proven highly appropriate to health education is the elaboration likelihood model (ELM) of Petty and Cacioppo (1986). This states that the influence of media output is the result of an interaction between message factors and the cognitive state of the recipient. According to the ELM, individuals are differentially motivated to attend to and process media messages as a consequence of their pre-existing beliefs and interests. They are more likely to attend to messages that are congruent with their pre-existing beliefs or that have personal relevance to them. Under these conditions, individuals engage in what Petty and Cacioppo refer to as central processing (see Figure 7.1). This involves active consideration of the media message, assessment of conclusions, and their integration within existing belief structures. Any consequent attitudinal change is likely to be both enduring and predictive of future behaviour. In contrast, recipients who are not interested in the issue or who hold incongruent beliefs are more likely to be influenced by non-message factors, including the credibility and attractiveness of the source. Identified as peripheral processing, any resultant attitudinal change is likely to be transient and not predictive of behaviour. Such individuals may be most responsive to emotional message appeals. As the ELM suggests that people with low issue involvement are more responsive to emotional appeals than reasoned argument, some have suggested that the role of emotion in health education may be as a motivator of those unaware of risks.

The weakness of the ELM is that although it provides a clear under-standing of methods that may be used to modify attitudes, evidence previously considered (see Chapter 3) suggests that such changes will have only a modest influence on behaviour. However, the other elements of the theory have been upheld in a largely laboratory-based, experimental literature.

An anecdotal example of how the credibility of the source of informa-tion may influence the reaction to a health education message is provided by the population reaction to a Polish government appeal to eat less meat and more vegetables, made when Poland was still under Soviet control. Following this appeal, meat sales increased dramatically as many people thought that the appeals indicated a future shortage and began panic-buying of meat. Another example of the importance of being aware of pre-existing attitudes, and how any media programme may either strengthen or weaken them, is illustrated by the negative effect of the initial British AIDS campaigns. This suggested that AIDS was an issue of

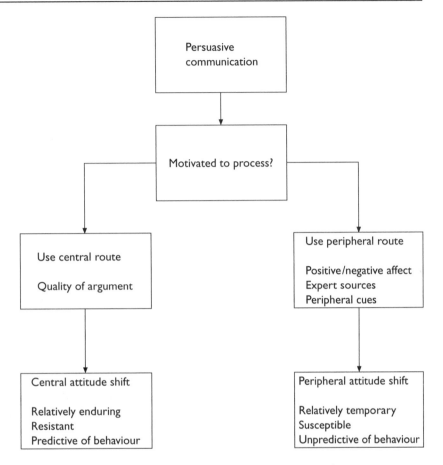

Figure 7.1   The elaboration likelihood model of attitude change

particular relevance to the 'three Hs': homosexuals, intravenous heroin users, and Haitians, the three groups in which the virus was first identified. Such messages served to increase anti-homosexual attitudes, and may have reduced condom use among the heterosexual community, as AIDS was not considered to be a relevant issue.

The health belief model

The health belief model suggests that measures to change behaviour should reduce the costs and increase the benefits of engaging in any new behaviour. They should also provide 'cues to action' to trigger any intended behavioural change. Such initiatives may occur at national or city level, for example by protecting green spaces in urban areas so they are available for recreational exercise, or through transport policies that encourage bicycle use and walking over the use of cars. They may also occur at a very local level: the provision of free condoms at night clubs affords one simple example.

Product labelling, including health warnings on cigarettes and nutritional information on food, is now used increasingly as a cue to encourage consumers to engage in health-enhancing behaviours. Unfortunately, nutritional information is not always understood by the public and is used infrequently, particularly amongst those with low income and education, whose food choices may be governed more by cost than quality. Similarly, health warnings on cigarettes appear to be ineffective in changing existing smokers' behaviour, although they may serve to prevent the uptake of smoking (Richards *et al.* 1989).

Environmental manipulations may form isolated interventions: they may also be incorporated into larger disease prevention programmes. The Heartbeat Wales programme (Nutbeam *et al.* 1993), for example, facilitated a number of environmental changes designed to reduce barriers and to cue appropriate behavioural change. Initiatives included encouraging food labelling and increasing the availability of 'healthy foods' in major retailers and local butchers, facilitating the establishment of 'healthy restaurants', and providing exercise trails in local parks.

Much social policy is premised, albeit implicitly, on the health belief model. The price of alcohol impacts on levels of consumption, particularly for wines and spirits. Beer consumption may be less sensitive to price. Increases in tobacco taxation may also form an effective measure in reducing consumption rates, with an estimated reduction in consumption of 4 per cent for every 10 per cent price rise. Taxation seems to be a particularly effective deterrent amongst the young, who are three times more likely to be affected by price rises than older adults.

Protection motivation theory

Protection motivation theory differs from the health belief model in that it emphasizes the importance of fear as a motivator, and self-efficacy as a mediator, of behavioural change. The influence of fear appeals on behaviour has been examined in a number of laboratory and field studies. Perhaps the most consistent finding is that fear appeals have only a modest impact on behaviour, particularly when no means of reducing any induced threat are provided. Even where significant and persistent health concerns are raised, behaviour change may not follow. The Australian 'Grim Reaper' campaign (Rigby *et al.* 1989), for example, dramatically raised audience awareness of AIDS and levels of health anxiety, but had no impact on AIDS-related knowledge or sexual behaviour. Rather than motivate behavioural change, moderate or high fear may actually interfere with change. Fear-arousing messages may result in increased resistance to the message, denial that a threat applies to the individual, and even increases in the targeted behaviour.

Fear messages may not always be counterproductive. Negative frames may make messages more memorable than positive ones, particularly where preventive action is simple and easily accessible. Meyerowitz and Chaiken (1987), for example, found that positive messages stressing the health benefits of breast self-examination had less influence on women's behaviour than negative messages concentrating on the potential dangers of failing to self-examine. Both negative and positive emotional messages may be more memorable when individuals can compare them to a message with the opposite emotional valence. It may be the contrast that is important, not the mood induced by one message in isolation.

Fear-based messages are most likely to change behaviour under conditions of low levels of perceived vulnerability, high self-esteem, when the means of avoiding the feared outcome are provided, the required changes are manageable, and individuals believe that they are capable of achieving them. Kreuter and Stretcher (1996), for example, allocated individuals screened for risk of CHD into one of three conditions: risk information, risk information combined with personalized strategies for behavioural change, or no information. Those in the combined intervention were 18 per cent more likely to change at least one risk behaviour over the six months following screening than those in the risk information only group. If relevant information is easily available, high fear appeals are more likely to trigger information-seeking than low fear appeals. Keesling and Friedman (1995) gave sunbathers high and low fear evoking pictures of melanomas and high and low levels of information about how to reduce risk for such outcomes. Participants in the high fear/low information group were more likely to seek additional information than those in the low fear/low information condition. Highlighting the need to develop interventions specific to differing target groups, they also found that individuals with high risk-taking personalities were less likely to seek out relevant information than those who were less risky.

Community programmes

The first major health promotion intervention aimed at a whole community, and involving more than simple advertising was the Stanford Three Towns Project (Farquhar *et al.* 1977). In this, two towns received a high intensity, year-long media campaign targeting CHD-related behaviours. In addition, a group of individuals at particularly high risk for CHD were identified in one town and, with their partners, received individual behavioural counselling on how to change their risk behaviours. These individuals were asked to disseminate their knowledge of risk factors and risk factor change to friends and colleagues. This combined intervention was expected to generate more change throughout the population than the media campaign alone. This, in turn, was expected to generate more

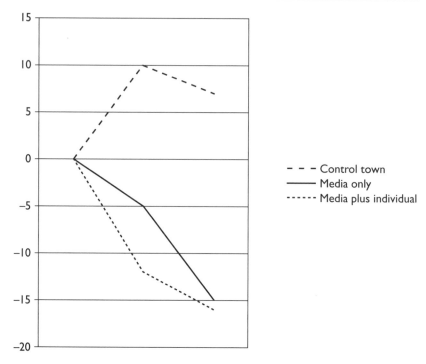

Figure 7.2   Changes in CHD risk scores following the Stanford Three Towns Project

changes than those in a town that received no intervention. The expected results were found (see Figure 7.2).

The European equivalent of this programme, the North Karelia project (Puska *et al.* 1985) was also considered a success. However, a dissenting voice was raised by one of the investigators, who argued that there was little evidence of any differences between the control and intervention areas that could be directly attributable to the intervention, and that all the project proved was that such an intervention was logistically possible.

Despite this reservation, a number of subsequent interventions have also targeted risk factors for CHD and have frequently met with less success than the initial programmes. The Stanford Five City Project (Farquhar *et al.* 1990) combined the methods used in the initial programme with an increased emphasis on community-initiated collaborative teaching programmes and environmental manipulations. The impact of the intervention in two cities was compared with changes in three control areas not receiving the intervention.

In a cohort followed for the duration of the study, knowledge of CHD risk factors rose in all samples but changed most in the intervention areas. Measures of total cholesterol, resting pulse and body mass index fell more in the intervention than control areas during the early years of the project. However, by its end no differences between the control and intervention area were evident. Only blood pressure and smoking rates differed at the end of the intervention. Nevertheless, in this analysis, risk for CHD was lowered by 16 per cent in the intervention population cohort in contrast to a 3 per cent fall among the control population. Unfortunately, this success was not replicated in the findings of a series of cross-sectional surveys conducted over the period of the project. In these, smoking rates did not differ between the intervention and control cities at any time and differences in risk levels for CHD did not vary between any of the communities.

A further example of a large-scale intervention aimed at CHD-risk reduction is afforded by the Minnesota Heart Health Programme (MHHP: Jacobs *et al.* 1986). This five-year intervention drew explicitly on social learning theory and persuasive-communications theory to develop its programmes. The mass media were used to promote awareness of the programme and to reinforce other educational components. However, the main foci of the MHHP was the provision of individual screening programmes in primary care settings, and direct contact with individuals through competitions, telephone support, classes in the community and the worksite, self-help materials and home correspondence programmes. In addition, the programme manipulated the environment to facilitate and maintain change through, for example, food labelling, healthy menus in restaurants and increased opportunities for physical recreation. Interventions aimed at smoking cessation included supportive primary care screening programmes, supportive telephone calls, worksite quit classes, home correspondence courses, Quit and Win competitions, and worksite manipulations including increased 'smoke-free' areas. Despite this sophisticated package of interventions, the effectiveness of the programme on smoking prevalence was marginal at best. Data on weight loss, another key intervention target for the programme was equally disappointing. Over the course of the trial the average adult weight in both intervention and control communities rose by nearly 7 lb, leading to the conclusion that the programme had little or no effect on levels of obesity.

The programmes described here are examples of a wider set of health promotion programmes but are not unrepresentative. Indeed, they are some of the most impressive programmes yet conducted. Their execution was impressive, yet their findings must raise a question as to their value. Against this background, some commentators remain strong advocates of the effectiveness of population approaches to health promotion; others are more cautious in their claims.

Worksite health promotion

An alternative strategy to attempting to influence whole communities has been to target smaller communities within them. Worksites form one such target. The programmes can be more focused, and typically achieve higher levels of programme recognition than community programmes. Most important of all, however, the workplace provides a closed system in which the environment can be manipulated to maximize the probability of behaviour change. Where this has been exploited, there is some evidence that environmental, social, or even economic manipulation can facilitate behavioural change. Where programmes have not done so, for example through workplace risk factor screening programmes, there is little evidence of any greater gain than that achieved in any other contexts (see Chapter 11).

Education and environmental manipulations

The Treatwell Program (Hebert et al. 1993) focused on changing dietary intake of fat and other nutrients to reduce the risk of cancer. It provided classes and food demonstrations for the workforce augmented by food labelling in worksite cafeterias, with the goal of reducing dietary fat to 30 per cent of total calories and to increase dietary fibre to between 20 and 30 grams per day. The intervention lasted a period of 15 months, and changes in diet following the programme were compared with those of a control worksite that did not receive it. By this time, modest but clinically insignificant reductions in fat consumption were found amongst participants in the active condition. There was no evidence of changes in consumption of dietary fibre.

Equally modest results were reported by the WellWorks programme (Sorensen et al. 1998). This study assessed the effects of a two-year long integrated health promotion programme focusing on dietary habits and cigarette smoking. It comprised three key intervention elements: joint worker/management participation in programme planning and implementation, consultation with management on worksite environmental changes, and health education programmes. Differences between intervention and control worksites were modest, but included reductions in the percentage of calories consumed as fat and increases in servings of fruit and vegetables and in total fibre consumption. No significant intervention effects were observed for smoking cessation.

The Take Heart programme (Glasgow et al. 1995) proved less effective. This programme provided screening programmes and an 18-month intervention involving a variety of environmental, educational and skills-based programmes in an attempt to modify workers' dietary and smoking habits. Smoking interventions included provision of self-help kits and group support meetings. Dietary interventions included written materials, presentations with food samples, and cooking demonstrations. Policy issues included the provision of no-smoking areas, increasing healthy food options in the cafeterias and vending machines, and stopping the sale of tobacco on site. The results were disappointing. After one and a half years of this programme, no differences between intervention and control sites were found on measures of smoking prevalence, dietary fat intake and serum cholesterol. The authors' 'inescapable' conclusion was that the Take Heart project did not improve employee health behaviours related to nutrition and tobacco use more than did repeated measures alone.

These are not isolated findings. Glanz *et al.* (1996) reviewed the effectiveness of ten worksite nutrition education programmes which used group education, group education plus individual counselling/instruction, cafeteria-based programmes, and group education plus cafeteria-based programmes. Sixteen worksite cholesterol programmes were reviewed in five categories: monitoring; individual counselling; group sessions or classes; mediated methods using print, audiovisual, telephone, self-help kits, and combined approaches. They concluded that evidence about a causal relationship between worksite nutrition and changed behaviour or improved health was lacking. Oldenburg and Harris (1996) were equally cautious in their conclusions about the effectiveness of worksite interventions. However, they noted that measuring the impact and effect of health promotion activity in the workplace is not an easy task. Most worksite intervention studies utilized inadequate study designs and poor measurement. In addition, high attrition rates and poor reach have also compromised their efficacy and effectiveness. Participation rates range from 32 per cent for health education programmes to 5 per cent for smoking cessation interventions, while onsite stress management programmes attract between 10 and 40 per cent of the workforce. Those who do attend are likely to be healthier and more concerned with health matters than non-attenders.

Economic incentives

One advantage of the workplace is that it can provide tangible non-health-related benefits for those taking part in any programme of change. Interventions taking advantage of this may prove more effective than the programmes so far reviewed. Glasgow *et al.* (1993) reported an intervention in which an incentive scheme for smoking cessation was combined with individual monthly monitoring of expired carbon monoxide levels. Abstinent smokers were eligible for monthly lottery prizes. Nineteen per cent of workers who smoked participated in the study. At the time of the final lottery draw, one year into the programme, 20 per cent of this group were no longer smoking. Such benefits are not universal, however, and programmes where participants lose money if they restart smoking have proven less successful. It seems that employees prefer schemes that reward success, not punish failure.

Social support

Social support may both change social norms towards those that support change and provide the opportunity for mutual help in achieving change.

Where it has been actively manipulated some gains have been reported. Brownwell and Felix (1987) manipulated social support through the development of teams in an attempt to increase participation and adherence to a weight reduction programme. Participants were organized into competitive teams and given relevant self-help manuals following a baseline weight assessment. Throughout the programme, the results from weekly weigh-ins were displayed in a prominent position at each worksite. After approximately 15 weeks, the average weight loss was 5.5 kg. This is an impressive reduction, in comparison to both other weight loss programmes and wider population trends, although longer-term maintenance may prove difficult to sustain.

A number of programmes have combined financial incentive programmes with social support. Koffman et al. (1998), for example, compared the effectiveness of a multicomponent smoking cessation programme alone, supplemented by incentives and team competition, and a standard smoking cessation programme. Six months after the programme, 41 per cent of participants in the incentive/competition programme were abstinent in comparison with 23 per cent of participants in the multicomponent programme and 8 per cent of those in the traditional programme. Six months later, the abstinence rates were 37, 30, and 11 per cent respectively.

Towards a new agenda for health promotion

Despite enormous financial and research commitment, much of the evidence reviewed has not shown even very sophisticated health promotion programmes to be effective in facilitating appropriate behavioural change. Some of the reasons for this apparent failure may, paradoxically, reflect the effectiveness of health promotion and its impact on the population as a whole. Most of the programmes described have taken place against a background of significant behavioural changes throughout the population. The prevalence of risk factors for CHD have changed markedly over this time, with significant increases in levels of exercise and reductions in smoking and dietary cholesterol. These changes were sufficient to lower rates of CHD in the USA by 22 per cent between 1968 and 1977.

Such changes have been facilitated by many small-scale health promotion projects and, perhaps even more importantly, by informal influences including access to a massive amount of information on health and healthy behaviours provided by the media. Behavioural change has been facilitated by changing social norms and environmental changes such as no-smoking areas and increased access to low cholesterol food items. The consequences of such changes are that, unless the campaign addresses a very new issue, most people who encounter health promotion programmes will have previously encountered much of the information given in any campaign. Those in the control areas are equally likely to encounter such information.

In the worst case, from an assessment perspective, control areas may engage in similar forms of health promotion to those in the intervention area. This was the fate of the Heartbeat Wales programme (Nutbeam *et al.* 1993) which measured changes consequent to a five-year intervention in Wales with those in a comparison area in England. Two major factors made comparisons between the two areas problematic. First, the government instituted a similar health promotion programme throughout England, including the comparison area, over the course of the intervention. Secondly, innovations such as food labelling that began in Wales were taken up by national supermarket chains and disseminated across their shops throughout the UK. It would be naive to assume that other programmes were insulated from such contamination. Accordingly, comparisons between intervention and control areas may underestimate any gains made as a consequence of a particular health promotion initiative. Any assessment of the effectiveness of health promotion should consider the role of both formal and informal health promotion in generating the population changes in behaviour evident over the past decades, not just comparisons between intervention and control areas of individual studies.

Nevertheless, these findings suggest that health promotion may have to change both its focus and methods if it is to prove more effective in changing behaviour than the background information that is already influencing much of the population. Research from other areas and relevant policy changes also suggest the need for change: in particular, the increasing understanding of risk factors for disease other than those traditionally considered by health promotion and the WHO's increasing emphasis on improving well-being. The final part of this chapter considers some possible issues that health promotion may have to address and some possible strategies it may, or is beginning to, adopt. They are not meant to be definitive and exclusive. However, they reflect the need for health promotion to develop further, both in the methods it uses and the issues it concerns itself with. Three differing pathways are suggested:

◆ targeting new risk factors;
◆ creating health-supporting environments;
◆ Increasing community involvement and letting it define the intervention targets.

Targeting new risk factors

Health promotion has traditionally focused on only a subset of behaviours that influence health, including diet, exercise, protective sexual behaviour, and alcohol consumption. Looking back to earlier chapters in the present text, a number of other factors have also been shown to be strongly associated with physical health, some of which may usefully form targets for future health promotion programmes. These include economic inequalities, social isolation, stress and depression, personal qualities such as hostility, membership of societal minorities, and work and unemployment factors. This section considers some of the ways in which one of these factors, socio-economic inequalities, may be addressed by those involved in health promotion.

The link between poor health and socio-economic inequalities has led some commentators to suggest that the most compelling intervention strategies to reduce health inequalities are likely to be social, economic and political. However, not all interventions that address economic factors need do so through financial means. Mays and Cochran (1988), for example, noted that it is very difficult for low-income ethnic minority women to refuse unsafe sex practices. Many lack power in intimate relationships because of economic dependence or are culturally excluded from decisions about contraceptive use. Such women may be helped by school and job training programmes. For similar reasons an important component in health and wellness programmes for pregnant teenagers is that the mother remains at school.

From an economic perspective, strategies to reduce health inequalities must include measures to reduce unemployment to the lowest possible level. The Swedish economic model identified a series of strategies that have proven effective in maintaining high levels of employment, including proactive employment exchange, high quality training aimed at providing skills required by the employment market, recruitment incentives for employers, and the right to temporary public employment in the last resort. Davey Smith et al. (1999) called for a series of differing economic measures. They argued for the implementation of 'affordable' basic income schemes as a means of ending poverty. These could take the form of a payment received by every person or household to provide a minimal income, with the amount paid based on age and family status. In addition, they suggested that all benefits to families with children receiving income support should be increased to avoid the next generation being disadvantaged from birth. They noted that one-quarter of all children are born to mothers under the age of 25 years, and that the government should ensure that those mothers under this age receive no fewer benefits than older individuals. It is beyond the scope of the present volume to comment on the strengths and weaknesses of various economic systems; however, economic systems do have significant implications for health and should, therefore, form a legitimate area of influence for those involved in promoting health.

Davey Smith et al. (1999) also identified a number of wider policy issues that would significantly impact on the health of the economically deprived, including reducing the mortality rate for pedestrian child deaths through the use of traffic calming measures, and improving child nutrition through increasing free school meals entitlement. These add to a list of policy factors compiled by the British Medical Association (1998,

Table 7.1 Some of the environmental factors identified by the British Medical Association as constituting a risk to health

Type of policy	Areas where policy changes may impact on health
Macroeconomic	Income distribution and level Changes in labour market Changes in cost of living, food and housing
Agriculture	Effect of subsidies on pesticide use and residues
Industrial	Use and promotion of toxic substances Occupational Health and Safety requirements Hazardous waste regulations
Energy	Nuclear fuel cycle Effects of 'smog'
Housing and social	Overcrowding Access to safe water Adequate waste collection and treatment Indoor water quality

see Table 7.1) that may influence the health of the population and in particular the more economically deprived.

In addition to changes in government policy, there is a need to develop strategies aimed at other processes that link socio-economic status and health. In Chapter 1, these were shown to include stress as a consequence of work factors. Changes in these processes may be brought about through interventions aimed at individuals or, more importantly, the wider working environment.

Initiatives that have addressed worksite stress have almost uniquely done so through the provision of programmes that teach stress management skills: that is, they help attenders to cope more effectively with the demands placed upon them. This chapter has already noted that such programmes frequently fail to attract those that are experiencing significant stress. However, they have a more fundamental flaw in that they fail to directly address issues relevant to work stress or the well-being of the majority of the workforce, and particularly those in blue-collar jobs.

One programme that did so was reported by Maes et al. (1998). Their intervention, conducted at a Dutch worksite, focused both on lifestyle change and modifying key aspects of the working environment in order to foster mental and physical well-being throughout the workforce. The first year of the programme followed a conventional pattern and focused on individual behavioural change through the provision of health education classes. In the second phase of the intervention, the programme became more innovative. It drew upon a substantial literature that has identified working conditions that appear to enhance both the well-being of workers and work production levels. These conditions include individuals working within their capabilities, avoiding short and repetitive performance tasks, having some control over the organization of work, and adequate social contact. With these factors in mind, Maes *et al.* attempted, within the constraints of production, to change the nature of each worker's job to bring it closer to the ideal. In addition, they trained managers in communication and leadership skills and identified methods through which they could recognize, prevent and reduce individual stress within the workforce.

Evaluation of the intervention involved following four groups of workers: those working in the intervention worksite, those in control sites, and participants and non-participants in the individual lifestyle-change programme. Their results indicated highly specific effects of each intervention. By the end of the individual intervention phase, participants in the lifestyle programme showed greater reductions in risk for CHD than those in the control group. However, by the end of the third year of the project, these gains were no longer evident. In contrast, the wider intervention was associated with increased quality of work and lower absenteeism rates in comparison with the control sites over the duration of the intervention. No data on 'stress' levels were taken by the research team. However, the data collected are indicative of positive changes in stress or job satisfaction levels.

An even simpler, but highly effective, intervention focusing on job spillover was conducted on one hospital ward in response to the nurses who had responsibility for child care arriving late and feeling 'stressed' at the beginning of their morning shifts. This was because the timing of the shift did not allow them to take their children to a childminder in time to get to work without rushing and at risk of being late. The ward manager's response to this was twofold. First, to start the shift half an hour later than previously. Secondly, to allow some flexibility in the time that individuals were expected to arrive on duty, and to record the 'handover' on audiotape so that late arrivals could easily obtain the information they needed to begin their work without another nurse having to take time out to brief them. This simple, responsive process made a significant difference to the effectiveness of the ward staff and the stress they experienced. Interventions that make a difference do not necessarily have to be complex, but they do have to be responsive to staff needs.

Creating supportive environments

Unhealthy environments have been characterized as those that threaten safety, undermine the creation of social ties, and are conflictual, abusive or violent. A healthy environment, in contrast, provides safety, opportunities for social integration, and the ability to predict and control aspects of that environment. These requirements present a significant challenge to future town and city planners and administrators. Those involved in health promotion should also be attempting to influence all aspects of environmental development in ways that increase its ability to sustain both mental and physical health. Issues relevant to health promotion vary from the design and architecture of 'safe' housing estates through to the planning and geographical location of shopping and leisure centres to transport policies that encourage cycling and walking. Such a process moves health promotion away from its traditional arena of high profile, targeted initiatives to one of consultancy, advising and even lobbying those involved in the development of public policy.

Evaluation of large-scale programmes focusing solely on the physical environment has proven difficult. Evaluation of the Healthy Cities movement serves as an example. Participating cities across the world were concerned with monitoring and improving environmental indicators of quality of life including unemployment, housing quality, democratic participation and education provision (Ashton 1992). Unfortunately, environmental changes were not instituted in a controlled manner and were not monitored effectively, making it impossible to establish any relationship between environmental changes and any changes in behaviour or health. Nevertheless, smaller-scale controlled trials of environmental manipulation attest to their potential effectiveness. Linegar et al. (1991), for example, measured the impact of environmental changes on exercise levels within the general population. Taking advantage of the closed community provided by a naval base, they established cycle paths, exercise equipment, exercise clubs and fitness competitions within the base. In addition, workers were given 'release time' from other duties while they participated in some physical activities. In comparison with a control area, where no such changes were initiated, significant increases in activity and fitness were found amongst both existing exercisers and previous non-exercisers.

Not all environmental interventions, however, have met with similar levels of success, including some attempts to establish restrictive smoking policies in the workplace. Gomel et al. (1993), for example, reported on the impact of a worksite smoking ban imposed on smoking both inside and outside the workplace of an Australian ambulance service. Before the ban was imposed, 60 per cent of the workforce smoked cigarettes: an average of 26 per day. Although the policy resulted in a reduction in smoking in the few days following its inception, salivary nicotine measures that provided biological verification of smoking levels showed a return to baseline measures within six weeks of the inception of the policy. These data are not atypical and a number of studies suggest that while such bans reduce the prevalence of smoking in the areas affected, there is little evidence that they reduce the prevalence of employee smokers. In addition, while an apparently logical leap, there is also little evidence that combining restrictive policies with the provision of smoking cessation groups is an effective approach. Accordingly, it appears that smoking policies may benefit non-smokers but have little influence on smokers themselves. Such findings may also suggest that restrictive policies that attempt to control behaviour may be less successful than those that provide the opportunity to engage in a wider set of behaviours.

Increasing community involvement

The models of health promotion so far considered have adopted a top-down approach. That is, they have been primarily informed by health policy makers, epidemiology and intervention theory. In total contrast to such interventions, the WHO has called for an increase in community involvement in health promotion. Such a move suggests that rather than the passive process through which the community typically receives health promotion, it should be actively involved in setting the agenda for, and developing, health promotion projects. This moves the community from being the recipient of external programmes developed from without to an active developer of initiatives from within. Such an idea is not new: Ross and Lappin (1967) identified community development as occurring when a community identified its needs or objectives, prioritized them and found the resources to work towards achieving them. In this context, the goal of health professionals is to work with communities in order to empower individuals within them to gain control over their lives.

The process of coming together as a community can be empowering and enhance well-being in itself. Individuals can develop feelings of empowerment through community or organizational involvement even if the community or organization fails to achieve any desired structural change. Participation can reduce feelings of hopelessness, and positively affect psychological health on measures such as social support, coping, problem-solving skills and personal competence. However, participation without a positive outcome may represent tokenism and, over an extended period, increase feelings of hopelessness. Members of the community are most likely to come together when they have an opportunity to share common experiences, develop emotional closeness and recognize that they have a common identity or destiny. They are most likely to take action when they have the necessary skills and resources and belong to organizations that have a task focus, clear roles for participating members and use democratic decision-making procedures.

The development of a viable community intervention starts with a reconnaissance phase in which the professional explores a community and how it operates. The professional needs to identify key individuals within the area and a group of people willing to work on a particular project, ideally determined by the group itself or from meetings with the wider population within the area. This group then takes action. Such a process makes formal evaluation of such programmes difficult to assess: the goal of the group is to benefit the community, not to provide a well controlled intervention trial. Nevertheless, Johnson (1988) provided an example of the process of development and implementation of a community programme working to reduce behavioural problems among the children of low-income Americans living in the Houston barrios. To gain the cooperation of the parents, the health workers first went from door to door asking parents about their aspirations for their children. These ideas were then taken to a group of parents for discussion. The parents were encouraged to form a Parent's Advisory Council that would facilitate and sanction the development and implementation of any interventions. The project's final goal and procedures were developed in collaboration with the Council. This validation and advice on how to approach possible participants was thought to increase participation rates in the intervention finally conducted.

A second example of such an initiative can be found in a CHD prevention programme in a British inner-city area. At the time, a series of health education classes known as Look After Yourself were proving a popular primary care intervention. However, while these were well attended, the participants were most frequently white middle-class women with sufficient time and resources to attend. In an attempt to encourage participation by other groups, health workers began to talk to the residents in the economically deprived areas of the city to find out why they did not attend these groups. Many single mothers reported that they would like to attend but were unable to find someone to look after their young children while they did so. In response to this, the mothers who lived in one block of flats formed a crèche that was supervised by different women each week so that all could attend the classes over the life of the project.

Not all community projects are successful. A study reported by Baumgarten *et al.* (1988) provides an example of a failed intervention. They reported on the outcome of a health promotion team's attempts to establish a mutual help network among elderly residents of a state-subsidised apartment in Canada. However, rather than improving matters, those taking part in the intervention reported higher levels of depressed mood and lower life satisfaction than a control group receiving no intervention. The probable cause of the worsening situation was that the people between whom the intervention team were trying to increase social interactions varied in religion and ethnicity and had a history of intergroup tension: not the ideal material for such a project. Such an outcome reflects a failure to fully engage the community in the instigation and development of the project, not a failure of the approach.

Summary and conclusions

Despite its critics, health promotion has proven an effective means of changing population behaviour. However, the agenda followed and methods used by health promotion may no longer be applicable to all behaviours and populations. This chapter called for a realignment and change of emphasis in the practice of health promotion: in particular, to focus more on emerging risk factors in a more systemic manner, targeting structural elements as well as individuals within the community, and involving the community in decision making in relation to its health targets and methods by which these may be met. Developments such as these should increase the role of health promotion as a political and economic force, which should be taken into account in a variety of policy strategies.

Further reading

Bennett, P. and Murphy S. (1997) *Psychology and Health Promotion*. Buckingham: Open University Press.

Naidoo, J. and Wills, J. (1994) *Health Promotion: Foundations for Practice*. London: Baillière-Tindall.

Part IV
Clinical interventions

Psychological interventions

Health psychology frequently seeks to explain the processes underpinning psychological factors relating to disease and health. On occasion, it also attempts to influence such processes, frequently through working with individuals using some form of psychological intervention. The goals of such interventions are generally twofold: to facilitate appropriate behavioural change and to help the individual to cope with particular demands that they are facing, typically as a result of disease or treatment factors.

This chapter provides a brief overview of the techniques and components of some of the more frequently used therapeutic approaches. The effectiveness of these approaches in a variety of medical settings and with differing therapeutic goals is reviewed in the next two chapters. As those involved in providing many of the interventions described may be from a variety of professional and therapeutic backgrounds, the chapter adopts the generic term of 'helper' to describe these various individuals.

The chapter introduces the following intervention strategies:

- ◆ **Client-centred counselling**
- ◆ Motivational interviewing
- ◆ Problem-focused counselling
- ◆ Cognitive-behavioural therapy
- ◆ Coping effectiveness training
- ◆ Emotional disclosure
- ◆ Self-management straining
- ◆ Operant conditioning

Matching interventions to individual characteristics

The goal of any therapeutic intervention is to bring about some form of change. The nature of that change may differ markedly according to the

Table 8.1 Type of intervention recommended for individuals in differing stages of change

Stage of change	Recommended intervention
Precontemplation	Motivational interview
	Operant conditioning
	Emotional disclosure
Contemplation	Problem-focused counselling
	Cognitive-behavioural therapy
	Client-centred counselling
Change	Self-management strategies
	Cognitive-behavioural therapy
	Coping effectiveness training

characteristics of the individual and the intended outcome of the intervention. Key targets in the context of clinical health psychology are changing behaviours that place an individual at risk of disease or disease progression, physiological mediators of disease, and mood where this may influence the individual's response to disease or even the course of that disease.

To treat all individuals as a homogeneous group with equal motivation to change their behaviour or enter a therapeutic alliance with a helper is inappropriate. Some people may actively seek help, be highly motivated to consider change and seek strategies by which this can be achieved. Others, such as those who take part in a routine screening programme, may be less willing to consider behavioural change. Although theoretically questionable, the 'stages of change' model of Prochaska and DiClemente (1986: see Chapter 3) provides some useful insights concerning matching interventions to differing levels of motivation to change. The model identifies five stages of behavioural change: pre-contemplation, contemplation, preparation for action, action, and maintenance. It also suggests that the goals of any intervention will necessarily differ according to the stage of change of the individual. For those in the pre-contemplation stage, a successful therapeutic outcome may be a shift towards more active consideration of change. For those already in the contemplation stage and beyond, the goal may be to develop strategies to facilitate change.

Individuals in the pre-contemplation stage rarely seek counselling. Accordingly, therapeutic techniques appropriate to this group have, until recently, received little consideration. Attempts at direct persuasion appear to have little influence on this group, and the challenge for those working with them has been to develop strategies to foster change. The most promising approach so far seems to be that of motivational interviewing (Miller and Rollnick, 1991). This approach contrasts strongly with approaches based on direct attempts to persuade individuals to change in that it is non-confrontational and does not involve the helper in an overt attempt to encourage change. For those in the contemplation or action stages, interventions may be more usefully focused on how to achieve change. For these individuals, interventions such as **problem-focused counselling** and **cognitive-behavioural interventions** may be most appropriate (see Table 8.1). Many of the interventions have specific techniques and differing underlying theories of human behaviour. However, many also draw upon a basic model of interaction with patients developed by Rogers in the 1950s and 1960s. It is at this point that the chapter starts.

Client-centred counselling

Carl Rogers (see, for example, Rogers 1967) argued that all individuals have a tendency to develop and grow in ways in which they choose: a process he called self-actualization. If they are prevented from doing so, the result is sadness, anxiety or depression. For many, the inhibition of the actualizing process begins in childhood. Children learn to gain the positive regard of others, and particularly their parents, by behaving in ways that please them and are rewarded. Subtle elements of this process can contribute to the process of pathology. In particular, phrases that signify both disapproval of bad behaviour and of the child engaging in that behaviour ('Your behaviour is bad, and I don't love you when you behave in this way') can lead the individual to place a negative value on themselves. In response to this, they associate their self-worth with their behaviour and others reactions to it: 'If I behave in a certain way my parents will love me'. In response to these beliefs, children tend to adopt the behaviour that will be rewarded and make them feel valued.[1]

The process of expressing love and affection contingent upon certain behaviour is known as providing conditional positive regard. It moves the recipient away from their own goals and needs, to adopt those of important others. According to Rogers, such a state is one of discontent and anxiety. The goal of therapy is to provide an environment in which the individual can identify their own life goals and how they wish to determine them: to place them on the pathway to self-actualization. Rogers stated that counselling does not rely on techniques or 'doing things *to*' the client; rather, the quality of the interpersonal encounter is the most significant element in determining effectiveness (Rogers 1967). The goal of the helper is to provide a setting in which the individual is not judged and can be free to explore new ways of being: that is, one in which they experience unconditional positive regard.

Rogers considered three conditions to be both necessary and sufficient for therapeutic change: the helper is integrated and genuine in their relationship with the client; the helper gains an empathic understanding of the client's perspective and communicates this to them; and the helper provides unconditional positive regard. Being genuine means that the helper shares feelings or gives feedback on how they feel as a consequence of what the client is telling them. Such feedback may be positive or negative, and shows the client that the helper is human with human feelings. It may involve expressions of sadness or even anger in response to individual's stories.

Empathy involves the helper in gaining an understanding of the individual's situation, problems, feelings and concerns, from *the client's* perspective and showing the client that they have achieved this level of understanding. The most frequent method by which this is achieved is through a process of reflection:

> *Client:*   After I was diagnosed with cancer, I just felt that he
>   could not or would not give me any support.
> *Therapist:* It feels like you were very disappointed or even angry at
>   his reaction . . .

Rather than a direct question, an empathic response can prove a powerful facilitator of further discussion and problem exploration. Note that empathy is not communicated through phrases such as 'I understand' or 'I know how that must feel'. Repetition of such trite phrases may prove alienating and inhibit progress in therapy. The final component of the therapeutic relationship is that the therapist is not judgemental, and does not repeat the past experiences of conditional positive regard.

Rogers argued that these three therapeutic conditions are both necessary and sufficient for therapeutic change. Most observers now agree that they are necessary, but not sufficient, for effective therapy. Accordingly, they have been integrated into a number of the therapeutic approaches described below.

Motivational interviewing

The primary goal of the **motivational interview** is to encourage individuals to explore their own, perhaps conflicting, beliefs about and attitudes towards a particular behaviour or behavioural change (Miller and Rollnick 1991). This process is intended to result in a state of cognitive dissonance in which the individual actively considers two or more sets of opposing beliefs and attitudes towards a particular issue. According to cognitive dissonance theory, this is an aversive state and motivates cognitive or behavioural work to reduce the discomfort. It may result in a rejection of the newly considered arguments. It may result in the adoption of new beliefs or behaviours: that is, progression through the stages of change.

The role of the helper is to facilitate this process, not to argue in favour of change or to directly attempt persuasion. The process is deliberately non-confrontational, and at its most basic provides the individual with the space to actively consider the benefits or disadvantages of behavioural change. It involves two key questions: 'What are some of the good things about your present behaviour ... ?', and 'What are the less good things about ... ?' The potential for resistance to discussion is diffused by a tacit acknowledgement that the behaviour in question has some benefits for the individual, and clients are asked to consider the benefits of change only when these have been reviewed. Following this, a similar process may be conducted in which the individual is asked to express any concerns they may have about their present behaviour, or about change itself. The results of all these discussions are then summarized and fed back to the individual by the helper in a way that highlights the dissonance process ('You find alcohol helps you cope with stress, but your drinking causes tensions with your partner'). Only if the person then expresses some interest in change does the interview progress to providing information on change or examining ways in which this could be achieved. Miller and colleagues do not consider the therapeutic approaches that can then be adopted: the motivational interview has done its work by this time. However, any approach used at this time will be action-focused and consider ways in which behavioural change may be facilitated.

The intervention is deliberately non-confrontational and utilizes methods central to the humanistic school of therapy, including actively engaging in a therapeutic alliance with clients through the use of empathy and a relatively non-directive approach.

Problem-focused counselling

One of the most widely used forms of counselling has been developed by Gerard Egan over the past three decades (see, for example, Egan 1990). Known as **problem-focused counselling**, it draws upon a variety of theoretical frameworks. It has strong similarities to humanistic therapy, in that Egan considers its primary goal to be one of helping the client towards an understanding of their problems and to identify their own goals and solutions to those problems. Like Rogers, he considers the quality of the relationship between helper and client to be a critical element of the therapeutic process. He states that helpers should be respectful and genuine in their relationships with their clients, express their feelings, and achieve and show high levels of empathy. In contrast to Rogers, however, he notes that issues relevant to problem-focused counselling are in the here-and-now, and that the process of counselling should be clearly structured.

Egan identified three stages through which the counselling process must proceed: (1) problem exploration and clarification, (2) goal-setting, and (3) facilitating action. This process may not always be linear: clients may identify new problems or differing priorities as counselling proceeds. Nevertheless, Egan argues that both client and helper need be aware of the stage they are in, and that only the successful completion of one stage will allow actions taken in subsequent stages to be effective. Egan also acknowledges that the process of change may require the use of resources or skills at present unavailable to the individual. Accordingly, the final stages of counselling may involve the client being taught skills, such as relaxation or assertiveness, in order to facilitate the desired change.

Stage 1: Problem exploration and clarification

The goal of the first stage of counselling is to ensure that both helper and client fully understand the problems that the individual is facing. Many people who seek counselling may feel so overwhelmed by a variety of problems and their emotional sequelae that they are unable to identify or prioritize specific issues that need resolving. It is essential that the helper does not repeat this error and that due attention is given to the process of problem identification. Health care workers all too frequently present 'standard solutions' to 'standard problems' without consideration of the actual problems faced by the individual. Overweight individuals are presented with diet sheets, people with arthritis are given standard information on limb mobilization, and so on, frequently with little consideration to the circumstances or history of the person receiving them. In the case of the overweight individual, for example, providing a diet sheet implicitly suggests that the problem is one of ignorance of the dietary changes necessary to lose weight, and that the solution is one of information provision. Rarely is the problem so simple.

Egan identified a number of strategies appropriate to each stage of the counselling process. In the first stage, these are primarily ones that promote the client's effective exploration of their problems, and include direct questioning, verbal prompts ('Tell me about . . .'), minimal prompts ('Uh-hu') and empathic feedback. Egan states that the use of open questions should be maximized, and that any direct question should generally be followed by a less directive method of encouraging consideration of the problem. Some examples of this process are given in a sample of dialogue involving a man recently identified as having high cholesterol levels but who has not been able to achieve the suggested dietary changes:

> *Helper:* So, you haven't been able to achieve your goal of changing your diet?
> *Mr B:* No. I'm just the same as before. No luck as usual.
> *Helper:* You've been here before then?
> *Mr B:* Yes. I don't know . . . It all seems such a problem. I set off with good intentions, and want to change my diet – but it all seems to fall apart. And I don't really know why.
> *Helper:* Hmmm. Perhaps it would help if we looked in a bit more detail at some of the times when things have gone wrong.

> *Mr B:* OK. Well, thinking back to yesterday, I asked my wife to get us a salad for dinner and then my kids started on and said they didn't want any more of the 'rabbit food' and I suppose I gave in and said we'd eat something different.
>
> *Helper:* You looked quite frustrated when you were telling me about that.
>
> *Mr B:* Well, it can get very annoying as it's often the kids or my wife that seems to decide what I eat. But they haven't got my problems. They don't seem to understand why I want to eat the things I do. They never compromise!

Note that in this brief example, the helper has begun to identify the factors contributing to Mr B's problems through the use of only one direct prompt, with the other interjections involving reflective feedback.

Stage 2: Goal-setting

Once the problems facing the individual are understood, the counselling process moves into its second phase. In this, the helper helps the client to identify how they would like the situation to be different. Note that *how* these changes may be achieved is not yet considered: the client has simply to identify what needs changing and how they would like things to be in the future.

This is typically expressed as a goal or series of subgoals ('I will run a marathon next year . . . I will start by jogging three times a week for twenty minutes'). Wherever possible, goals should be behaviourally defined, precise and manageable ('I will jog immediately after work on Monday, Wednesday and Friday'): achievable goals encourage change by enhancing self-efficacy; failure can reduce self-efficacy and exacerbate the problem. The goal of the helper at the beginning of this stage is to move the client from a process of problem exploration to one of planning future changes. In order to mark this shift in direction, Egan suggests that a bridge between the two phases be constructed. This may be achieved by providing a summary of the problems that the individual is facing, followed by questions with a new focus: how would you like things to be different? An example of the bridging process is provided below.

> *Helper:* Let's look at the situation as you've described it to me. You've told me about a number of things that get in the way of your attempts to change your diet. These include the children demanding their 'old' food such as burgers for tea, and you having to sit down with them and eat them too.
>
> *Mr B:* Yes, I think you're right. That seems to sum up the problem. I guess I really need to change some of these things – although how I do that I'm not sure.

Helper: Well, let's leave the how till later. I wonder which of these various problem areas you would most like to change, and how you would like things to be different.

Stage 3: Facilitating action

The final stage of the problem-focused approach involves the client thinking through how their goals may be accomplished. It may be necessary to consider a variety of strategies, and clients are often asked to brainstorm a variety of solutions before a final strategy, or set of strategies, is decided upon. It is important that the client develops their own strategies, for which they take responsibility, and that the helper does not provide formal, expert advice. However, where the client is bereft of ideas, suggestions can be made in a non-directive way, for example through the use of phrases such as, 'One person I saw in a similar situation tried . . . I wonder how useful that may be in your situation?'

Not all clients need complete the entire counselling process. Many will gain sufficiently from input at stages 1 or 2 that they do not need further help. As noted previously, they may also shift from stage to stage in a less structured manner than has been implied. Nevertheless, the Egan framework provides a transparent and simple approach that is applicable to many of the problems faced by those having to change their behaviour in the context of health and health problems.

Smoking cessation as a form of problem-solving counselling

Smoking cessation is a highly specific intervention, but of great importance to clinical health psychology. There are many methods through which successful smoking cessation can be achieved. However, one of the most useful intervention packages draws strongly on the problem-solving model of Egan, albeit implicitly, in that it involves setting goals and subgoals, identifying potential barriers to achieving these goals and strategies by which they may be overcome. It typically follows five stages: establishing motivation, identifying smoking triggers, cutting down, stopping, and relapse prevention.

Motivation is typically enhanced through the use of motivational interview techniques. These may both benefit those already contemplating change as well as shift those in the pre-contemplation stage.

The next stage is one of planning and a gradual reduction in the number of cigarettes smoked. Planning involves both smoker and helper gaining a clear understanding of when and why the individual smokes each cigarette: whether they are a function of habit, nicotine dependence, and so on. This process can be aided by the completion of a diary each time a cigarette is smoked, recording the reasons for smoking that particular cigarette and how difficult it would have been not to smoke it. Once the individual becomes aware of the triggers to their smoking, they can begin to develop strategies that will help them cope with the absence of any particular cigarette. These strategies may be developed through brainstorming or rehearsal and may include avoiding triggers to smoking (for example, not taking coffee breaks at work with people who smoke), specific strategies to be used when triggers cannot be avoided (for example, concentrating on non-smoking elements of a situation, or perhaps chewing gum), and gaining support from family and friends. During this period, the smoker may also reduce the number of cigarettes they smoke each day, starting with those that are the easiest to cut out.

The third stage involves a phased reduction in the number of cigarettes smoked until a level of about twelve cigarettes per day is reached. Dropping below this level is seldom beneficial as it results in blood nicotine levels dipping below the level required to prevent withdrawal symptoms. Each cigarette smoked then relieves this discomfort, establishing a powerful negative reinforcement schedule. As a consequence, the majority of smokers who try to quit using this approach fail to move beyond this stage (Cinciprini *et al.* 1994). By the end of this stage the smoker is working towards a 'quit day', beyond which they stop smoking completely.

The fourth stage involves maintaining abstinence. About half of those who quit smoking experience some degree of withdrawal and strong cravings for a cigarette. These 'symptoms' may last up to two weeks, although they are most severe in the first two to three days after cessation. Smokers who are highly nicotine dependent may benefit from the use of nicotine substitutes at this stage: those whose smoking is predominantly habitual will benefit less (see Chapter 11). Dependence can be evaluated during the planning stage and preparations made for their later use. Continued use of any strategies found helpful during the cutting down phase may also help both nicotine-dependent and habitual smokers to cope with the problems faced following cessation. In addition, personalized methods of dealing with cravings may be helpful.

Problem-solving skills may also be involved in the development of strategies to reduce the risk of relapse. The main issues at this stage are anticipating and developing strategies to reduce the risk of relapse in high-risk situations, and cognitive restructuring to deal with self-defeating attributions following isolated lapses ('I've had one cigarette. I've failed to keep off the ciggies, so I may as well have another': see below).

Stress management training

Cognitive-behavioural therapy involves a series of procedures designed to influence the behaviour, cognitions and emotional state of the individual. Not all cognitive behavioural therapy techniques are applicable to all conditions. This section focuses on those relevant to helping people cope with either acute or chronic distress. Other behavioural strategies are considered later, under the rubric of self-management programmes.

Unlike the counselling process described by Egan, the cognitive behavioural therapist is seen as an 'educator', teaching new skills to help people to cope with stress. Nevertheless, the process adheres to the principles identified by Rogers and Egan: the client is applying new skills to help solve old problems. Accordingly, the goal of the therapist is both to educate and to maintain client responsibility for thinking problems through, and in particular to think how the techniques taught apply to their situation and how best to use them.

The initiator of the stress response is usually an environmental event that triggers a series of psychological processes. The first of these involves a cognitive appraisal of the event. Lazarus and Folkman (1984) suggested that the event is assessed in terms of its threat potential and the individual's perceived ability to cope with the threat. Where the threat potential of an event is high and the perceived ability to cope with it low, the individual will experience the event as stressful. Others, such as Beck (1976), talk in more general terms of 'stressogenic' cognitions: that is, thoughts that are unrealistic and distort reality in ways that increase the perception of stress associated with an event. In both cases, cognitive content is directly associated with emotional states such as anger, anxiety and depression. Stress-engendering cognitions may also increase physiological arousal. At low levels of stress, this is usually evidenced through increased muscular tension. Higher levels of arousal may evoke a wide constellation of symptoms, including palpitations, sweating and shaking. An additional outcome of the stress process involves engaging in 'stressed' behaviours, including avoidance of feared situations, agitation, loss of temper, use of alcohol or drugs to reduce the experience of stress, and so on.

Each of the components of the stress processes may form the target of stress management procedures. Triggers can be identified and modified using problem-focused counselling strategies: cognitive distortions through a number of cognitive techniques some of which are described below, high levels of muscular tension through relaxation techniques, and 'stressed' behaviours through consideration and rehearsal of alternative behavioural responses.

Relaxation training

Unlike meditation, which provides a period of deep relaxation and 'time out', the goal of teaching relaxation skills is to enable the individual to relax as much as is possible and appropriate both throughout the day and at times of particular stress. This reduces levels of physical tension and other symptoms of sympathetic over-arousal. The use of relaxation techniques may also lead to an increase in actual or perceived control over the stress response: a valuable outcome in itself, as perceptions of loss of control contribute to the stress process. There is some evidence that relaxation may also enhance access to more calm and constructive thought processes, although this is a relatively weak effect.

Relaxation skills are best learned through three phases: learning relaxation skills, monitoring tension in daily life and, finally, using relaxation at times of stress.

Learning relaxation skills

The first stage of learning relaxation skills is to practise them under optimal conditions. Initially, a trained practitioner should lead the client through the process, and this initial process be augmented by continued practice at home, typically using taped instructions. Continued and regular practice over a period of days or even weeks is important at this stage, as the skills need to be overlearned in order to permit their effective use *in vivo*.

The relaxation process most commonly used is a derivative of Jacobson's deep muscle relaxation technique. This involves alternately tensing and relaxing muscle groups throughout the body in an ordered sequence. As the individual becomes more skilled, the emphasis of practice shifts towards relaxation without prior tension, or relaxing specific muscle groups whilst using others, in order to mimic the circumstances in which relaxation will be used in 'real life'. The order in which the muscles are relaxed varies, but a typical exercise may involve the following stages (the tensing procedure is described in brackets):

- Hands and forearms (making a fist)
- Upper arms (touching fingers to shoulder)
- Shoulders and lower neck (pulling up shoulders)
- Back of neck (touching chin to chest)
- Lips (pushing them together)
- Forehead (frowning)
- Abdomen/chest (holding deep breath)
- Abdomen (tensing stomach muscles)
- Legs and feet (push heel away, pull toes to point at head: not lifting leg)

Monitoring physical tension

At the same time as practising relaxation skills, individuals can begin to monitor their levels of physical tension throughout the day. Initially, this provides an educative effect, helping them to identify how tense they are during the day and what triggers their tension. As they move through the practice stage, monitoring may help to identify future triggers and provide clues as to when the use of relaxation procedures may be particularly useful. This may entail the use of a 'tension diary' in which the individual typically records their level of tension on a of numerical scale (0 = no tension, 10 = very high levels of tension) at regular intervals through the day.

In vivo relaxation

After a period of monitoring tension and learning relaxation techniques, individuals can begin to integrate them into their daily lives. At this stage, relaxation involves the individual in monitoring and reducing tension to appropriate levels while engaging in everyday activities. Relaxation is best used initially at times of relatively low levels of excess tension. The consistent use of relaxation techniques at these times can prepare the person to cope with times of greater tension. An alternative strategy that many find useful involves relaxing at regular intervals (such as coffee breaks) throughout the day.

Cognitive interventions

Most theorists agree that cognitive processes lie at the heart of the stress process, and more particularly that stress arises at least in part from faulty cognitive processing. They suggest that we each interpret events and make judgements as to their cause and future implications. Stress or distress can arise when individuals fail to make rational appraisals of such events, and instead make judgements that are biased and distorted.

'Stressogenic' cognitions

Two levels of cognitions involved in the stress process can be identified. Surface cognitions are the thoughts of which we are aware and can consciously evoke and change. A second order of cognition can also be identified. Cognitive schemata provide a template, or set of fundamental beliefs, that guide our interpretation of the world and, hence, our surface cognitions. We are usually unaware of such schemata, although they may be accessed at times, such as during the counselling process. Price (1988) for example, suggested that the schemata underlying Type A behaviour are low self-esteem and a belief that one can gain the esteem of others only by continually proving oneself as an 'achiever' and capable individual. These underlying beliefs underpin more conscious competitive, time-urgent or hostile thoughts.

Cognitive strategies

Two strategies for changing cognitions are frequently employed. The first, and simplest, was developed by Meichenbaum (1985) and is aimed at surface cognitions. Self-instruction training involves interrupting the flow of stress-provoking thoughts and replacing them with more realistic or 'coping' ones. These typically fall into one of two categories. The first act as reminders to use any stress-coping techniques that the person has at their disposal ('You're winding yourself up here – come on, calm down, use your relaxation'). The second form of self-instruction is more akin to reassurance, reminding the individual that they can cope effectively with their feelings of distress ('Come on, you've dealt with this before – you should be able to again'). To ensure relevance to the individual, and that they can actually evoke these thoughts at times of stress, Meichenbaum suggests that particular coping thoughts should be considered and rehearsed, wherever possible, before the stressful events occur.

A more complex intervention involves identification and challenging the veracity of stress-engendering thoughts (Meichenbaum 1985). It asks the individual to consider such thoughts as hypotheses, not facts, and to assess their validity without bias. It may involve consideration of both surface cognitions and cognitive schemata. This rational examination of issues may draw on a number of lines of evidence. This is shown in the following dialogue between Alan, recently diagnosed as having had an MI, and a health care worker:

Alan: That's my lot now – I just know I'm for the dump now . . . I'm sure I'll lose my job – I've always said they need younger men than me . . . and my wife is going to be seriously unhappy about that.

Helper: Those feel like big issues to be dealing with. Can you tell me why you feel you might lose your job?

Alan: Well, many people do, I guess.

Helper: Well, some people do, but by no means all. What sort of a job do you have?

Alan: I'm a manager in a large transport company.

Helper: Oh, in a large company like the one you work for, I guess a number of people go off ill at some time. How does the company treat them? Do you know?

Alan: Not too badly, actually. Most people do OK.

Helper: Do they often give them the sack?

Alan: No, that would be crazy – they'd lose some valuable workers and have to get in new people who would not be half as good at the job. Probably have to pay them more as well.

Helper: So, as far as you know, the company tries to keep people on even if they are ill.

Alan: Well, yes. But I've had a heart attack – surely that's got to be different.

Helper: Why should it be? The heart can recover like any other part of you. Do you think that you won't be able to walk? Talk to people? Do the things your job requires?

Alan: Well, no . . . I suppose I would have the physical ability.

Helper: So, you'd have the ability to do the work and the firm has a good reputation for keeping people on.

Alan: OK, OK. Perhaps it won't be that bad after all, now I come to think of it.

Here, Alan is encouraged to question the assumptions behind his anxieties, not simply to accept them as true. The intention of therapy would be to teach him to engage in a similar internal dialogue when faced with similar situations in the future.

Stress inoculation training

Meichenbaum (1985) suggested that the various strands of cognitive-behavioural therapy could be combined into a simple iterative learning process. He combined these strands in two ways. First, he suggested that when an individual is facing a stressor, they need to keep three processes under review: check that their behaviour is appropriate to the circumstances, maintain relaxation, and give themselves appropriate self-talk. In addition, he suggested that where a particular stressor can be anticipated, the opportunity should be taken to rehearse these actions before the event itself. Once in the situation, the planned strategies should be enacted. Finally, after the situation has occurred, time should be given to review what occurred and to learn from successes or failures.

Coping effectiveness training

A recent variant of stress management training has been drawn from coping theory by Chesney and Folkman (1994). While utilizing many of the principles of stress management, it differs in that it teaches a metastrategy for choosing between coping strategies in order to maximize their effectiveness. **Coping effectiveness training** involves teaching individuals to 'fit' their coping strategies to the characteristics of the stressful situation encountered. The intervention has three elements: training in appraising the demands of the situation, emotion- and problem-focused coping, and gaining appropriate social support.

Appraisal training teaches people to identify the causes of recurring stresses, and to distinguish between changeable and unchangeable aspects of these situations. Situations identified as changeable are dealt with using active coping techniques such as problem-solving and communication skills. In contrast, the negative emotions associated with situations considered to be unchangeable can be dealt with using emotion-focused strategies including cognitive restructuring, relaxation and the use of humour. A third strand of coping effectiveness training involves not just learning how to gain social support, but learning how to match social support with the demands of the situation.

Emotional disclosure

The stress management strategies so far described are probably the treatment of choice for individuals coping with long-term stress or facing acute stressful situations. Two alternative approaches for helping individuals to cope with high levels of distress following particularly traumatic incidents are now increasingly being used. Both utilize a strategy of encouraging **emotional disclosure**, one through verbal, the other through written channels. The first involves a process known as psychological debriefing (Bisson *et al.* 1997). This requires skilled therapeutic input, encouraging the individual to explore the nature of the trauma and its personal meaning in some depth. A more gentle strategy, known as 'written disclosure' affords an alternative (see Pennebaker and Seagal 1999). This involves the individual in writing about the event, usually over four to five occasions. This approach may prove equally effective, although comparative studies are lacking.

Several mechanisms have been proposed to explain how emotional disclosure reduces distress. The most widely supported view is outlined in inhibition theory (Wegner *et al.* 1987). This suggests that attempts at inhibition of a particular thought, in this case linked to memories of the traumatic situation, may paradoxically increase the likelihood of it recurring. Attempts at suppression lead to rebounding thoughts and ruminations. Repeated intrusive thoughts can lead to significant emotional distress, cognitive disturbance, increased errors in everyday functioning, and physical health problems. It is thought that emotional disclosure breaks this suppression–rumination cycle.

While such strategies may be of benefit to some individuals, some important caveats should be noted. The short-term effects of both interventions are usually negative, including a worsening of mood and increased obsessive rumination about the traumatic event. In addition, following any stressful or traumatizing event there is a natural period of recovery, lasting weeks or even months. There is evidence that the use of intense verbal therapy too early in this recovery period may interfere with this process and worsen rather than improve the long-term prognosis (Bisson *et al.* 1997). Accordingly, such interventions may benefit individuals who have experienced symptoms of post-traumatic stress disorder for some extended period of time, but not those who are experiencing short-term traumatic distress. That is not to say that patients who wish to express distress should be discouraged from doing so; rather, they should not be placed in 'therapeutic' situations in which issues are formally identified and discussed in depth.

Self-management training

Reflecting an increasing emphasis in patient responsibility for their own care, self-management programmes have become an increasingly popular intervention, particularly in the USA. Their goal is to shift responsibility for the management of chronic conditions, such as arthritis and diabetes, from the physician to the patient. **Self-management training** is based on social cognition theory (Bandura 1986: see Chapter 3) and draws on a variety of cognitive behavioural techniques. It assumes that one can learn self-management skills from practice and watching others, and that success in achieving change will lead to increased confidence in their use and their continued application. Accordingly, the core of self-management training is a structured, progressive skills training programme which ensures success at each stage before progression to the next.

There are a number of elements to self-management training (Lorig 1996). One of the most important is that participants develop their own plans for the management of their condition. These provide behavioural goals and indicate skills that may be needed to achieve them. Participants are taught to monitor their condition, so they are aware of the impact of these management plans on their condition. They are also taught a variety of disease-specific management skills as well as more generic skills such as relaxation or cognitive restructuring. Practice and integration of these skills into the life-context of participants is achieved through the use of rehearsal, problem-solving discussion and role play. Once decisions about management are made, they are implemented, their effectiveness monitored, and management strategies either maintained or modified as appropriate.

A self-management programme that draws heavily on cognitive behavioural strategies, focusing on the control of chronic pain is described below. Such programmes typically involve two stages. The first is an educational phase which familiarizes participants with a biopsychosocial model of pain and that the goal of the intervention is to help them to cope more effectively with their pain, not to make it go away.

The second phase involves training in a variety of pain-coping skills, including relaxation, activity pacing, pleasant activity scheduling, visual imagery, distraction techniques, cognitive restructuring, problem solving and goal setting. Relaxation may be generalized throughout the body or focused on specific muscle groups whose tension is contributing to the pain. Distraction techniques involve focusing on elements other than the pain. Formal techniques include self-hypnosis, meditation and the use of pleasant imagery. More simply, distraction may involve learning to focus on non-pain-related elements of any situation that the individual is in rather than those that are pain-related.

Activity pacing involves a certain amount of problem solving. The individual has to identify, prioritize and maintain a level of activity that keeps them mobile and actively engaged in events, but which is not so excessive that it contributes excessively to pain or tiredness and inhibits future activity. Cognitive restructuring involves identifying and modifying cognitive distortions that may contribute to the experience of pain or pain behaviours. Finally, pleasant activity scheduling involves identifying and engaging in activities that the individual enjoys. This may enhance mood and reinforce distraction from pain-related cognitions and behaviours. Specific routines may also be useful to counter the pain resulting from disorders such as rheumatoid arthritis: daily flexibility exercises, for example, may maintain or enhance mobility and reduce pain. Determining which of these strategies to use, and when, can be facilitated through discussion, role play or behavioural rehearsal.

Operant conditioning

Operant theory states that if behaviour is followed by some form of reward its frequency will increase or be maintained (Skinner 1953). If it is not rewarded, or followed by an unpleasant outcome, the behaviour will occur less frequently. A number of schedules of reinforcement and punishment have been developed. In the simplest, the individual is rewarded or punished after each episode of behaviour. This results in rapid learning, but when the contingencies change and the expected outcome no longer occurs, behavioural extinction can also be rapid. When behavioural rewards or punishment are intermittent, learning is slower (it takes time to work out the behaviour-outcome contingencies) but, once established, behaviour is much more stable.

Hospital staff frequently inadvertently establish such reward schedules. Patients may be given analgesia only after a number of requests; they may gain the attention of staff only by frequently trying to attract their attention. In such conditions, they may learn to hassle staff and become 'difficult' patients. Sick role behaviour can also be established as a consequence of rewards for behaving in a 'sick' manner: expressions of sympathy or being excused responsibilities may follow the expression of pain or discomfort. Operant procedures can also be used to change such behaviour. A number of strategies may be employed, typically the rewarding of behaviours considered appropriate and not responding to those considered inappropriate.

Some of the best examples of **operant conditioning** in a hospital setting have been reported by Fordyce (see for example, Fordyce 1982). He reported a number of case examples of the operant treatment of pain behaviours. In a typical case, staff would provide analgesia at a fixed time interval rather than when requested by the patient, removing it as a reinforcer for excessive pain behaviours. They would also provide social contact, and talk to the patients independently of any complaints or expressions of distress. In this way, the contingencies between complaints and staff behaviour were broken. A similar strategy has been used to modify the behaviour of patients who show inappropriately high use of health care services. The recommended intervention with such patients is that one doctor provides regular appointments at agreed times, during which the patient is encouraged to discuss issues and concerns they may have. Between these appointments, no appointments are made unless there is a clear medical need agreed by the doctor.

A final example of the use of operant conditioning is afforded by its use as a component in the treatment of the irritable bowel syndrome (IBS). Part of the multimodal intervention that Latimer (1981) suggested for the treatment of individuals with IBS involved working with relatives to stop them reinforcing excessive or inappropriate illness behaviours. This intervention can be made acceptable to both patients and their relatives by suggesting that relatives' talking about the patient's condition or responding in other ways, however sympathetically, increases the patient's awareness of their symptoms. Ignoring, or not asking about their condition is therefore not a sign of not caring, but one of not wanting to remind the individual of their condition.

Informal interventions

This chapter has focused on formal therapeutic techniques. However, informal interactions between health care workers and patients provide the opportunity for maximal impact on the psychological well-being of the majority of patients.

One of the simplest ways of reducing distress in hospital is the appropriate provision of information. For many patients, being fully informed of what will happen to them is a key element of maintaining control and morale. Accordingly, appropriate psychological care should aim at maximizing the amount of desired and relevant information given to patients and their relatives. This involves three stages: an initial check of the person's present level of knowledge and what they want to know; information exchange; and an accuracy check making sure that new information has been understood and remembered.

The initial check can form part of the daily provision of care. Patients should be routinely asked if there is information they want to know, and checks made to ensure that the knowledge they already have is accurate. This check should be conducted with some subtlety to ensure the individual does not feel they are being interrogated: 'I know you spoke to Dr Jones yesterday about things. But I don't know exactly what she told you. Could you tell me what you talked about? If you thought of any questions as a result of your talk, perhaps I could answer them now.'

The second stage of the process is the provision of information. This should be expressed clearly and in short, simple sentences. The language used should be appropriate to the patient. Information should be given in a structured way, using the primacy effect to enhance memory of key information. Diagrams and notes may also be used to facilitate memory (see also Chapter 6). Following the provision of information, it is important to check whether the information has been understood and remembered. This should be assessed, again, as subtly as is possible.

Nichols (1984) argued that a care environment that is conducive to the expression of emotion, both negative and positive, is essential to the good psychological care of physically ill patients. He argued that three criteria must be met before this is possible: the ward or clinic environment must be psychologically 'safe'; staff must give patients permission for the expression of emotion; and staff must be able to react appropriately to any emotional expression. Making the patient feel safe involves treating them with respect and making it clear that the expression of emotions, whether positive or negative, is acceptable. Giving permission for the expression of emotion involves gentle questioning, showing empathy, allowing time for the expression of emotion, and, most of all, not trying to allay or inhibit the expression of distress. Finally, and perhaps most importantly, the interaction needs to take place in a ward or unit that places a priority on providing appropriate psychological care. It should not be rushed or seen as an addition to the processes of care, engaged in only when other more appropriate tasks have been completed.

Summary and conclusions

This chapter has identified a number of therapeutic strategies, each with a different name and theoretical rationale. In many ways, the unstructured approach of Rogers is separated by a substantial theoretical gulf from the cognitive behavioural or self-management approaches. Yet even these approaches acknowledge the need to engage the patient in the process of therapy: treating them with warmth, empathy and respect while giving them responsibility for their own progress. Other approaches have significant overlap. In particular, self-management approaches draw heavily on cognitive behavioural techniques, and interventions given both labels are frequently indistinguishable. Consideration of these formal interventions should not overshadow the importance of informal communication. These may influence the psychological well-being of the majority of patients and have a wider impact than the specialist interventions experienced by a minority.

Further reading

Lorig, K. (1996) *Patient Education: A Practical Approach*. Newbury Park: Sage.

Hawton, K., Salkovskis, P.M. and Clark, D.M. (1989) *Cognitive Behaviour Therapy for Psychiatric Problems: A Practical Guide*. Oxford: Oxford University Press.

Rollnick, S., Mason, P. and Butler, C. (1999) *Health Behaviour Change. A Guide for Practitioners*. Edinburgh: Churchill Livingstone.

9 > Assessment issues

One of the strengths of the applied psychology disciplines is that the interventions they conduct are based on sound empirical research and can be justified by empirical evidence. These criteria are now increasingly being demanded by health care providers, with clinicians being increasingly required not only to justify their choice of treatment but also to show evidence of personal effectiveness in the application of that treatment.

Assessment of the effectiveness of the work of clinical and health psychologists calls for the use of psychological measures. However, we are not the only discipline to consider psychological measures as important outcomes. Quality of life, as well as quantity of life, is now an issue concerning medical practitioners. This important change of emphasis in outcome measurement has resulted from a number of pressures. The WHO defines health in terms of social, psychological and physical well-being, marking an important move from health being regarded as merely the absence of illness. Perhaps even more important has been the acknowledgement that some chronic diseases, such as rheumatoid arthritis, cannot be completely cured and that treatments should aim to minimize the disability associated with the disease process. Equally important has been the acknowledgement that, for a small number of diseases, including some cancers, the treatment may be so devastating that the decision to intervene should be premised on consideration not only of survival time but also the quality of life during and after the period of treatment.

A further indication of the need to identify and influence psychological factors is because of the effect that these factors have on disease and rehabilitation. Depression and anxiety have consistently been found to influence recovery from a variety of illnesses, in terms of both risk for disease progression and poor adherence to treatment or rehabilitation programmes. Similarly, patients' differing self-efficacy beliefs, their illness and treatment representations, or factors such as the social support available to them, may need to be taken into account in the development of maximally effective interventions. Accordingly, there are a number of areas where psychological assessments are critical to appropriate health care, including:

◆ measuring the quality of life associated with disease and its treatment;

◆ identifying those at risk for poor illness outcome owing to psychosocial or personality factors;

◆ identifying those who are psychologically distressed;

◆ measuring the behavioural and psychological outcomes of any intervention.

This chapter briefly reviews each of these areas. The review can consider only a few of the many measures available; the interested reader should consult the further reading list at the end of the chapter for reviews of a wider set of measures. The following domains are considered:

◆ Quality of life

◆ Pain

◆ Affect

◆ Coping with illness

◆ Individual differences

◆ Health behaviours

Measuring quality of life

Traditional measures of the effectiveness of medical interventions have focused on outcomes including changes in future morbidity, disease progression, or more pragmatic indicators such as hospital readmission. Some have argued that these measures are both necessary and sufficient for the evaluation of the effectiveness of any intervention. However, these 'objective' outcomes are not always related to patient-based reports: 'good' medical outcomes do not necessarily equate to 'good' patient outcomes. These differences indicate the need to measure both types of outcome, particularly in the case of chronic diseases where medical treatment can result in only a partial or temporary amelioration of symptoms.

The choice of measure is not simple, and the clinician or researcher attempting to measure psychological outcomes frequently faces a confusing choice from a plethora of scales measuring apparently similar constructs. Any scale must be both valid and reliable. That is, it must measure what it claims to, and must measure this reliably and consistently. An equally important attribute is the sensitivity of the measure to change. This attribute is an important criterion in the choice of instruments measuring the outcome of clinical interventions: a lack of sensitivity may result in failures to detect beneficial interventions.

Initial attempts to measure the impact of disease on quality of life focused almost exclusively on functional status: the degree of limitation resulting from the disease. The New York Heart Association indices, for example, graded people following MI as 'dead' or 'alive' with four grades of complications. Similarly, the American Rheumatism Association functional classification distinguished just four grades of disability, from 'complete functional ability' to 'largely or wholly incapacitated'. Such measures provide no indication of the effects of the condition on physical, social, economic or psychological functioning.

More recently, attempts have been made to measure the impact of illness on various life domains, under the general rubric of measuring quality of life. The WHOQOL Group (1998) defined this as the individuals' perception of their position in life in the context of the culture and value systems in which they live and in relation to their goals, expectations, standards and concerns. In other words, quality of life cannot simply be derived from an individual's ability to engage or otherwise in a series of behaviours or activities. It incorporates an evaluation of the individual's satisfaction or dissatisfaction with the abilities they have and the activities they can engage in. It is generally thought to encompass all or most of the following:

Psychological

◆ Depression
◆ Anxiety
◆ Adjustment to illness

Social

◆ Personal and sexual relationships
◆ Engagement in social and leisure activities

Occupational

◆ Ability to carry out paid employment
◆ Ability to cope with household duties

Physical

◆ Pain
◆ Mobility
◆ Sleep
◆ Appetite and nausea
◆ Sexual functioning

Choice of a measure lies between general and disease-specific measures. Both have their advantages and disadvantages. Good disease-specific scales provide sensitive measures of change in particular medical conditions, often, but not universally, more so than general measures. What the specific measures gain in specificity they often lose in terms of narrow focus, and they may fail to measure factors such as social support, coping, life satisfaction and mood. Their use also precludes comparisons of quality of life with other patient groups. For these reasons, many commentators suggest the optimum measure is a disease-specific measure combined with scales from more general measures.

Three widely used 'traditional' measures of quality of life are considered below, as well as a new approach. Following that, some of the disease-specific measures that have been used to measure the quality of life of people who have cancer and CHD are described.

Sickness Impact Profile

The Sickness Impact Profile (SIP) comprises 136 statements with yes and no responses (Bergner *et al.* 1981). Each item has a dichotomous response format and contributes to one of twelve scales: walking, body care and movement, mobility, work, sleeping and rest, eating, housework, recreation, emotion, social interaction, alertness and communication. The first three scales can be combined to form a 'physical scale', which closely resembles a disability measure. The others contribute to a psychosocial scale.

Studies of the SIP's internal and test/retest reliability have generally found both to be high, although a review by Anderson *et al.* (1993) reported that the strength of correlation between SIP scores and measures of clinical status varies between 0.4 and 0.6: a figure the authors suggested may not be high enough to justify its use in studies of health care interventions. In addition, the sensitivity of the SIP has been challenged, and although a number of studies have found it to be sensitive to changes over time, many have found it less sensitive than other widely used instruments, including SF-36 (see below). Perhaps the most problematic aspect of the SIP is that it takes between 20 and 30 minutes to complete, and many less able patients find it tiring to complete. According to Bowling (1997) its use has been rejected in a number of British trials of patients with CHD in favour of the Nottingham Health Profile (Hunt 1984).

Nottingham Health Profile

The Nottingham Health Profile (NHP) is divided into six sections: sleep, energy, pain, social isolation, emotional reaction and physical mobility. Its sensitivity is compromised, as is the SIP's, because of its yes/no answer format. In addition, the sections may not be independent: the pain and mobility scale scores, for example, tend to be highly correlated. Nevertheless, the brevity of the NHP has made it the instrument of choice in a number of outcome studies. It has been shown to correlate well with clinical judgements and biological markers of disease severity in populations as diverse as cardiac transplantation patients, those with arthritis, and elderly patients involved in a community exercise programme. It has generally held up well in comparisons with other instruments. In one study with arthritis patients, Fitzpatrick *et al.* (1989) compared the NHP with a disease-specific measure of quality of life in arthritis and the Beck Depression Inventory (see below). Patients with rheumatoid arthritis scored higher than controls on the NHP scales of energy, pain, mobility and sleep. In addition, energy, pain, mobility and emotions scales of the NHP correlated significantly with the parallel scores of the disease-specific measure, clinical assessments and the BDI. Five of the six scales of the NHP were stable on retesting. Only the social scale of the NHP did not correlate with the matching scale of the disease-specific measure and was relatively unstable over time.

The NHP has proven sufficiently sensitive to measure changes in fracture patients following treatment, following lung and heart transplant, and acute viral inflammation. However, its sensitivity following less dramatic changes in populations with chronic diseases such as arthritis and respiratory disease has been questioned. In a direct comparison of the sensitivity of the SIP and NHP, Taylor *et al.* (1998) followed a cohort of patients, taking measurements six weeks and six months following MI. Four SIP subscales showed a moderate sensitivity to change: body care and movement, emotional behaviour, work and eating. Other SIP, and all the NHP subscales, had lower sensitivity indices.

Short Form-36

The Short Form-36 (SF-36) is a widely used measure. The product of the US Medical Outcomes Study (Ware *et al.* 1993), it comprises 36 items forming eight subscales: physical functioning, role limitations due to physical health problems, social functioning, bodily pain, mental health, vitality, and perceived health changes over the previous year. Each scale has its own scoring format, varying from dichotomous responses (yes/no) to six-point scales. The subscales are not summed together to produce a total score. It takes between five and ten minutes to complete. Population norms are now available for both the USA and Europe.

The SF-36 has proven an effective measure of health status. It can discriminate between different surgical groups, younger and older patients receiving surgery, patients with physical and mental health problems, and patients with low back pain, menorrhagia, peptic ulcer and varicose veins. Kvien *et al.* (1998) compared the utility of the SF-36 with a disease-specific measure in a group of over one thousand patients with rheumatoid arthritis. They reported strong correlations between the SF-36 and

Table 9.1   Domains measured by various measures of quality of life

Sickness Impact Profile	Nottingham Health Profile	Short Form-36
Sleeping and rest	Sleep	
Alertness	Energy	Vitality
	Pain	Pain
Social interaction	Social isolation	Social functioning
Emotion	Emotional reaction	Mental health
Mobility	Physical mobility	
Walking		
Body care and movement		
Eating		
Housework		Role limitations due to physical functioning
Recreation		
Communication		
		Physical functioning
		Perceived health changes over past year

subscales of the disease-specific assessment on all measures of gross physical functioning. Only on measures of specific arthritis symptoms, such as hand/finger function, did the SF-36 fail to capture the impact of the disease. However, the SF-36 was more sensitive than the other measure to low levels of physical disability.

The reliability of the SF-36 varies across studies and study populations. In a large review of the relevant studies, Ware *et al.* (1993) reported that measures of internal reliability varied between 0.55 and 0.90 and test/retest coefficients varied between 0.43 and 0.90. Gatchel *et al.* (1998) concluded that the low reliability coefficients and limited score levels achievable by the SF-36 gave it only limited clinical utility on an individual patient basis. Nevertheless, it is one of the most widely used generic measures of quality of life.

Table 9.1 summarizes the domains measured by the three tools discussed in this section.

Schedule for the Evaluation of Individual Quality of Life

The Schedule for the Evaluation of Individual Quality of Life (SEIQoL) differs radically both conceptually and in the process of measurement from the three instruments so far considered (see, for example, O'Boyle *et al.* 1992). Its authors argue that satisfaction with life is a consequence of being able to do the things one values, not those considered important by others. As a result, the SEIQoL adopts an idiosyncratic approach to assessment. Respondents are asked to identify five facets of life that are most important to them and to rate their level of functioning on each. They are then asked to indicate the relative weight or importance they attach to each and how satisfied they are in that domain. Accordingly, an individual's final score may be based on scales that differ from those of others. In addition, the scales from which a final score is derived may change over time.

The complex abstract information processing required to complete the SEIQoL make it inappropriate for some populations, such as the elderly or seriously ill. The time taken may also prevent its use in large surveys. However, smaller-scale surveys have shown the instrument to be acceptable to patients and to demonstrate good reliability (McGee *et al.* 1991).

Disease-specific measures

Cancer

Despite the positive tone of the opening comments of this chapter, few papers reporting the outcome of clinical trials involving patients with cancer have measured quality of life. In the 1980s, for example, only 3 per cent of trials reported in surgical journals did so. While this figure has undoubtedly risen in the decade following, there is still resistance to its measurement by some. Green (1997), for example, in summing up a journal debate on the value of measuring quality of life in cancer patients noted that some surgeons consider it to be an irrelevant outcome measure. His more moderate conclusions were that when comparing treatment regimens for a disease such as cancer, three measures must be considered. First, the primary endpoint: how long do patients survive? Secondly: how well do patients function? Only third in importance was, how well do patients feel? Clearly, some remain to be convinced of the value of measuring quality of life.

European Organization for Research on Treatment of Cancer

The goal of the European Organization for Research on Treatment of Cancer (EORTC) group was to develop a brief, standardized measure of quality of life for use with all cancer patients (see, for example, Aaronson 1993). Its measure addresses a number of issues, including cancer-specific disease symptoms, treatment side-effects, psychological distress, physical functioning, social interaction, sexuality, body image, global health, and the financial implications of the illness. The original questionnaire incorporated 42 questions, from which 36 were selected for the final measure. A second rationalizing of items reduced the instrument to a 30-item questionnaire, known as the QLQ-C30. This forms the core of a modular approach, with 13 different disease-specific symptom modules combining with the QLQ-C30 to provide a full assessment.

The questionnaire is acceptable to most patients and takes about ten minutes to complete. It is able to discriminate between patients having different types of cancer, and its factor structure has been independently verified. Its subscales correlate moderately to strongly with the equivalent scales on the SIP. Not surprisingly, correlations between the EORTC and other cancer-related measures are stronger than those with more generic measures of quality of life. In addition, it achieves good test/retest reliability. Nevertheless, Ringdal and Ringdal (1993) suggested that the measure would gain psychometric strength by using between three and four items to measure each of its dimensions. They were particularly critical of the six one-item measures that address factors such as sleeplessness and financial problems.

Rotterdam Symptom Checklist

Along with the EORTC measures, the Rotterdam Symptom Checklist (RSC) has proven a popular measure of quality of life in patients with cancer (De Haes *et al.* 1990). It comprises 38 items, measuring physical toxicity, social functioning, physical activity and psychological adjustment to disease. Participants rate 30 symptoms on four-point Likert scales. The remaining items, except for the last one which measures the individual's overall quality of life, assess daily activities. The questionnaire takes between five and ten minutes to complete. Tests of validity and reliability are relatively sparse. However, these indicate that it has good test/retest reliability, was able to classify correctly 75 per cent of patients assigned a psychiatric diagnosis by clinical interview, and appears to be sensitive to changes in condition over time. Some have suggested that it may usefully be supplemented by an additional measure of mood. However, the consensus appears to be that it is a useful scale with good validity and ease of use.

Coronary Heart Disease

A review by McGee *et al.* (1999) identified 32 cardiac rehabilitation interventions that measured psychosocial outcomes. Arguing that the best instruments to use in this population are those with proven sensitivity to change, they identified five useful measures from these reports. Two were general scales measuring mood (the Beck Depression Inventory and State Trait Anxiety Inventory: see below). The other three have been developed specifically for use with cardiac patients: the Global Mood Scale (Denollet 1993: see below), the Health Complaints Scale (Denollet 1994), and the Heart Patients Psychological Questionnaire (Erdman 1982).

Health Complaints Scale

The Health Complaints Scale (HCS) comprises two scales measuring somatic and cognitive health complaints frequently reported by cardiac patients (Denollet 1994). The twelve somatic complaints include chest pain, dyspnoea and fatigue. The twelve cognitive items include concerns about health, fears of disability and lack of worth. Items were drawn from pre-existing instruments as well as being designed specifically for the scale. The model on which the scales were based was supported by confirmatory factor analysis, and both scales have high internal reliability and adequate test/retest reliability. The measure is also sensitive to change: perhaps more than more generic models of patient distress. Despite the scale's psychometric strength it has yet to be widely used in studies of cardiac patients.

Heart Patients Psychological Questionnaire

The Heart Patients Psychological Questionnaire (HPPQ) comprises 52 items, each with a dichotomous response (yes/no) combined into three scales: well-being, subjective invalidity and displeasure (Erdman 1982). It has been validated in a number of studies, has shown high internal and test/retest reliability and is able to discriminate between stroke and cardiac patients. Denollet (1993) followed a group of 162 men with CHD who took part in a cardiac rehabilitation programme, taking measures with the State Trait Anxiety Inventory (Spielberger *et al.* 1983: see below) and the HPPQ disability and well-being scales. The scores of participants who showed high levels of distress at the beginning of the intervention had fallen significantly on all measures by its end. However, the magnitude of change in HPPQ scores was substantially greater than those of the State Trait Anxiety Inventory. Among patients with low levels of distress, only the HPPQ scales showed significant changes over time.

Measuring pain

The simplest way of measuring pain is through the use of visual analogue or numerical rating scales. Most clinicians working with pain patients prefer the latter, with scales typically ranging from no pain (0) to the worst possible pain (100). The advantage of such measures is that they are quick and simple to administer and score. One disadvantage is that some patients find it difficult to conceptualize pain as a number, although numerical rating scales correlate strongly with other intensity measures (see, for example, Jensen *et al.* 1986). Another simple approach is provided by verbal rating scales, in which patients rate their pain on a list of adjectives indicating increasing pain. This method is also simple, although the more limited range of responses, and patients' tendency to use middle adjectives more than endpoints, make them less sensitive than visual analogue or numerical rating scales.

McGill Pain Questionnaire

A more sophisticated assessment strategy is provided by the McGill Pain Questionnaire (MPQ: Melzack 1975). This comprises 78 terms describing the quality and intensity of the pain; these are typically presented as 20 clusters of between three and five similar descriptors. Shorter versions of the scale do exist. Respondents circle the descriptive clusters that correspond to their pain experience. The questionnaire has four subscales. The sensory and evaluative subscales rate the intensity and type of pain experienced. The third scale measures the emotional response to the pain, while the fourth captures a number of miscellaneous items. Depending on its length, the questionnaire takes between 2 and 15 minutes to complete. Scoring is based on the number of descriptors circled and the weights assigned to these descriptors. The MPQ is one of the most widely used measures of pain. Despite this, studies of its validity or reliability are scarce. It was able to accurately classify 77 per cent of patients with varying pain syndromes into the appropriate diagnostic category. It has modest test/retest reliability.

Measures of affect

Beck Depression Inventory

The Beck Depression Inventory (BDI) is one of the most widely used measures of depression (Beck *et al.* 1961). It comprises 21 items, each of which has a four-point scoring system of severity. Although Beck argued that the instrument should be used only as a measure of the severity of depression once it is diagnosed, the scale has normative scores that are indicative of both normal and depressed states: 0–9 normal; 10–15 mild depression; 16–19 moderate; 20–29 moderate/severe; 30+ severe. The scale is generally considered to have high validity. It compares well with interview-based psychiatric diagnoses, with 97 per cent agreement within one category of severity (Beck *et al.* 1961), and has good split-half and test/retest reliability. It also appears to have moderate to good sensitivity. Beck suggests that the BDI represents one underlying syndrome of depression comprising highly interrelated factors: negative attitudes to self, performance impairment and somatic disturbance. The latter means that the BDI may overestimate depression scores in patients with debilitating physical illnesses.

Hospital Anxiety and Depression Scale

Despite its name, no question in the Hospital Anxiety and Depression Scale (HADS) refers to hospital or any other element of health care (Zigmond and Snaith 1983). It was given this name because it is short and easy to use in hospital settings. It comprises 14 items divided into two subscales measuring depression and anxiety. The particular strength of the HADS is that it specifically avoids items that measure physical manifestations of depression, which may lead to score inflation and inappropriate categorization on measures such as the BDI. The depression scale is considered to measure anhedonic depression, which the authors argue is the central pathological element of depression and responds well to antidepressant medication. Scores of 7 or less are considered to be non-cases, 8 to 10 as doubtful, and more than 11 as definite cases. It is easily understood by and acceptable to patients.

Original item selection for the scale was based on clinical experience and it was validated entirely on a sample of individuals with a psychiatric diagnosis. Nevertheless, it has performed reasonably well in tests of validity and reliability. Independence from items that mimic mental health problems as a consequence of physical health problems, such as tiredness or fatigue, was confirmed by Zigmond and Snaith (1983) who found that HADS scores in physically ill patients who did not have a mood disorder were similar to those of a normal sample. Factor analyses have both confirmed and disconfirmed the two-factor structure of the measure and internal reliability scores have been modest. Despite these drawbacks, the scale's brevity and respondent acceptability have resulted in its frequent use.

Global Mood Scale

The Global Mood Scale (GMS) measures positive affect, characterized by energy and sociability, and negative affect, comprising fatigue and malaise (Denollet 1993). It was developed specifically for heart patients and has two ten-item scales, each consisting of a list of one-word mood descriptors. Response is using a five-point Likert scale. Fatigue was chosen as a factor within negative affect as many cardiac patients deny negative moods but do report feelings of fatigue, which, in turn, is associated with distress. Development of the GMS involved its being given to nearly 500 men following infarction who either entered a rehabilitation programme or acted as no-intervention controls. It proved internally reliable, consistent over time, and correlated significantly with other measures of mood. In addition, scores changed on those patients who entered the rehabilitation programme, with less change evident among those in the control group. Importantly, the fatigue scores did not correlate with cardiorespiratory fitness, so were not simply capturing an element of the disease process.

State Trait Anxiety Inventory

The present version of the State Trait Anxiety Inventory (STAI) is widely used. Its development was reported by Spielberger et al. (1983). Two scales are available: a trait version, measuring a general tendency towards anxiety, and a state version, measuring transitory feelings of anxiety. Each scale has 20 items: those of the state measure have an attached four-point intensity scale, those of the trait measure have an equivalent frequency scale. Each scale takes less than five minutes to complete. The scale is well regarded, sufficiently so that Bowling (1995), reporting varying strengths of association with other measures of anxiety, concluded that the lower values probably reflected weaknesses in the other scales. Test/retest data suggest the questionnaire is highly reliable. Despite the relative brevity of the STAI, the need for an even shorter measure of anxiety led Marteau and Bekker (1992) to develop a six-item state anxiety scale based on the STAI. Their scale achieved high reliability and validity coefficients, and its scores were able to discriminate between various patient groups, suggesting acceptable sensitivity.

Novaco Anger Inventory

One of the first psychometric measures of anger, the Novaco Anger Inventory (NAI) comprises 90 statements describing anger provoking incidents (Novaco 1975). Respondents report the degree to which each incident would anger or provoke them, using a five-point Likert scale. It has high internal reliability coefficients. However, a test/retest reliability coefficient as low as 0.17 has been reported and the scale has not been found to correlate with self-report ratings of anger in imaginary and role play simulations, or the number of anger-provoking incidents experienced during a two-week period. These weaknesses, and its length, have meant that the scale has been largely replaced by ones developed subsequently, the most popular of which are those of Spielberger and colleagues.

Spielberger Anger Scales

The State Trait Anger Scales (STAS) were designed to assess the intensity of anger as an emotional state and individual differences in anger proneness as a personality trait (Spielberger *et al.* 1983). Trait anger reflects the dispositional tendency to experience anger. State anger measures the intensity of anger experienced at any one time. Those high in trait anger also score highly on the state anger measure whenever annoying or frustrating conditions are encountered. The STAS is shorter than the Novaco scale, having 20 items in each scale and has good internal and test/retest reliability.

When measuring anger, it can be useful to know not just how often an individual feels angry, but also how they express that anger. The two most frequently measured responses are anger suppression (anger-in), in which the individual inhibits the outward expression of an angry response, and anger-out, where anger is expressed and directed at others. Different modes of expression may have implications for underlying physiological responses to stress. They may also be useful indicators of change following an intervention. In response to these needs, Spielberger *et al.*

(1985) developed the Anger Expression Scale, which measures three dimensions of anger response: anger in, anger out and anger control. All three dimensional scores have good internal reliability.

General Health Questionnaire

The General Health Questionnaire (GHQ) was designed to be a screening questionnaire for psychiatric disturbance of recent onset (Goldberg and Williams 1988). It is not intended to measure longer-standing problems as its questions focus on 'recent' changes between the respondent's usual and present state. Nor is it intended to measure change. Despite these technical considerations, it has been used as an outcome measure in a number of intervention trials, with sensitivity ranging from poor to good. The GHQ focuses on general symptoms of psychiatric morbidity, in particular depression and anxiety, although the psychoses may also be detected. The original GHQ comprised 60 items, although 30, 28, 20 and 12 item versions have also been developed. Each item has a four-point scale of severity. Two methods of scoring this scale have been developed. The method recommended by Goldberg involves assigning scores of 0 or 1 to one of four response categories provided for each item (0–0–1–1), where zero is considered to indicate the absence of symptoms and one to indicate their presence. Others have used the scale as a Likert scale, assigning scores of 0, 1, 2 or 3 to each response. Goldberg and Williams (1988) suggest there is little to be gained by using this scoring format and most users have adopted the simpler scoring method.

As the GHQ is intended to be used as a screening instrument for psychiatric morbidity, it provides varying cut-off scores above which there is a 50 per cent chance of the individual being assigned a psychiatric diagnosis. As physically ill people score highly on the GHQ, they are over-represented among false positives, and Goldberg and Williams suggested raising the threshold criterion for such people. The GHQ achieves reasonable validity when compared with psychiatric interview, and correlates significantly with the BDI. In addition, it has good internal and test/retest reliability and acceptable validity and sensitivity. However, in a direct assessment of its strengths relative to the HADS in a study with patients with cancer, Ibbotson et al. (1994) compared the screening performance of the GHQ-28 and the HADS against a structured psychiatric interview. Although the performance of the GHQ proved acceptable, the HADS did best in those free of disease, in treatment, and when the disease was judged to be stable.

Coping with illness

According to Leventhal (e.g. Leventhal et al. 1997), the initial response to the onset of illness is to identify the nature of the threat faced, so that appropriate coping strategies can be engaged (see Chapter 4). This is typically represented along five dimensions: disease identity, cause, consequences, timeline and controllability. Until recently, each dimension has been measured using a variety of different scales, including those acknowledged as relevant to the domain in question, semi-structured or open-ended interviews and 'self-made questionnaires'.

Illness Perceptions Questionnaire

In response to this somewhat chaotic situation, Weinman *et al.* (1996) constructed the Illness Perceptions Questionnaire (IPQ), a questionnaire addressing each of the five illness representation components. The identity scale has 12 core symptom items which can be added to when exploring specific illnesses. There are ten items in the cause dimension, three in the timeline scale, eight in the consequence scale and six in the control/cure scale. It elicits the same number of or more items than interview and has high internal and test/retest reliability in groups of patients with diabetes, chronic fatigue syndrome, chronic pain, renal disease and MI. The scale has good discriminant validity, being able to distinguish between different patient groups by their dimension scores. Subsequent studies have shown it to have predictive utility: it is able, for example, to discriminate between those patients who will and will not attend cardiac rehabilitation classes. This version of the scale does not address the emotional aspects of the response to illness; a revised version of the IPQ, in development at the time of writing, will do so.

Measures of coping

Most measures of coping address similar behavioural and cognitive responses to threat, although the level of complexity addressed by each questionnaire varies markedly. Some measures focus on just two dimensions of coping, with each subsuming a variety of related strategies. Others address more complex models of coping, trading parsimony for a more detailed description of the strategies used (see Table 9.2).

Ways of Coping Questionnaire

The original measure of coping, the Ways of Coping Questionnaire (WCQ) comprises 50 items plus 16 'fill items' and 8 empirically derived scales (Folkman and Lazarus 1988: see also Table 9.2). It is a state measure, with respondents reporting their use of coping strategies with reference to a particular event that occurred in the previous week. Test/retest reliabilities were not reported in the paper describing its development. Lazarus argued that high stability should not be expected as individuals adjust their coping strategies to the differing requirements of

Table 9.2 Taxonomies of coping, and questionnaires, developed by various research groups

Lazarus and Folkman (1984)	Endler et al. (1998a)	Carver et al. (1989)
Ways of Coping Questionnaire	CHIP	COPE
Confrontive coping	Distraction	Active coping
Distancing	Palliative	Planning
Self-control	Instrumental	Suppress competing activities
Seeking social support	Emotional preoccupation	Seek instrumental support
Accepting responsibility		Seek emotional support
Escape/avoidance		Positive reinterpretation
Planful problem solving		Restraint coping
Positive reappraisal		Acceptance
		Turn to religion
		Vent emotions
		Denial
		Behavioural disengagement
		Mental disengagement
		Alcohol/drug disengagement

each situation. More problematic is that the WCQ has a weak factor structure. Factor analyses on data from different samples have resulted in varying factor structures and numbers of derived factors.

Folkman and Lazarus encouraged researchers to adapt the WCQ to the specific needs of the population under investigation. Dunkel-Schetter *et al.* (1992) did so by adapting it to the demands of cancer patients. The Ways of Coping with Cancer questionnaire comprises 49 items from the WCQ, some of them reworded asking specifically about how patients cope with the demands of a diagnosis of cancer. A factor analysis yielded five factors: seek and use social support, cognitive escape/avoidance, distancing, focus on the positive, and behavioural escape/avoidance.

COPE

Based on a theoretical model of coping and subsequently validated through factor analysis, the COPE, developed by Carver *et al.* (1989) comprises 13 subscales (see Table 9.2). Although Carver is cautious about the use of factor scores, they can be derived. These are problem-focused coping, emotion-focused coping, venting emotions, behavioural disengagement and mental disengagement.

The questionnaire has 52 items and has both trait and state versions. The internal consistency coefficients are generally high and it has good test/retest reliability. A shorter version of COPE, known as Brief COPE has been developed, comprising only two items per coping strategy and collapsing some of the scales; for example, combining behavioural and mental disengagement into one 'disengagement' scale. This has obvious advantages when brevity is important. However, Endler et al. (1998a) have criticized the full COPE for the psychometric properties of its four-item scales, and the internal consistency coefficients of some of the two-item scales are only modest. A compromise between the two measures has been reported by Bennett et al. (2000) who added the item most strongly loading on each scale from the full COPE to the two-items of the Brief COPE. The resultant three-item scales evidenced more consistent internal reliability than the two-item scales.

Coping with Health Injuries and Problems

Most measures of coping consider how individuals respond to a variety of unspecified stressors. One exception to this approach is Coping with Health Injuries and Problems (CHIP), which measures coping strategies in response to health problems and injuries (Endler et al. 1998a). It measures four coping dimensions: distraction, palliative, instrumental, and emotional preoccupation coping. Endler et al. (1998b) examined CHIP's temporal stability and internal reliability by administering it to a sample of 50 men with prostate cancer and 110 women with breast cancer on two occasions, with an interval of two weeks between assessments. The mean scale scores at both times were virtually identical. The internal consistency reliability was also high.

Individual differences

A number of individual differences have been shown to influence the development or course of disease. Some, such as Type A behaviour, hostility, or Type C behaviour may influence the course of disease directly (see Chapter 1). Others, such as negative affect, hardiness and health optimism may impact on health indirectly by governing behaviour related to health and health threats. Here, three measures of individual differences are reviewed: measures of negative affect, health optimism, and hostility.

Positive and Negative Affect Scales

Watson et al. (1988) identified two dominant dimensions constantly found in studies of the structure of mood: positive and negative affect. Positive affect reflects the extent to which a person feels enthusiastic, active and alert. Negative affect measures a variety of aversive mood states, including anger, contempt, disgust, fear and nervousness. If considered as a trait, positive affect corresponds to Eysenck's extroversion factor, and negative affect to neuroticism. The Positive and Negative Affect Scales (PANAS) comprises two ten-item scales measuring both constructs, which are considered to be orthogonal. Internal and test/retest reliability analyses have been conducted on scores based on several different assessment timeframes, including 'right now' to 'in general' or 'during the past year'. High test/retest reliability coefficients were found for them all, and were high enough for the longer timeframes to suggest that the scales can be used as trait measures of affect. This is now the predominant use of the scale. It has also been adapted for use with children, and a shorter ten-item scale has been developed and validated in a sample of over 2500 adults (Mackinnon *et al.* 1999).

Life Orientation Test

In contrast to the PANAS, the Life Orientation Test (LOT) is a measure of dispositional optimism (Scheier and Carver 1985). This is thought to moderate factors more proximal to behaviour such as efficacy expectations and coping. Individuals high in optimism are likely to engage and maintain effort in achieving desired goals, and be less bothered by minor physical symptoms, recover more quickly from surgery and report higher quality of life than low scorers. The LOT has 20 items, including four filler items intended to disguise the nature of the assessment. It has good psychometric properties. However, Smith *et al.* (1989) noted that LOT scores were highly correlated with scores of negative affectivity, and that the relationship between LOT scores and symptom-reporting was no longer significant after controlling for neuroticism. In response to these criticisms, Scheier *et al.* (1994) argued that when a sufficiently large sample size was employed, the degree of association between neuroticism and optimism, while moderate, was insufficient to suggest that the two scales were measuring the same construct. Nevertheless, for theoretical reasons, they took the opportunity of this reanalysis to shorten the LOT by removing two items considered to measure coping strategies rather than dispositional factors. The psychometric properties of this shortened scale were acceptable.

Hostility

Hostility is a poorly defined, indeed multiply defined, construct. However, a consensus seems to be developing that considers it to have three components: cognitive, affective and behavioural. The cognitive component comprises negative beliefs about others. The hostile person considers others to be untrustworthy, undeserving and immoral. Pervading non-specific suspicions are considered to represent cynicism, while more specific hostile attributions consider the actions of specific people to be antagonistic. Emotional elements include anger, annoyance, resentment and contempt. The behavioural component involves both verbal and physical aggression.

Questionnaire methods

The most widely used measure of hostility is the Cook and Medley Hostility (Ho) Scale (Cook and Medley 1954). It was taken from the Minnesota Multiphasic Personality Inventory Scale used to identify teachers who had difficulty getting on with their students. Accordingly, some of the items in the scale do not directly address hostility. Nevertheless, the majority of items are thought to tap into the cynical hostility component, with a smaller number of items dealing with hostile affect, and even fewer with hostile behaviour. It has predictive utility: a number of cross-sectional and longitudinal studies using the measure have shown a relationship between Ho scores and the subsequent development of CHD (see Chapter 1). A second recognized measure of hostility is the Buss–Durkee Hostility Inventory (BDHI: Buss and Durkee 1957). It has seven subscales, simplified by factor analysis into two factors. The first incorporates the resentment and suspicion subscales, and represents 'neurotic' hostility. The second includes measures of expressive and affective hostility. Like the Ho Scale it has been shown to be predictive of CHD, although the number of studies using this measure is much fewer.

Both measures suffer from being self-report: respondents may under-report their hostility levels in order to represent themselves in a socially acceptable manner. This self-representation bias may have distorted the apparent relationship between hostility and the development of CHD in a number of studies. McCranie et al. (1986), for example, found no relationship between Ho scores obtained from students applying for medical school and subsequent levels of CHD. However, their average Ho score was almost half the average for this cohort when measured in less biasing circumstances. The apparent relationship between hostility and disease may have been strongly distorted as a consequence of the response biases of candidates wishing to impress potential future teachers. One way of reducing this bias is to make the items appear as socially acceptable as possible. Here, the Ho seems better than the BDHI, with statements such as 'I strongly defend my own opinions as a rule' being easier to endorse than 'People who continually pester you are asking for a punch in the nose'. However, a better way of avoiding such biases is to base judgements of hostility on observed behaviour.

Interview methods

Although a number of specialist interviews have been developed, the best known remain the structured interview (SI) developed by Rosenman (see Chesney *et al.* 1988) and the videotaped structured interview (VSI) used by Friedman to measure Type A behaviour (see, for example, Friedman and Powell 1984). The SI involves an interview lasting about ten minutes in which the participant is asked about their behaviour and attitudes in general and when under pressure or provoked. The respondent's verbal responses and behaviour during the interview are recorded on audiotape and later subjected to analysis. Originally, participants were assigned a global rating based on the degree of Type A behaviour reported or evident during the interview. More recently, component scoring schemes have been developed to quantify the expression of specific elements of Type A behaviour, including anger and 'potential for hostility' (Chesney *et al.* 1988). Inter-rater reliability is generally high among experienced raters, but not among those with less experience, and the interview and assessment both require significant training and time. The VSI is a separate instrument developed by Friedman and Powell (1984). As its name suggests, assessments are made of behaviour videotaped during an interview. Participants are scored on a continuum, derived by combining scores on 35 psychomotor indicators of Type A behaviour, with the derived scales measuring hostility, time urgency and 'pathophysiologic' indicators. The complexity and time involved in these assessments makes them inappropriate for many researchers and clinicians. Nevertheless, they are considered the 'gold standard' against which pencil and paper assessments should be judged.

Health-related behaviours

Obtaining valid measures of health-related behaviour in its everyday context is remarkably difficult. Validation of measures is almost impossible other than through covert observation of those who have completed questionnaires. Obtaining objective measures against which to validate instruments has proven problematic. Biological measures provide only crude indicators of behaviour: physiological markers of smoking or alcohol, for example, are both highly intrusive and verify whether or not an individual is smoking or drinking, but not how much. Other than extremely controlled laboratory measures, measures of exercise or calorie consumption are equally difficult to achieve. Accordingly, health behaviours are typically measured using self-report. The one exception to this has been in the study of smoking cessation, where biological markers of nicotine metabolism are easy and cheap to identify. Salivary nicotine levels indicate whether or not an individual has been smoking, but not how much they have smoked. Expired carbon dioxide provides a cheaper but less reliable measure, as it may be contaminated by levels of the gas in the atmosphere: walking in car-polluted air may result in levels indicative of low levels of smoking. A cautionary note is that when compared with self-report, levels of disagreement of up to 20 per cent are not unusual.

Measures of the frequency of health-related behaviour have typically employed self-report measures. The questionnaire used by Norman *et al.* (1998) was not atypical. In this, cigarette smoking was measured by asking respondents to indicate the number of cigarettes they smoke in a typical day. Alcohol consumption was measured by providing a series of unit equivalents (one short = one unit) and asking respondents to report a typical week's alcohol consumption measured in units. A more accurate estimate may be obtained by asking people to report their consumption separately for each day in the previous week. Fewer conversion errors will occur if respondents report the actual drinks they had rather than attempt the conversion. Diet may be measured both in terms of the frequency of eating different foodstuffs and choices between various similar foodstuffs (for example, full fat versus low fat milk). Some measures also attempt to measure the size of typical helpings. An alternative, and highly accurate, measure of consumption is afforded by the use of diaries and weighed portions of food. However, this method so distorts behaviour that it rarely reflects participants' behaviour when they are not completing such records.

Levels of exercise can be assessed by measures of the frequency of planned exercise. In the Norman *et al.* study these were divided into three levels: vigorous, moderate and mild (each with examples). Respondents were asked to indicate how many times they engaged in each type of exercise over a typical week. Other measures have taken into account more general exercise choices. The Stanford study, for example, rated activity by measuring whether respondents 'usually participated' in taking stairs rather than the elevator, walking instead of driving short distances, parking a distance from destination and walking, walking during lunch hour or after dinner, or leaving a bus before one's destination in order to walk (Sallis *et al.* 1988).

Diaries can provide a useful measure of behaviour and are often used as assessments in clinical interventions. They may not only incorporate a measure of the behaviour being monitored but also allow the individual to provide a wealth of additional information that may help them to plan any behavioural change. These may include the circumstances in which the behaviour occurs or the thoughts they have before, during or after the behaviour in question. A simpler measure of behaviour is afforded by measures such as the General Preventive Health Behaviours Checklist (Amir 1987). This assesses whether or not the respondent has engaged in behaviours as diverse as smoking, getting a regular medical check-up or eating snacks. However, the subjective nature and lack of focus of some of the items (I get enough sleep; I get enough exercise) make this and similar instruments inappropriate as measures of change.

Summary and conclusions

Psychosocial outcomes are increasingly seen as relevant in the context of the care of patients with physical health problems. However, the would-be researcher or clinician wishing to evaluate patient outcomes is faced with a plethora of measures purporting to measure the same construct. Choice of measure is far from easy and is frequently governed by factors such as familiarity and ease of access to measures, as well as by more scientific criteria. However, psychometric and theoretical issues should take precedence over these more pragmatic ones, and it behoves those using these instruments to use those that are most applicable to the question and population being addressed. This chapter has reviewed some of the better known measures addressing psychosocial issues and identified some issues to consider when choosing relevant instruments. However, it has only touched upon the range of instruments available. Those seeking a wider review of these instruments would benefit from reading texts reviewing specific issues in more detail.

Further reading

Bowling, A. (1995) *Measuring Disease*. Buckingham: Open University Press.
Bowling, A. (1997) *Measuring Health: A Review of Quality of Life Measurement Scales*. Buckingham: Open University Press
McDowell, I. and Newell, C. (1996) *Measuring Health: A Guide to Rating Scales and Questionnaires*. Oxford: Oxford University Press.

Improving quality of life

Medical science has progressed significantly in the past decades. Lives are now saved when they would previously have been lost. However, such improvements are not without their costs. Some treatments may provide additional life, but carry significant costs for the patient. Some people may have to live with chronic diseases that medicine cannot fully control. Both problems have brought those practising medicine to face the same issue: that the quality of life of patients should be an important consideration in any treatment plan. Decisions about whether to commence or continue some treatments are now premised not only on the length of life such a treatment will confer, but also on the quality of that life. In addition, where illness or disability is chronic, increasing attention is being given to the psychosocial concomitants of the problem and interventions are being developed to maximize patient quality of life.

This chapter reviews evidence of the effectiveness of such interventions. The review is not all-encompassing: its aim is to provide some evidence of the relative effectiveness of differing interventions. Some studies, which combine several therapeutic approaches and where the relative effectiveness of each intervention is unclear, are not reported. This approach provides some clarity of issues but means, inevitably, that some multimodal interventions are ignored.

The chapter focuses on a number of approaches including:

♦ Information provision

♦ Cognitive-behavioural interventions

♦ Coping effectiveness training

♦ Problem-solving counselling

♦ Operant approaches

♦ Self-management

♦ Emotional expression

These interventions are considered in the context of helping people both to manage their illness more effectively and to cope with the emotional distress associated with chronic disease. The effectiveness of these and some other approaches in the context of risk behaviour change is considered in the following chapter.

Information provision

Diagnosis and concerns about prognosis and treatment raise significant anxieties, and many patients want information about their condition and its treatment. Rahn *et al.* (1998), for example, asked women receiving radiotherapy for breast cancer to identify what best helped them to cope with their diagnosis and treatment. Ninety-four per cent stated that the most important factor was being kept well informed about the treatment they were receiving. Accordingly, a number of interventions to improve mood or change behaviour have done so by providing information about the cause, course, treatment or progression of a condition. In addition, patients are frequently given information in an attempt to help them manage a chronic condition effectively.

Changing knowledge

There is a substantial body of evidence that patient education programmes can enhance knowledge of a condition or treatment, at least in the short term. However, some negative findings have also been reported. Pruitt *et al.* (1993), for example, compared the effectiveness of a three-session radiotherapy outpatient education programme with a no-intervention control. The content of the course included factual information about cancer and radiotherapy, common concerns and coping strategies, and how to communicate with the health care team. Neither group showed any improvement in relevant knowledge. Another study compared the effectiveness of educational cardiac rehabilitation programmes in two hospitals. While knowledge scores rose in one hospital, they actually fell in the other. Unfortunately, details of the programmes were not provided, but the data strike a cautionary note.

Changing behaviour

Even where increases in knowledge are achieved, they may not impact on behaviour or symptom control: a number of studies have found only marginal relationships between knowledge and symptom control. In contrast, Bill-Harvey *et al.* (1989) reported significant gains following a six-week series of classes for 'low literacy' outpatients with osteoarthritis.

Participants in the active intervention increased their exercise levels and use of adaptive equipment relative to those in a no-treatment control group. Despite the potential benefits for some, the inconsistent findings following information provision have made a number of commentators question its benefits as the sole method of facilitating behavioural change, and information provision now frequently forms one element of multi-component interventions.

The failure of some educational interventions may, however, not reflect the potential impact of such interventions. They may indicate an inadequate or inappropriate method of information provision. This may be illustrated using studies of the written provision of information. Reid *et al.* (1995), for example, evaluated the impact of a widely available diabetes pamphlet. Immediately after reading it, participants could recall an average of only 8 of the 108 ideas in it. Many readers lacked appropriate reading skills. In addition, the topics that they thought were important differed from the topics that a physician thought were important. That one pamphlet had 108 ideas in it suggests that the demand on the readers was very high, and the authors acknowledge that many participants found it difficult to read. Here, there may be some confusion between the medium and the message: the medium can only be effective if it is used appropriately. Ley (1997) suggested that about one-quarter of published medical leaflets would be understood by only 20–30 per cent of the adult population.

Changing mood

Even simple information about the context of care can prove an extremely valuable means of improving mood. A tour of a clinic, the provision of general information about treatment, and the opportunity to pose questions with an oncology counsellor have been found to be highly effective in reducing stress prior to chemotherapy in patients recently diagnosed as having cancer. Further benefits of the provision of appropriate information on anxiety in the context of acute hospital procedures are discussed in Chapter 6. Hospital-based interventions may also contribute to longer-term reductions in anxiety. Tooth *et al.* (1998), for example, found an educational intervention given prior to angioplasty resulted in gains on measures of patient anxiety at four months postsurgery and, in comparison with no treatment, improved partner quality of life ratings at eleven-month follow-up assessment.

Information does not necessarily have to be given in conventional form. Taylor *et al.* (1985) allocated cardiac patients undergoing treadmill exercising into one of three conditions. In the first, they underwent the test on their own. In the second they undertook the test in the presence of their partner. In the third condition, the partners both observed the patients' exercise and underwent a treadmill test themselves. Subsequent levels of partner anxiety and patient engagement in exercise differed according to the degree of spouse involvement, with those in the 'exercise alone' condition faring worst and those in the active intervention faring best. This is an important finding as there is consistent evidence that the partners of men who have an MI experience more anxiety than the men themselves and that this may adversely impact on their rehabilitation.

Information versus other strategies

Despite the benefits for some of information provision, it may not necessarily provide the optimum intervention. A number of studies have compared the effectiveness of educational programmes with alternative treatment approaches. Decker and Cline-Elsen (1992) compared the effectiveness of an education and counselling intervention with that of relaxation training and imagery in a group of patients receiving either curative or palliative radiotherapy. Only the latter group showed reductions in measures of tension, depression, anger and fatigue.

Additional gains following a cognitive-behavioural programme were also found by Campbell *et al.* (1996). They compared the effectiveness of educational and behavioural instruction programmes for patients with non-insulin-dependent diabetes. The goals of the intervention were improved diet and weight reduction. Both types of intervention proved equally effective in facilitating weight reduction. However, those in the behavioural programme evidenced greater or more rapid reductions in diastolic blood pressure and cholesterol levels. They also reported the highest treatment satisfaction levels.

A third study examined the relative benefits of an education and exercise programme alone or in combination with a cognitive-behavioural intervention in the treatment of chronic lower back pain. Immediately following the intervention, the combined intervention resulted in significantly greater improvements on measures of functional impairment, use of active coping strategies, self-efficacy beliefs and medication use. These differences were maintained at six-month follow-up.

Not all comparisons support the superiority of cognitive-behavioural over educational interventions. In a direct comparison of the two interventions in the treatment of fibromyalgia, Nicassio *et al.* (1997) compared a ten-week education programme that presented information on a range of health-related topics without emphasizing skill acquisition with a behavioural intervention focused on the practice of a variety of pain-coping skills. Although improvement across time was found on measures of depression, self-reported pain behaviours, observed pain behaviours and myalgia scores, no differences were found between the behavioural and education conditions. Nevertheless, the majority of studies have shown didactic educational programmes to be less effective than more interactive or skills-based programmes.

Stress management and other cognitive behavioural interventions

Stress has been identified as a factor contributing to the onset or exacerbation of a variety of conditions (see Chapter 2). Not surprisingly, a number of interventions have focused on teaching stress management procedures in an effort to control the symptoms of these disorders. These have proven effective in conditions as diverse as chronic obstructive airways disease and atopic dermatitis. Stress management procedures have also been found to impact on the distress associated with severe conditions, including HIV infection and AIDS.

Diabetes

There are theoretical reasons to presume that relaxation may prove an effective element in any programme of diabetes control. Stress often precedes periods of reduced adherence to self-care behaviours and may be associated with inappropriate changes in eating patterns. In addition, stress hormones reduce insulin sensitivity and should, theoretically, be accompanied by elevations in blood glucose: although in practice such a relationship is far from consistently found. Accordingly, some studies have found relaxation to be an effective intervention in reducing blood glucose levels. However, others have had more disappointing results, and some have even reported increased numbers of hypoglycaemic episodes following the use of relaxation techniques in previously well controlled diabetics.

The findings of Aikens et al. (1997) give some insight into the complex issues underlying these contradictory findings. They randomly allocated non-insulin-dependent diabetics to either six group sessions of progressive muscle relaxation and imagery or routine medical care. All participants were assessed before and after the 8-week intervention, and again at 16 weeks follow-up. Somewhat paradoxically, they found that participants in the relaxation group who had low pre-intervention stress levels evidenced a greater improvement in blood glucose levels than did those with higher levels of stress. Retrospective analysis revealed that those participants who were particularly stressed and who rated their glucose as more stress-responsive practised relaxation less between sessions than less stressed and non-stress-responsive patients. The authors speculated that the least anxious and stress-responsive patients benefited from group-based relaxation training. More anxious individuals may have needed individually administered interventions.

Just as relaxation has not been shown consistently to help diabetic symptom control, so stress management programmes have met with mixed success. Boardway et al. (1993) randomly assigned adolescents with diabetes to a stress management group or standard outpatient treatment.

The treatment programme was substantial, comprising ten sessions over the first three months of the programme, followed by three additional monthly sessions. By the end of the programme, participants in the stress management group reported less diabetes-related stress but did not differ from the comparison group on measures of metabolic control or regimen adherence. Such results suggest a specificity of treatment effect, and that effective control of stress and increased metabolic control may best be achieved through differing interventions or a combined self- and stress-management intervention. The effectiveness of one such programme was reported by Mendez and Belendez (1997). During twelve sessions with diabetic adolescents, participants were involved in blood glucose discrimination training, role-playing, relaxation exercises, self-instruction and problem-solving strategies. In comparison with a no-treatment control group, the intervention group showed improvements in adherence to the recommended regimen, in skills and frequency of glycaemic analyses, and a reduction in blood glucose estimate errors. Changes on stress-related variables included reductions in daily hassles and unease in social interactions. These gains were maintained for over a year following the end of the intervention.

Disorders of the gut

Perhaps the earliest report of a controlled evaluation based on the principles of stress management was reported in the mid-1930s in a group of patients with peptic ulcer disease. Participants were allocated to medical treatment alone or in combination with psychological treatment. The psychological treatment comprised small group meetings held for seven days a week over a period of six weeks, and included an educational phase and instruction in what would now be referred to as distraction and positive self-talk techniques. The intervention also attempted to stop reinforcement of previously rewarded illness-related behaviours. Amazingly, given the intensity of the programme, 32 of the original 47 participants completed the intervention and evidenced substantial long-term reductions in symptoms.

More modern evidence of the effectiveness of stress management procedures was provided by Brooks and Richardson (1980). They compared a stress management programme with a placebo intervention in the treatment and prevention of relapse in individuals with peptic ulcer disease receiving antacid medication. Immediately following the intervention phase, the benefits of the intervention were limited to participants who reported high levels of anxiety and low levels of assertiveness at baseline. This group experienced significantly fewer days of symptomatic pain and consumed less medication than their equivalents in the placebo condition. It was, however, in the long term that the strength of the intervention was most convincing. Over a three and a half year follow-up period, fewer participants in the active intervention experienced recurrences, they attended hospital less frequently, and fewer had surgery than those in the placebo group.

The majority of studies of the effectiveness of stress management procedures have targeted the irritable bowel syndrome (IBS), and several have shown the procedures to be more effective than no intervention. However, IBS patients appear to respond positively to any intervention, even one considered to be a placebo. Accordingly, only studies where all participants receive some form of intervention permit the effects of specific interventions to be compared. Such studies have met with mixed results. Stress management has been shown to be equally or more effective than medication or a placebo psychotherapy condition in both the short and the long term (see, for example, Whorwell *et al.* 1987). In contrast, Payne and Blanchard (1995) failed to find consistent gains on measures of IBS symptoms when comparing stress management with an attention control. They also found no benefit of stress management procedures when compared with pseudomeditation and EEG alpha-wave feedback. There have been a number of other negative findings, perhaps because IBS has multiple aetiologies not all of which are associated with stress (see Chapter 2). Future interventions perhaps need to be careful to target individuals where there is a clear relationship between IBS symptoms and stress.

Arthritis

A number of studies have shown stress management to be effective in the treatment of the symptoms of rheumatoid arthritis. O'Leary *et al.* (1988), for example, found that stress management training was more effective in improving measures of pain, joint movement and self-efficacy than standard medical treatment alone, both immediately after the intervention and at four-month follow-up. These gains were associated with immune changes, including greater numbers of suppressor T cells, and reduced joint inflammation. Parker *et al.* (1995) compared a 10-week stress management intervention followed by an additional 15-month maintenance phase with usual care. The stress management group evidenced significant improvements on measures of helplessness, self-efficacy, coping, pain and health status. Beneficial effects were still detectable at the 15-month follow-up evaluation.

In a study comparing the additive effect of stress management and a family support intervention, Radojevic *et al.* (1992) randomly allocated patients with rheumatoid arthritis to one of four conditions: a family support group, stress management alone or in combination with a family support group, or no treatment. The stress management interventions resulted in greater improvements in joint examination pain, swelling severity and the number of swollen joints than either of the other two conditions both immediately following the intervention and at follow-up. These benefits may have been made as a consequence of increased mobilization and exercise undertaken by those in the stress management group.

Cancer

A cognitive-behavioural intervention designed specifically for use with cancer patients has been developed by a clinical team in the Royal Marsden Hospital in London. Adjuvant therapy is a brief, focused therapy that identifies significant problems, teaches cognitive and behavioural strategies for solving them, and aims to induce a positive fighting spirit. The first study to evaluate its effectiveness compared it with routine care (Moorey et al. 1994). Matched for levels of psychopathology at the time of entry, patients in the active intervention evidenced significantly less psychological distress by its completion than those in the control group. At one-year follow-up, rates of anxiety were 19 per cent in the active intervention group and 44 per cent among control patients: rates for depression were 11 and 18 per cent, respectively. Following this success, the same team compared the effectiveness of adjuvant therapy against a counselling intervention with patients experiencing an adjustment reaction to their illness. The adjuvant therapy proved more effective in improving measures of distress, coping with cancer and in engendering fighting spirit than the counselling, both immediately following the intervention and at four-month follow-up.

In an evaluation of a more traditional cognitive behavioural intervention, Fawzy et al. (1993) compared the effectiveness of a stress management intervention and usual care in a group of patients with stage I or II malignant melanoma whose tumour had been surgically excised. Both immediately after the intervention and at six-month follow-up only the active intervention group evidenced improvements on mood. They also evidenced substantially higher T- and NK cell counts. Similar gains in mood have been found in a number of other studies, and have been shown to match the gains of pharmacological therapy (Holland et al. (1991).

Chronic pain

Chronic pain, lasting six months or more, may result from disease or traumatic processes. It may be exacerbated by a variety of psychological or psychophysiological processes including inappropriate catastrophizing cognitions (see Chapter 4) or muscular tension initially used to prevent excess movement in an affected part of the body itself contributing to the problem. These aetiological features suggest that relaxation or more wide-ranging stress management strategies may help people to cope better with their pain.

A number of studies have shown relaxation alone, or in combination with biofeedback procedures, to be more effective than no intervention in the treatment of conditions including headache, chronic back pain and arthritis. However, relaxation has not always proven more effective than placebo. Silver and Blanchard (1978), for example, assigned patients with both tension and migraine headaches to either relaxation with biofeedback or a pseudomeditation condition. The level of clinically significant improvement found in the relaxation condition was higher than that in the pseudomeditation condition (51 versus 37 per cent), but this difference was not significant.

Stress management programmes build on relaxation to provide a wider range of coping skills upon which patients may draw. Often they are delivered through a multidisciplinary pain management programme involving elements such as education sessions, goal-setting, graded activity training, pacing, applied relaxation, cognitive techniques, social skills training, drug reduction methods and contingency management of pain behaviours. Johansson et al. (1998) found this type of intervention to produce short-term gains relative to a no-treatment control group on measures of cognitive catastrophizing, pain behaviours, take-up of occupational training and leisure-time activity, and sustained gains on measures including pain intensity, pain interference, life control, mood disturbance, physical fitness and use of analgesics. Keel et al. (1998) found similar stress management procedures to be more effective than relaxation in the treatment of fibromyalgia.

Nicholas et al. (1992) reported a study of the effectiveness of cognitive treatment with and without relaxation training, and behavioural treatment with and without relaxation training in patients with chronic lower back pain. All conditions, including a standard treatment control, also received physiotherapy and a back pain education programme. Participants in the combined interventions improved significantly more than those in the standard treatment conditions on measures of pain intensity, self-rated functional impairment and pain-related dysfunctional cognitions. However, progressive relaxation training did not add to the benefits of either the cognitive or behavioural treatments. Work by Rokicki et al. (1997) offers one explanation of these findings. They found that the therapeutic gains subsequent to relaxation training were primarily as a result of cognitive changes, not a direct effect of changes in muscle tension. These apparently different therapeutic approaches may work, at least in part, through a common pathway. Certainly, the centrality of relaxation as an intervention with chronic pain can be questioned.

HIV

Stress management programmes have generally proven effective as a means of reducing distress in individuals with HIV or AIDS. Fawzy et al.

(1989), for example, assigned men with a diagnosis of AIDS into either a stress management programme or a 'usual care' group. After the ten-week programme, men in the active intervention reported greater reductions in anxiety and depression than those in the control group. Lutgendorf et al. (1997) also found significant benefits following a ten-week stress management programme relative to a no intervention condition. The programme was designed to increase participants' ability to cope with the distress of symptomatic HIV and their use of social support. By the end of the programme, participants reported greater use of cognitive coping strategies such as positive reframing and social support in comparison to those in the control condition. Both these factors were associated with improvements on measures of anxiety and depression.

Coronary Heart Disease

A number of studies have evaluated the effects of relaxation or stress management in reducing distress in cardiac patients, with some success in terms of changes of anxiety, depression and other measures of quality of life. However, not all programmes have proven effective. Collins and Rice (1997) failed to find any benefit of relaxation in an unselected group of individuals without evident anxiety at the beginning of the treatment programme. However, where care has been taken to ensure that all participants had the potential to gain from such an intervention the outcome has been more positive. Oldridge et al. (1995), for example, randomly assigned patients with mild to moderate anxiety or depression scores to either a usual care condition or an eight-week stress management programme. Even in this selected population, only those participants whose anxiety scores were above the mean evidenced significant reductions in anxiety.

As well as targeting day-to-day stress, programmes using stress management procedures to reduce the frequency of episodes of angina have focused on the use of these procedures at the time of an angina episode, in an attempt to reduce the sympathetic drive contributing to coronary vasospasm. One of the first studies to explore the effectiveness of this approach was reported by Bundy et al. (1994). They assigned patients with stable angina to either a stress management programme or routine care. Participants in the stress management programme reported reductions in the frequency of angina symptoms, were less reliant on medication and had improved exercise tolerance relative to those receiving routine care. A much larger study, involving hundreds of participants, was reported by Gallacher et al. (1997). They compared a less intensive intervention, involving three group meetings and a distance-learning stress management programme, with a no-treatment control condition. At six-month follow-up they found a significant reduction in stress-, but not exercise-related, angina.

Coping effectiveness training

Based on cognitive behavioural principles, coping effectiveness training (CET) teaches participants to match their coping efforts to the characteristics of the stressor they have to cope with (see Chapter 8). Its strong theoretical basis and use of reliable strategies, albeit in a novel manner, suggest that it may prove a highly effective intervention. However, supportive data are limited.

Perhaps the earliest intervention to use the title CET was reported by Chesney and Folkman (1994) in a study of forty HIV positive men who were randomly allocated into either a coping effectiveness training programme or a waiting list control. Those in the active intervention gained significantly on measures of depression and morale at six-week follow-up. Gains were primarily attributable to reductions in self-blame coping and a shift towards the use of more active coping strategies including planful problem solving and positive reappraisal. The intervention they developed drew upon the work of Telch and Telch (1986) who had earlier reported a larger study, with cancer patients randomly allocated to one of three conditions: group coping skills, support group therapy, and no treatment. Participants in the coping intervention evidenced greater gains on measures of anxiety, depression, anger, vigour and fatigue immediately following the intervention than those in the support group. In addition, they reported more confidence in their ability to cope with medical procedures, communicate with physicians, and engage in social and leisure activities. Unfortunately, high attrition rates, including the death of several participants, precluded longer-term assessment of the treatment effects.

Contrary to the theoretical rationale of the intervention, King and Kennedy (1999) reported significant gains in mood following CET in a group of patients with spinal injuries in the absence of any changes in their use of coping strategies. The authors considered the possibility that their method of measuring coping was not sufficiently sensitive to capture changes in the use of coping strategies. However, they concluded that changes in mood may have been consequent to changes in participants' appraisals of their disability and their perceived ability to cope with it.

Problem-solving counselling

Several studies have shown counselling to be an effective intervention for people with different illnesses. Problem-solving counselling techniques may be implicit in many of the interventions so far discussed and in the client-centred approach increasingly being adopted within medical consultations (see Chapter 8). However, some studies have been more explicit in the use and evaluation of problem-solving counselling. De Vellis *et al.*

(1988) examined the effect of a preliminary psychosocial interview that assessed participants' arthritis-imposed lifestyle problems and identified the potential resources that might be mobilized to cope with them. In addition, half those attending took part in a supplementary one hour long problem-solving intervention based on the principles of Egan's counselling process: problem identification, identification of potential strategies of problem resolution and selection of 'best' solutions, followed by a two-week follow-up meeting to assess the need for any further intervention. All participants reported significant reductions in symptom severity, including measures of stiffness, fatigue, swelling and pain, and impairment in physical activities. However, there was no between-group difference on any measure used in the study. It is possible that counselling is not effective in this context or that it added little to the initial interview which began the counselling process.

More positive results were reported by Maisiak et al. (1996). They compared telephone counselling with telephone symptom monitoring and usual care, over a nine-month trial period in a large group of patients with both osteo- and rheumatoid arthritis. In comparison with usual care, participants in the counselling, but not the symptom monitoring group, evidenced significant gains on a wide-ranging measure of quality of life. The number of medical visits by patients with osteoarthritis in the counselling group was also significantly reduced in comparison with baseline levels.

Operant approaches

Few randomized controlled trials have evaluated the impact of operant approaches on the control of symptoms, and most of these have focused on the control of pain. However, what data there are suggest that this may form a useful intervention. In the 1970s, several single case studies (see, for example, Fordyce 1992) showed that differential reinforcement of non-pain- and pain-related behaviours resulted in significant clinical gains and reductions in the use of pain medication. Larger-scale studies have since complemented these findings. In one such study, Lindstrom et al. (1992) compared the effectiveness of an operant approach against a usual care treatment condition in aiding blue-collar workers to return to work following a diagnosis of lower back pain. Participants in the operant condition took part in a programme of gradually increasing exercise, with appropriate rewards for achieving behavioural targets. They returned to work significantly earlier than did the patients in the control group.

A number of studies have compared the efficacy of operant and stress management procedures in the treatment of chronic pain. Nicholas et al. (1991) found that both treatments reduced reports of pain, but that operant procedures had greater immediate effects on medication use and significant others' ratings of functional impairment. The same trend was found by Turner and Jensen (1993), but by six and twelve months follow-up participants in the stress management intervention had continued to gain and neither group differed at these times. Evidence that the two approaches used together may combine to be a more effective treatment was provided by Vlaeyen *et al.* (1995). They allocated patients with lower back pain into either an operant condition, one in which they received cognitive therapy to reduce catastrophizing cognitions, and a combined intervention involving an operant approach combined with either relaxation or cognitive therapy. Follow-up assessment occurred at six months and one year after termination of treatment and revealed significant improvements on measures of pain and health behaviours, pain cognitions and affective distress in all conditions. However, participants in the combined interventions fared better than those in the single-intervention conditions.

Operant procedures have also been incorporated into multi-component treatment programmes for other disorders. Latimer (1979), for example, identified three inter-related sets of symptoms that occurred in patients with the irritable bowel syndrome: bowel symptoms, pain as a consequence of muscular spasm associated with these symptoms, and illness-related behaviours such as complaints or expressions of pain. The latter, he argued, were shaped by reinforcement over the course of the illness. He suggested that as well as more general stress management procedures, any treatment programme should also include procedures to change this reinforcement process. Bennett and Wilkinson (1985) attempted just such a procedure. However, most of the families of the participants in their study were no longer rewarding such behaviours (some were heartily sick of them) and the reinforcement process did not form an important contributor to the success of the intervention. Nevertheless, operant procedures form an important potential intervention in the treatment of problems associated with any chronic illness.

Self-management

Self-management procedures encompass a variety of strategies and methods. Central to this approach is education, training and rehearsal in methods of control over behaviour and the disease process (see Chapter 8). While many programmes would not give themselves the title of 'self-management' they embody these principles and are included in this section. This definition of self-management encompasses some programmes described as educational, but excludes those based solely on the provision of information.

Arthritis

One of the first research groups to apply self-management principles to health care was led by a research team at Stanford University, USA. They initially ran groups focusing on the management of single conditions, of which one of the first was for individuals with arthritis (Lorig and Holman 1993). The Arthritis Self-management Program was a six-week programme incorporating education about arthritis, modelling and problem solving related to techniques of disease control including mobility exercises and cognitive reinterpretation of symptoms. Although the study had no control group, there was some evidence of the programme's efficacy, as 20 months after attending the programme participants reported a decreased number of visits to the physician, reductions in pain and a modest reduction in disability. Three years later, in a summary of the relevant literature, SuperioCabuslay *et al.* (1996) reported that compared with drug treatment alone, self-management interventions provided additional benefits of 20–30 per cent on measures of pain relief in both osteoarthritis and rheumatoid arthritis, 40 per cent in functional ability in rheumatoid arthritis, and 60–80 per cent in the reduction of tender joint counts in rheumatoid arthritis: impressive benefits in a population with a chronic progressive disorder.

Chronic conditions

Following their work with specific conditions, the Stanford group explored the impact of a generic intervention aimed at people with a variety of chronic conditions. Lorig *et al.* (1999) reported the outcome of nearly one thousand patients attending a self-management programme with a variety of diagnoses, including CHD, lung disease, stroke and arthritis. Participants were randomly allocated to either a generic six-month programme or a waiting list control. When compared with those in the control group, participants in the active intervention demonstrated improvements on measures including exercise, cognitive symptom management, communication with physicians, self-reported health, fatigue, disability, and social or role limitations. They also had fewer hospitalizations and days in the hospital. No differences were found on measures of pain or physical discomfort, shortness of breath or psychological well-being. Nevertheless, these data suggest that self-management groups may prove an effective intervention, at least in the short term, with patients who have any one of a number of conditions.

Asthma

Self-management procedures have proved equally effective in helping both adults and children control the symptoms of asthma. Perez *et al.*

(1999), for example, evaluated the effects of a self-management educational programme on children aged between 7 and 14 years and their parents. The children were given information on the nature of asthma and its treatment, and given practice in the appropriate use of inhalers and cognitive behavioural strategies to help them to cope with panicky thoughts. Their parents received two talks and an information brochure. By the end of the programme, both children and parents in the intervention group showed significant gains on measures of asthma knowledge, while the children evidenced improvements in their use of self-management strategies and on an index of asthma morbidity: changes not found in a usual-care control group. Younger children benefited most from the programme, possibly because they had previously developed fewer coping strategies than the older children had.

In a study evaluating the effectiveness of different treatment components, Vazquez and Buceta (1993) compared a self-management programme with the same programme combined with relaxation and a usual treatment control group. Overall, participants in the self-management condition evidenced the most reductions in their subjective assessments of attack intensity. However, those in the combined intervention whose asthma was triggered predominantly by emotional stimuli showed significant decreases in attack duration and improvements in peak expiratory flow rate in comparison with similar patients in both other groups.

HIV

One of the most complicated conditions to manage is that of being HIV positive. Not surprisingly, self-management programmes have been developed to help such individuals to cope with the complex demands of their condition. Gifford *et al.* (1998), for example, randomly assigned men with symptomatic HIV infection or AIDS to either a seven-session self-management group or a usual-care control group. The self-management groups used interactive methods to provide relevant information and a number of disease self-management skills, including symptom assessment and management, medication use, physical exercise and relaxation skills. They also taught them communication skills in order to help their communication with their doctors. Following the intervention, the number of significantly troubling symptoms reported by those in the intervention group fell, whilst it increased in the control group. Similarly, perceived efficacy in coping with symptoms was maintained in the intervention condition, but fell in the control group.

Diabetes

Control of insulin-dependent diabetes requires a complex self-management regimen. Diabetics have to monitor and vary both the amount of carbohydrate consumed and the insulin used in injections according to blood glucose levels measured prior to each insulin dose. Each of these variables will vary according to the metabolic demand placed on the individual as a function of factors including levels of exercise and stress. Accordingly, diabetics have to make frequent complex dosage decisions. Failure to make the correct decisions may result in hypo- or hyperglycaemic episodes in the short term and increased health-damaging effects in the long term. In order to facilitate diabetic control, many treatment centres focus on teaching appropriate self-management skills.

In an evaluation of such a programme, Langewitz *et al.* (1997) examined the effectiveness of what they termed intensified functional insulin therapy. This incorporated both an educational component in which patients learned through direct experience how they reacted to factors (such as exercise or diet) that impacted on their blood glucose levels; and a problem-solving component in which they developed specific strategies to cope with these situations. In comparison to baseline measures, participants evidenced significant improvements in blood glucose levels and the number of hypoglycaemic episodes in the following year. In addition, they reported more moments free of disease-specific strain.

Despite the gains made by such programmes, a cautionary note about their implementation within a primary care setting was provided by Pill *et al.* (1998). They found diabetic patients initially benefited from a self-management programme conducted with their general practitioners. However, although the clinicians involved in the study were highly enthusiastic at the beginning of the study, by two years into its implementation only 19 per cent were applying the method systematically and at this time the intervention was not able to demonstrate significant biochemical or functional improvements.

Innovative methods of self-management

Teaching self-management techniques does not necessarily depend on contact between those providing and receiving the intervention. Glasgow *et al.* (1996) provided diabetics with a touchscreen computer-assisted assessment designed to provide immediate feedback on key barriers to dietary self-management, and to enhance goal setting and the use of problem-solving strategies. Follow-up components to the single-session intervention included telephone calls and interactive video or videotape instruction as needed. This intervention produced greater improvements than usual care on a number of measures of dietary choice at follow-up.

A fun example of the use of information technology was reported by Brown *et al.* (1997). They examined the impact of an interactive video game designed to improve self-care among children and adolescents with diabetes. Participants were randomly allocated to an educational group or a control group. In the game, players take the role of animated characters who managed their diabetes by monitoring blood glucose, taking insulin injections and choosing foods, while setting out to save a diabetes summer camp from marauding rats and mice. Those who played the game evidenced improvements relative to the control group on measures of diabetes-related self-efficacy, communication with parents about diabetes, and self-care behaviours. They also made fewer unscheduled visits to the doctor.

Emotional expression

At a time of emotional distress, interventions that focus on providing emotional support are likely to be of benefit: indeed, this is the key element of the emotional care discussed in Chapter 8. Few controlled studies have evaluated the outcome of this approach in patients with physical health problems. However, those studies that have been conducted testify to its value.

The simplest method of examining the effects of emotional disclosure is to use the protocol developed by Pennebaker and Seagal (1999). In this, participants write or talk in an unstructured way about the stresses or upsets they have experienced, typically for 20–30 minutes a day over three or four consecutive days. Kelley et al. (1997) examined the effects of such a protocol in patients with rheumatoid arthritis. Participants were randomly assigned to talk privately either about stressful events or about trivial topics for four consecutive days. Disclosure resulted in an immediate increase in negative mood. Two weeks later, the groups did not differ on any health measure. However, by three-month follow-up patients in the emotional disclosure condition reported less affective disturbance and better physical functioning in daily activities than those in the 'trivia' condition. These findings mirror those of other studies where the gains of emotional disclosure are typically in the medium to long term, not immediately following the intervention.

Other studies have reported on more complex methods of facilitating emotional expression. Forester et al. (1993), for example, randomly assigned patients receiving radiotherapy either to group psychotherapy or to a standard treatment control group. The supportive psychotherapy groups comprised ten weekly sessions, each lasting 90 minutes. By four weeks after the end of radiotherapy, the patients who received group psychotherapy reported less emotional distress and somatic preoccupation and fewer physical symptoms then those in the control group.

In another study of patients with cancer, Capone (1982) randomly allocated women newly diagnosed with some form of gynaecological cancer to a structured counselling condition or usual treatment. The intervention provided information on surgery and treatment, promoted the expression of participants' feelings related to diagnosis, and attempted to enhance self-esteem, femininity and interpersonal relationships. It also provided information on methods to reduce sexual anxiety when resuming intercourse for those to whom this was relevant. In comparison with those in the no-treatment condition, women who received this intervention had fewer difficulties in social relationships and in returning to work or housework following surgery, fewer episodes of depression (3 versus 19 per cent at second follow-up), less strain on their marital relationship as a consequence of illness, and fewer sexual difficulties. Group social support and emotional expression have also been found to benefit cancer patients in the longer term (see, for example, Spiegel *et al.* 1981). These findings are discussed in the next chapter.

Summary and conclusions

A number of therapeutic approaches have proven effective in helping people both to cope emotionally and to engage in behaviours to control the symptoms of their condition. Information may be of benefit to some individuals in some situations, but may not be appropriate for all. Self-management approaches incorporate many behavioural or cognitive behavioural strategies. Their effectiveness is now widely acknowledged, although in some cases their benefits may only last as long as attendance at a programme continues. Similarly, stress management procedures have been shown to be effective in helping people to cope with the emotional sequelae of illness. The dominance of these approaches should not hide the potential benefits associated with the less frequently used approaches, including operant approaches, emotional expression and CET, all of which may contribute significantly to patient well-being.

Further reading

Camic, P.M. (ed.) (1998) *Clinical Handbook of Health Psychology: A Practical Guide to Effective Interventions.* Berlin: Hogrefe & Huber.

Risk behaviour change

As evidence has accumulated that a number of disease processes are mediated by behaviour, so psychologists and others have begun to identify strategies to facilitate risk behaviour change – and hence reduce risk for disease or disease progression. The disease most strongly associated with behaviour over the past decade or more has been coronary heart disease (CHD). Indeed, the majority of primary prevention programmes, attempting to delay or prevent the initial onset of disease, have been aimed at changing risk factors for CHD. With the onset of AIDS, the agenda of primary prevention has changed considerably and significant efforts are now being given to reduce the prevalence of risky sexual behaviours. A further recent development has been advances in the identification of genetic markers of risk for future disease, which has raised a number of psychological and ethical as well as medical issues.

The agenda of secondary prevention, which attempts to slow the progression of disease has again focused primarily on CHD, although encouraging data on the effects of psychological treatments on immunologically mediated diseases such as cancer and AIDS are also reviewed.

The aim of this chapter is to review the evidence of the effectiveness of a number of therapeutic approaches used both in primary and secondary care settings and to draw some conclusions about their relative effectiveness. For this reason, as in the previous chapter, it is led by intervention rather than disease type. Such a review cannot hope to be all-encompassing, and studies selected are those that provide some measure of the effectiveness of specific types of intervention. Those that combine several therapeutic approaches, and where the relative effectiveness of each intervention is unclear, are generally not reported unless they are particularly important.

The chapter considers the following intervention approaches:

◆ Screening programmes

◆ Educational programmes

◆ Self-help approaches

- ◆ Behavioural programmes

- ◆ Relaxation and stress management

- ◆ Motivational interviewing

- ◆ Social support

- ◆ Operant conditioning

- ◆ Counselling

Screening programmes

The past decade has been associated with a substantial shift of resources towards the prevention of disease in many western countries. One manifestation of this movement has been the establishment of programmes screening for risk of disease. Some programmes, such as cervical screening, may lead to medical intervention should risk factors be identified. Others may require individual behaviour change to reduce risk for disease. Still others, including genetic screening programmes, may require individuals to make decisions potentially affecting future generations' health. Whilst the impact of screening on any one individual's health is likely to be modest, the numbers of people involved mean that such programmes may result in substantial changes in population rates of disease.

Screening and advice

Coronary risk

A number of community health promotion programmes have utilized screening programmes as part of a wider set of preventive strategies (see Chapter 7). However, the largest evaluation of their effectiveness as a single intervention is provided by the OXCHECK study (OXCHECK Study Group 1994). This study followed a population of over five thousand adults who were offered either a screening health check or formed a no-intervention control condition. The health check involved an assessment of participants' risk for CHD and advice on any necessary behavioural changes. Those who took part in this procedure had lower blood pressure and serum cholesterol levels between two and three years following the intervention than those who did not. However, the between-condition differences in cholesterol levels were significant for women but not for men, and no differences on measures of smoking or body mass index were found. Assessment of risk factor change closer to the time of screening was not conducted.

Evidence of shorter-term gains was reported by Redman *et al.* (1995). They measured the effectiveness of a single session in which participants received feedback of their cholesterol level combined with either brief written material or a brief educative phase and more extensive written information. At four-month follow-up, serum cholesterol levels had fallen significantly in both groups: in the feedback condition by 0.5 mmol/litre and by 0.84 mmol/litre in the more extensive intervention group. A similar pattern of results was found by Russell *et al.* (1979) in a study comparing the effectiveness of family doctor's advice to stop smoking with the same advice combined with an additional leaflet describing methods of cessation. At one-year follow-up, 3 per cent of those in the advice-only condition and 5 per cent of those in the advice-plus-leaflet condition were abstinent. These rates compared with a 0.3 per cent abstinence rate in a no-treatment control condition.

A number of more recent studies have failed to find any changes in smoking levels following similar procedures. Slama *et al.* (1990), for example, randomly assigned family doctors' patients to one of three conditions: 'simple advice', a structured behavioural change programme, and a control group. Participants in the simple advice group received a brief statement of advice from their family doctor accompanied by three pamphlets. Those in the structured intervention group were given information on behavioural and cognitive strategies to facilitate quitting. Validated smoking levels did not differ across conditions. These findings may reflect changes in the population of smokers now targeted by such programmes. In the early 1970s a much higher percentage of the population smoked cigarettes than in the late 1980s and messages about the health costs of smoking were fairly novel. In the decade between these studies, many smokers stopped smoking and, of those who continue to smoke, a majority has tried to stop smoking – perhaps on many occasions. This population may be much more difficult to influence than the target population of ten years previously.

Screening and counselling

Coronary risk

Screening interventions followed by some form of counselling may be more effective than screening alone. In a test of this hypothesis, Rose *et al.* (1980) compared the effectiveness of screening alone or in combination with three additional sessions as part of a smoking cessation programme. At five-year follow-up, 7 per cent of participants in the extended programme had quit smoking: none of those who received the single interview was abstinent. The corresponding figures for men found to be at high risk of CHD were 12 and 0 per cent, respectively. Similar gains following extended interventions have been reported for other CHD-related behaviours, including exercise and dietary cholesterol.

Perhaps the largest study of the effects of a screening and counselling programme was conducted in the UK. The Family Heart Study Group (1994) evaluated the impact of a screening procedure similar to that of the OXCHECK group combined with further counselling at between two- and six-monthly intervals over the following year. By the end of the follow-up period, and in comparison with a control group, participants' levels of cigarette smoking were lower by 4 per cent, average blood pressures by 5 mmHg, weight by 1 kilogram and serum cholesterol by a clinically insignificant 0.1 mmol/litre. These differences were greater than those reported by the OXCHECK group, albeit measured closer to the time of screening.

Genetic screening

Recent medical advances have led to the establishment of screening programmes for genes carrying risk of future health problems. Some, such as the genes for Huntingdon's chorea, may affect future generations. Others, including those for breast or bowel cancer, have more direct implications for health. One strand of the relevant work has focused on changes in knowledge following screening. Evans et al. (1994), for example, followed over five hundred women who received information on their risk of breast cancer. Before being given the information, 16 per cent of the women screened understood the population lifetime risk of breast cancer. This figure rose to 33 per cent following screening. Accurate assessment of personal risk rose from 11 to 41 per cent. Participants were significantly more likely to retain information if they were sent a post-clinic letter or if they initially overestimated their personal risk. In a similar population, Watson et al. (1999) found that information provision resulted in a modest shift in the accuracy of perceived lifetime risk, but 77 per cent of women continued to overestimate their risk of breast cancer.

In a possible foretaste of future preventive interventions, Audrain et al. (1997) used knowledge of risk for disease as a strategy to motivate risk behaviour change. They randomized smokers to one of two smoking cessation interventions: counselling, or counselling combined with biomarker feedback about genetic susceptibility to lung cancer. Participants in the latter group were more than twice as likely to make a quit attempt than those in the counselling group. However, 30-day cessation and follow-up smoking rates revealed no between-intervention differences. Fortunately, an initial increase in depression scores among those given genetic susceptibility feedback was not maintained over time.

Psychological impact of screening

Screening is not a neutral process. It has the potential to benefit individuals; it also carries the risk of psychological harm. Some individuals told that they had high blood pressure following a screening programme, for example, were more anxious about their health and had twice as many days off in the year following screening than in the previous year. Even where no health problem is found, people may respond to the process of screening with some anxiety. Stoate (1989), for example, reported that levels of anxiety rose amongst a significant number of participants following screening for high cholesterol in a general practitioner's clinic, even when they were told that they carried no risk for CHD. It seems that the implicit message of screening, that we may carry risk for disease, is enough to raise health anxieties in vulnerable individuals. Such findings suggest that the use of genetic information to motivate behavioural change (see Audrain *et al.* above) should not be conducted without considerable ethical debate.

Not surprisingly, false positives also carry high levels of psychological morbidity. Three months after mammography screening, Lerman *et al.* (1997) found that 41 per cent of women with a benign lesion continued to worry about breast cancer, whilst 25 per cent reported more widespread emotional problems. Screening may also prove ineffective in reducing pre-existing anxieties. Watson *et al.* (1999) found high levels of cancer-specific distress amongst women at risk for breast cancer prior to genetic screening: 28 per cent of participants reported that they worried about breast cancer 'frequently or constantly' and 18 per cent stated that worry about breast cancer was 'a severe or definite problem'. Levels of cancer-specific distress were unchanged following counselling.

Educational programmes

Education alone

The majority of educational programmes have been established in secondary prevention settings, particularly with patients who have had an MI or some form of surgery to increase blood flow to the heart muscle. The aim of such interventions is to reduce risk of the disease progression as a consequence of low levels of exercise, smoking or high fat diets.

Coronary Heart Disease

The majority of cardiac rehabilitation education programmes incorporate provision of information about cardiac disease, its treatment and the need to change behaviour to reduce risk of disease. They are frequently accompanied by a structured programme of gradually increasing exercise. There is little evidence that this short-term exercise component has any impact on risk of reinfarction: only long-term programmes lasting years do so. However, the psychological benefits can include improvements in mood and efficacy beliefs.

Short-term behavioural change is not guaranteed. Wrisley and Rubenfire (1988), for example, reported that patients found to have high cholesterol levels following an MI were no more likely to reduce their fat intake after participation in an educational programme than if they did not attend the programme. Other studies have found that didactic educational programmes focusing on smoking cessation, dietary management and regular physical activity added to exercise programmes result in few behavioural changes over and above those resulting from participation in the exercise programme alone.

Educational programmes versus others

Coronary heart disease

A number of studies have compared the effectiveness of educational programmes and behavioural programmes in which participants are taught and practise new skills and behaviour. In one study, Gomel *et al.* (1993) allocated 400 factory workers identified as having at least one risk factor for CHD into one of three conditions: no-treatment control, risk factor education or behavioural counselling. Participants in the risk factor education group were provided with standard advice on the life-style changes required to reduce risk for heart disease, an educational resource manual and videotapes containing information on how to modify risk factors for heart disease. Behavioural counselling involved partici-pants in up to six lifestyle counselling sessions based on the stages of change model. In the preparation stage, reasons for and against change were identified. Participants also monitored behaviours contributing to their risk for CHD, identified high-risk situations and developed coping strategies for dealing with them. In the action stage, short- and long-term goals for risk factor change were determined and strategies for achieving them considered. Finally, strategies for maintaining behavioural change and avoiding relapse were discussed. As in the education group, participants were provided with a resource manual. Overall, gains in the behavioural group were significantly greater than those in the education group on measures of cigarette smoking, blood pressure, body mass index and percentage of body fat throughout the follow-up period. By one-year follow-up, the smoking cessation rate was 7 per cent in the behavioural group, while none of the participants in the education group had given up smoking.

Behavioural programmes have also proven more effective than educa-tional programmes in patients who already have CHD. Oldenburg *et al.* (1989) compared the effectiveness of a behavioural and educational cardiac rehabilitation programme in a large group of post-MI patients. Participants in the education condition received a didactic programme focusing on behavioural risk factor change as well as medical informa-tion. The behavioural programme incorporated group work in which participants considered how they would incorporate any changes into their own lives, and rehearsed any behavioural plans. Both interventions were compared with a group that received a standard medical intervention, involving outpatient appointments with their physician. There was a clear benefit from attending the behavioural programme, with participants in this group improving more on a variety of measures of mood and risk behaviour up to eight months after the end of the programme.

Self-help approaches

Perhaps the simplest method of facilitating behavioural change is through the provision of self-help materials. Such materials can provide substantial information and, in some cases, a structured approach to achieving behavioural change. Self-help approaches can prove effective in well motivated populations. In a review of formally evaluated self-help smoking cessation programmes, for example, Klesges et al. (1989) reported average initial cessation rates of 31 per cent and that 26 per cent of participants maintained their cessation in the longer term. These statistics compare well with the outcomes of more formal interventions.

The most ambitious programme using self-help materials was reported by Fries et al. (1992). They followed a cohort of over 100,000 individuals enrolled in a health programme provided by their insurance company. Participants were asked to complete a simple health status questionnaire. They were then sent individual programmes, based on their responses to these questionnaires, that identified future health goals and how these could be achieved. Reassessments made six months later indicated significant reductions in risk for CHD among participants relative to changes in the general population. However, the potentially coercive nature of a health programme provided by the participants' own insurance company, and the potential bias in participants' responses to questionnaires and behaviour preceding any biochemical assays, suggests that these results should be considered with caution.

In an attempt to promote behavioural change in cardiac patients, Heller et al. (1993) sent MI patients an education package focusing on diet, exercise and smoking. Over the subsequent four months, participants were sent monthly newsletters containing further information and contacted twice by telephone. By the end of the programme, 450 patients had participated in either the intervention or the control group. The only difference between the groups at this time was on a measure of dietary fat, which was significantly lower in the intervention group. The groups did not differ on measures of frequency of regular exercise, smoking status or cholesterol levels.

The impact of another distance-learning package was reported by Lewin et al. (1992). They compared the effectiveness of a comprehensive home-

based programme known as the Heart Manual with a placebo package
of information and informal counselling. The Heart Manual provided
a structured rehabilitation package, focusing on the progressive change
of risk behaviours and teaching stress-reduction techniques. Participants
were contacted by telephone on three occasions over the six-week period
in which the manual was to be used in order to encourage adherence to
the programme. Over the following year, participants in the active intervention evidenced better psychological adjustment and had less contact
with their family doctors and fewer hospital readmissions than those
in the control group. No data have been reported on any behavioural
changes, which were the main target of the intervention. Nevertheless,
the appeal of such a cost-effective intervention has led to the Manual
being adopted by many rehabilitation programmes throughout the UK.

Self-help versus other approaches

A number of studies have reported comparisons between self-help and
other therapeutic approaches. Cinciprini *et al.* (1994), for example, compared a self-help smoking cessation programme with a structured group
intervention. The structured programme included baseline monitoring
of smoking levels followed by a structured reduction in the number of
cigarettes smoked and a specific quit date. Cognitive behavioural interventions and relapse prevention training involved behavioural rehearsal
of non-smoking skills in a relapse prone environment. Participants in the
self-help condition were given the American Cancer Society 'I Quit Kit',
that covered similar issues to the cognitive behavioural phase of the
active intervention. By 6-month follow-up, 53 per cent of the 'live' smoking group were abstinent and 41 per cent were abstinent at 12-month
follow-up. Only 6 per cent of the self-help group quit and remained
abstinent. Less clear-cut differences were found by Decker and Evans
(1989), who compared a 'by mail' smoking cessation course with a series
of five weekly meetings combined with a telephone hotline. One-year
abstinence rates in each intervention were 37 and 41 per cent respectively.
No between-group differences in cessation rates were found by Owen
et al. (1989) in a comparison of a sophisticated smoking cessation correspondence course and a control intervention comprising brief information on smoking cessation.

Behavioural programmes

A number of studies have incorporated behavioural or cognitive behavioural principles into a programme of behavioural change. The most
frequent strategies used by such groups involve teaching and rehearsal

of new skills and consideration of plans of how these may be acted upon in real life. Such interventions strongly resemble the self-management interventions discussed in Chapter 8. This section reviews some of these studies, focusing on programmes aimed at reducing risk of CHD or disease progression and HIV infection. The first part of this section focuses on studies that have examined changes in physiological processes or disease endpoints. It then considers the effect of different interventions on risk behaviours.

Hypertension

Antihypertensive medication has proven effective in the treatment of high blood pressure. However, side-effects are prevalent and a number of studies have found minimal reductions in CHD-related morbidity amongst those whose blood pressure is only mildly raised. Accordingly, a number of non-pharmacological approaches have been used to reduce blood pressure, particularly among such individuals. Some interventions have focused on behavioural strategies, and one such by Stamler et al. (1989) allocated overweight hypertension-prone individuals to either a monitoring condition or one in which they were directed to eat a low fat diet, reduce their alcohol intake to two drinks per day, and increase their exercise to three periods of 30 minutes per week. Although only a minority of participants achieved all the dietary and behavioural goals set during the five years of the trial, the incidence of hypertension was more than twice as high in a monitoring condition than in the intervention group (19.2 versus 8.8 per cent).

In a study of the effectiveness of a combined pharmacological and behavioural intervention, Elmer et al. (1995) allocated mildly hypertensive persons to one of five pharmacological or placebo interventions in combination with an intervention involving both individual and group counselling sessions. These focused on modifying diet and alcohol intake and increasing levels of exercise. The intervention adopted an approach based on social learning principles. Participants were, for example, taught to recognize and modify cues that led to overeating, modify their attitudes towards eating, and worked with their spouses to foster social and marital support for any changes made. At one-year follow-up, all the intervention groups evidenced significant behavioural change. Seventy per cent remained below baseline weight, alcohol intake was reduced by 1.6 drinks per week and reported leisure physical activity increased by 86 per cent over baseline measures. These changes were associated with clinically significant reductions in blood pressure that were maintained up to four-year follow-up.

Coronary Heart Disease

Some of the most dramatic research findings in the field of coronary risk reduction have been reported by Ornish and his colleagues. In their first study, Ornish et al. (1983) compared the cardiovascular status of a small group of patients with CHD following participation in a 24-day retreat with a matched group of patients receiving usual care. The intervention involved eating a very low fat and cholesterol diet, the use of relaxation-based stress management techniques, and a mild aerobic exercise programme. Those in the intervention who changed their lifestyle were able to achieve a 44 per cent increase in duration of exercise on a treadmill. Most participants also evidenced improved cardiovascular status, a reduction in the number of episodes of angina and a 20 per cent reduction in low density lipoproteins: all significantly greater than any changes in the comparison group.

In a subsequent study, patients with angina were assigned to a similar programme but of a longer duration (Ornish et al. 1990). It began with a week-long retreat followed by twice weekly meetings over a period of four years. At each meeting, participants took part in a graded exercise programme, practised stress management techniques, had a low fat meal and participated in a support group meeting. By the end of the first year, most participants had made substantial behavioural changes and these were reflected in reductions in weight and angina frequency. Stenosis of the cardiac arteries reduced from an average of 40.0 per cent to 37.8 per cent in the intervention group while rising from 42.7 to 46.1 per cent in the comparison group. Despite a fall-off in adherence to the programme, levels of atherosclerosis in the intervention group continued to regress, albeit more slowly, over the next three years, while they continued to progress in the comparison group.

Perhaps even more dramatic than the findings of Ornish et al. were the results of the Recurrent Coronary Prevention Program in Type A men who had experienced an MI (Friedman et al. 1986). Participants were allocated to one of three groups: cardiac rehabilitation, Type A management, and a usual-care control. The rehabilitation programme involved small group meetings over a period of four and half years in which participants received information on medication, exercise and diet, as well as social support from the group. The Type A management group received the same information in addition to engaging in a sustained programme of behavioural change involving training in relaxation, cognitive techniques and specific behavioural change plans. Evidence of the effectiveness of this process was compelling. Over the four and a half years of the intervention, those in the Type A management programme were at half the risk of further infarction than those in the traditional rehabilitation programme, with total infarction rates over this time of 12 and 6 per cent in each group. Even more impressive were the rates of reinfarction among those who changed their behaviour, regardless of group assignation, after one year into the trial. Such individuals evidenced a reinfarction rate of 3 per cent: the reinfarction rate among those who did not change their behaviour was 21 per cent.

Evidence reviewed in Chapter 2 suggests that depression substantially increases risk of infarction or reinfarction. Such a relationship suggests that interventions that reduce depression will also reduce risk of reinfarction. Although few studies have explored this hypothesis, the available data suggest that this will indeed prove to be the case. Black *et al.* (1998), for example, allocated MI patients found to be experiencing significant distress to either usual care or a psychiatric evaluation plus one to seven sessions of behavioural therapy. Thirty-five per cent of participants in the active intervention were hospitalized with cardiac symptoms in the following year, in comparison with 48 per cent of those in the usual-care group. Some caution, however, has to be given to interpretation of such findings. While treatment for depression may result in changes in cardiac processes, it is possible that these changes are more indicative of mood-related changes in the perception of symptoms and help-seeking behaviour.

Smoking cessation

One area of particular interest to those involved in smoking cessation has been the relative effectiveness of pharmacological and behavioural cessation methods. Two methods of smoking cessation that specifically address nicotine dependence – nicotine gum and nicotine patches – have become widely used in the past decade. The gum is the less effective of the two methods, perhaps because of its deliberately unpleasant taste and variable nicotine absorption rates. Its effectiveness has been found to be no better than placebo and it is best when used in combination with psychological support of some kind (Lichtenstein and Glasgow 1992). Nicotine patches that deliver nicotine transdermally and provide more consistent levels of nicotine through the day appear to be more effective. Nevertheless, pharmacological interventions should not be the first-line intervention for some groups of individuals, such as pregnant women or those with CHD. In addition, they may not be the optimal tool for all smokers. Some smokers may smoke predominantly out of habit, some due to an addiction to nicotine. Accordingly, the same therapeutic approach may not be optimal in both groups.

Evidence of the differential effectiveness of interventions matched to the 'type' of smoker was provided by Hall *et al.* (1985), who assigned high and low nicotine-dependent smokers to either an intensive behavioural intervention, nicotine gum, or a combination of both approaches. At one-year follow-up, 50 per cent of the high-dependence smokers in the combined intervention were not smoking. This compared with abstinence rates of 28 per cent in the nicotine gum condition and 11 per cent in the cognitive behavioural intervention. In contrast, low-dependence smokers benefited more from the behavioural intervention, which achieved one-year abstinence rates of 47 per cent in comparison with rates of 42 and 38 per cent in the gum and combined intervention conditions, respectively.

The question of the relative effectiveness of pharmacological and behavioural approaches may soon be considered a 'non-issue'. Only half the studies that report the use of nicotine patches show sustained levels of cessation following withdrawal of the patches. As a consequence, a number of commentators have argued that the best long-term results are likely to be achieved by a combination of pharmacological and behavioural interventions, particularly those that focus on teaching relapse prevention skills. Although the impact of this approach may not have proven as effective as was first hoped, it still appears to benefit many of those who are taught such skills. Stevens and Hollis (1989), for example, followed outcomes in over seven hundred adult smokers who took part in a four-day intensive intervention. Three-quarters of the group were able to quit and were assigned to either training in relapse training skills, group discussion, or no further treatment. Group discussion proved no more effective than no treatment. However, the relapse prevention programme resulted in significantly better long-term cessation rates: 41 versus 33 per cent cessation.

Sexual behaviour

A simple behavioural task proved an effective addition to a safer sex education programme evaluated by Weisse et al. (1995). In their study, a group of young adults took part in an AIDS prevention workshop aimed at reducing embarrassment while purchasing condoms and encouraging their use. Half of this group then participated in an exercise involving the purchase of condoms at local shops. Immediately after the workshop, all the participants evidenced greater knowledge about AIDS and more positive attitudes towards the use of condoms than before attending. However, only those who participated in the exercise reported less embarrassment during the subsequent purchase of condoms.

Other studies have compared the effectiveness of behavioural and educational programmes in reducing sexual risk behaviour. Kelley et al. (1994), for example, found a behavioural intervention involved risk education, training in condom use, practising sexual assertiveness, problem-solving and risk trigger self-management to be more effective than an educational programme conducted with women considered to be at high risk of HIV infection. At three-month follow-up, women in both conditions reported having a similar number of sexual partners. However, women in the behavioural intervention reported that more of their partners used condoms, and on more occasions. Similar levels of success following skills training have been found in 'hard to reach' groups. One such programme involved hard drug users. In it they practised skills relating to condom use, needle sterilization, and changing a number of high-risk sexual and drug-related behaviours. Participants in this group evidenced better skills in condom use and sexual communication and reported fewer incidences of sexual risk behaviour over the following months than those in an information-only group.

Behavioural interventions need not be time-consuming. The Talking Sex project found a single discussion and skills training group to be as effective as its four-session equivalent. Neither need they be conducted 'live'. O'Donnell *et al.* (1995) compared the effectiveness of a number of video-based interventions designed to promote safer sex amongst attenders at a sexually transmitted disease clinic. Participants were randomly allocated to one of three groups: no-treatment control, video, or video plus interactive group 'skill-building session'. The latter comprised a 20-minute meeting in which barriers to condom use were identified and addressed through the provision of information, discussing condom options and practising condom negotiation skills. All those participating in the study were provided with coupons redeemable for free condoms at a local pharmacy. In comparison to the control condition, those who saw the video were more likely to redeem condom coupons (21 versus 28 per cent). Participation in the interactive sessions further increased redemption rates to 40 per cent.

Relaxation and stress management training

Hypertension

Blood pressure is, in part, mediated by changes in sympathetic activity. High levels of sympathetic activity cause the peripheral blood vessels to constrict and the heart to pump harder, resulting in increased blood pressure. Chronically raised blood pressure is assumed to be, at least in part, a consequence of stress-related surges in blood pressure countering homeostatic attempts to lower blood pressure and incrementally increasing resting levels of blood pressure. Such a model suggests that reductions in sympathetic activity should minimize any blood pressure surges, reducing peak blood pressures and facilitating homeostatic attempts to control blood pressure.

Early studies of the effects of relaxation showed it to be superior to no or minimal treatment control conditions in reducing clinical measures of blood pressure. Ambulatory data from Agras *et al.* (1983) confirmed that such gains were generalized through the working day. Early comparisons with other interventions generally supported the effectiveness of relaxation, although the more the alternative intervention provided a means to reduce stress effectively, the less apparent the difference. Irvine *et al.* (1986), for example, found a placebo treatment involving mobility and flexibility exercises proved less effective than relaxation in reducing blood pressure up to three months following the intervention phase. In contrast, Wadden (1984) failed to find any difference between relaxation and cognitive therapy either immediately after intervention and at five-month follow-up. Cognitive and relaxation-based interventions may combine to maximize blood pressure reductions, perhaps because both work in different ways to reduce stress and change behaviour.

Despite such positive findings, a number of authors have suggested that even the findings of controlled studies overstate the effectiveness of relaxation or stress management procedures in controlling blood pressure. Their argument goes as follows. Measurement of blood pressure evokes a mild stress response, part of which involves a small but clinically significant rise in blood pressure. Repeated measurements result in a habituation process, which may take many measurements to achieve. Stress management procedures may speed this process of habituation, resulting in different rates of habituation across the intervention and control groups. Accordingly, between-group differences in blood pressure may indicate different degrees of habituation to blood pressure measurement rather than meaningful differences in underlying blood pressure. To combat this potential confound, such critics argue that any treatment effects should be measured following an extended series of baseline measures that permit habituation to occur. Where such a method is used, the treatment gains associated with relaxation or stress management are attenuated, leaving Eisenberg *et al.* (1993) to conclude that cognitive behavioural interventions for essential hypertension are superior to no therapy but no more effective than credible placebo interventions or to self-monitoring alone.

Secondary prevention

Relaxation methods have also been used in an attempt to reduce the extent of disease progression in people who have evidence of disease: with some success. Appels *et al.* (1997) compared the effects of a relaxation and controlled breathing programme with a no-treatment control in an attempt to reduce the risk of further medical intervention following coronary angioplasty. The intervention resulted in a 50 per cent reduction in risk of further intervention or a new coronary event in comparison with that carried by participants in the no-treatment group. A similar study compared the effect of an exercise training programme alone or in combination with individual instruction in relaxation and breathing in a group of post-MI patients. The relaxation intervention induced a slower breathing pattern that was associated with beneficial effects on measures of resting heart rate and arrythmias.

A larger study of stress management techniques has also resulted in significant clinical gains. Blumenthal *et al.* (1997) randomly assigned over one hundred patients with CHD to a four-month programme of exercise or stress management training. Patients living at a distance from the site of the intervention formed a non-random, usual-care comparison group. Myocardial ischaemia was reassessed following treatment, and patients were contacted annually for up to five years in order to document cardiac events, including death, non-fatal myocardial infarction and cardiac revascularization procedures. Those in the stress management group were significantly less likely to have a cardiac event over this period, showing a relative risk of 0.26 in comparison with that of controls. The risk of an event among patients in the exercise group was not significantly lower than for those in the control group. Results such as these challenge the orthodoxy of exercise programmes forming the intervention of choice in cardiac rehabilitation programmes.

Immune function

There is growing evidence that stress management may improve the immunological status of patients with cancer or who are HIV positive. Lekander et al. (1997), for example, allocated patients receiving chemotherapy for ovarian cancer to either relaxation training or a usual-care control condition. After two months' training, the intervention group showed some immunological benefits, evidencing higher lymphocyte and white blood cell counts than those in the control group: suggesting a lower susceptibility to infection. No significant effects were found on natural killer (NK) cell activity (see Chapter 2). Fawzy et al. (1993) compared the effectiveness of a multicomponent intervention and no treatment in a group of patients with stage I or II malignant melanoma who had had a tumour surgically excised. The intervention involved six weekly group meetings in which participants received health education and training in stress management and problem-solving skills. Participants in the active intervention evidenced substantially higher T-cell and NK cell counts than the controls. Six years later survival levels were significantly greater in the intervention group than in the control group. Similar findings were achieved by Gruber et al. (1993) following a stress management programme in women following radical mastectomy. Despite no differences in reported levels of distress, women in the active intervention evidenced increased NK cell activity and an increase in both numbers and responsiveness of circulating lymphocytes following the intervention.

Populations with HIV have evidenced similar gains following stress management procedures. Antoni et al. (1991) allocated gay men who were tested for their HIV status, but unaware of the findings, into either a group stress management intervention, aerobic exercise, or a no-treatment control group. Blood assays were taken three days before and one week after participants were notified of their HIV status. Not surprisingly, seropositive individuals in the control group evidenced significant increases in depression and reduced CD4 and NK lymphocyte counts between the measurement times. Those in the active interventions showed no such decrement. In a study of the effectiveness of a longer intervention conducted by the same research group (see Antoni et al. 1991), the effects of a ten-week stress management programme on mood and immunological parameters in symptomatic HIV seropositive gay men were compared with a waiting-list control condition. Those in the active intervention reported significantly greater gains on a number of measures of mood and distress than those in the control group. In addition, they evidenced decreased herpes simplex virus-Type 2 (HSV-2) immunoglobulin G antibody titres. However, neither group displayed changes in HSV-Type 1 antibody titres or in CD4+ or CD8+ cell numbers.

In total, these studies clearly show that stress management may impact in a positive way on a number of markers of immune function. Whether or not these changes are sufficient to impact on the course of a disease process remains to be shown consistently. However, there have been some promising results (see, for example, Fawzy *et al.* 1993). Some other studies that have attempted to increase social support, and therefore indirectly influence stress levels, have also met with some success, although this is no means universal (see below).

Motivational interviewing

As noted in Chapter 8, the motivational interview is intended to shift individuals from a state of precontemplation to one of contemplation or action in order to increase their likelihood of engaging in any required behavioural change. Accordingly, an appropriate outcome measure in any assessment of the method's effectiveness may be the number of individuals who engage in a programme of behavioural change as a consequence of its use. However, most interventions have considered the longer-term benefits of motivational interviewing, measuring changes in behaviour at some time remote from the interview itself. While one would hope that higher numbers of attempts at behavioural change would translate into higher levels of actual behaviour change at follow-up, this method provides a conservative measure of the effectiveness of the interview process.

Addictive behaviours

One of the first studies of motivational interviewing was reported by Bien *et al.* (1993). They randomly assigned outpatients involved in a substance abuse treatment programme to receive either a brief motivational intervention or a placebo interview in addition to standard outpatient treatment. Participants who were given the motivational interview evidenced a better clinical outcome at three-month follow-up on measures of total alcohol consumption, peak blood alcohol level and number of days abstinent. However, by six-month follow-up any differences were no longer significant. Other studies have subsequently reported a similar pattern of results in people with alcohol problems and cigarette smokers. Colby *et al.* (1998) compared the effects of brief advice to stop smoking with a motivational interview in a group of hospital patients. Participants in the latter condition reported more attempts to quit and immediate reductions in smoking, suggesting that the motivational interview did facilitate immediate behavioural change. However, any between-group differences in smoking rate did not differ at three-month follow-up. Longer-term benefits have been found when motivational interviewing formed a component of a wider set of interventions including telephone contact and nicotine replacement, with six-month cessation rates of up to 70 per cent in post-myocardial infarction patients.

Exercise

In an interesting alternative to the motivational interview, Marcus *et al.* (1998) compared the effectiveness of self-help materials tailored to the stage of change of each individual with a more general self-help programme. The programme took place in eleven worksites, where over 1500 employees were randomized into one of two conditions: the provision of printed self-help exercise promotion materials matched to the individual's stage of motivational readiness for exercise adoption, or standard materials. Thirty-seven per cent of those receiving the motivationally tailored intervention reported an increase in exercise levels; 27 per cent of the standard intervention did so.

Motivational interview versus others

HIV

As noted above, motivational interviewing is not meant to form a primary treatment: it is intended to be a method of engaging individuals in a treatment programme. Nevertheless, Baker *et al.* (1994) compared the effectiveness of a six-session cognitive behavioural programme, a motivational interview lasting 60–90 minutes, and a no-treatment control condition in an attempt to reduce HIV risk-taking behaviours among injecting drug users enrolled in methadone programmes. At one-month follow-up, there was evidence of a lower rate of needle-risk behaviour (sharing and cleaning) in the group given cognitive behavioural therapy. There was no indication that the motivational interview was of greater benefit than the usual methadone treatment and neither intervention appeared to reduce sexual risk behaviour.

Other interventions

The chapter so far has considered the impact of some of the most frequently used psychological interventions. However, a number of other therapeutic approaches to risk reduction have been taken, including the use of social support, operant conditioning and counselling.

Increasing social support

Smoking cessation

Social support has proven a powerful adjunct to other interventions requiring behavioural change, including smoking cessation programmes (see also above). West *et al.* (1998), for example, reported on the benefits of a 'buddy system' for individuals attempting to quit smoking. All those involved in the study attended a nurse-led smokers' clinic. Smokers in the buddy condition were paired with another smoker trying to give up at the same time to provide mutual support between clinic sessions. The percentage of smokers still abstinent at the end of treatment was significantly higher in the buddy condition than the solo condition: 27 per cent versus 12 per cent, respectively. A further study by Digiusto and Bird (1995) randomly allocated smokers to either social support or self-control interventions. Their findings emphasized the need to tailor interventions to the specific needs and characteristics of the target population: the social support treatment proved most effective for participants who already had high baseline self-control orientation scores and those with high self-efficacy scores.

Cancer

One of the most influential results of any intervention with patients with cancer was reported by Spiegel *et al.* (1981). In a study intended to influence quality of life in cancer patients, they randomly assigned women with breast cancer to either an active treatment programme or a no-treatment control. The active intervention involved weekly support groups that emphasized building strong supportive bonds, expressing emotions, dealing directly with fears of dying, improving relationships within the family and active involvement in decisions concerning treatment. To the surprise of the investigators, women in the active intervention lived an average of 18 months longer than those in a no-treatment control despite being well matched for disease status at the beginning of the trial. Retrospectively, this has been seen as an attempt to reduce Type C behaviour and replace it with the fighting spirit of Derogatis and colleagues (see Chapter 1). Unfortunately, an attempted replication of the study met with only modest success. Gellert *et al.* (1984) compared the effectiveness of the programme developed by Spiegel *et al.* with a standard treatment condition in a matched sample of breast cancer patients. Although their data showed trends towards a survival gain in the intervention group (by an average of 11 months: 96 versus 85 months), these differences were not statistically significant. Other negative findings have also been reported. Accordingly, increasing social support has yet to be convincingly shown to impact on disease outcomes in patients with cancer.

Operant conditioning

Smoking cessation

Smoking is, at least in part, an operantly governed behaviour. The individual smokes in the expectation of cognitive, emotional or physiological changes. In this way, cigarette smoking is highly reinforced over thousands of learning trials. Smoking may be triggered by internal (craving, mood) or external (using the telephone, coffee break) cues. Scheduled smoking is an approach to cessation that attempts to weaken the associations between smoking and such cues. The method developed by Cinciprini and colleagues (1994) involves a three-week process of scheduled smoking during which the number of cigarettes is gradually reduced before full cessation is attempted. During this phase, smoking is governed by the passage of time rather than the smoker's wishes or urges. A cognitive behavioural approach combined with this reduction regimen proved more effective than the same intervention combined with either an uncontrolled gradual reduction or no planned reduction prior to quitting on measures not only of immediate cessation rates but also of sustained abstinence. One-year abstinence rates were 44, 18 and 22 per cent respectively.

Counselling

Coronary heart disease

The impact of a cost-effective counselling intervention with cardiac patients was reported by Frasure-Smith and Prince (1985). In the Life Stress Monitoring Program, they followed a cohort of over 450 patients who had an MI, allocating them into a usual-care control group or a low contact intervention. In the latter, they received monthly telephone contact for a period of one year, during which they completed a measure of psychological distress. If they scored above a criterion score, they were offered a home visit by a specialist nurse. The action taken by this nurse could vary according to the circumstances encountered: the majority of contacts involved teaching and providing reassurance by supplying information. Half those in the intervention condition had at least one contact with the nursing team over the period of the intervention. These individuals had an average of 6 hours' contact with the team nurses. By the end of the intervention, the total mortality rate in the control group was 9 per cent, while that of the intervention group was 5 per cent: a significant difference. Four years following their MI, differences in mortality between the two groups did not differ, although the rate of reinfarctions did: total morbidity rates in the intervention group were 15 per cent compared with 25 per cent in the control group. While these data were encouraging, they should be viewed with some caution. The proportion of white-collar workers in the intervention group was significantly greater than that in the control group. Accordingly, the intervention group may have been at less risk of reinfarction than the control group. Owing to methodological constraints, these differences could not be statistically partialled out, and the interpretation of the results must be considered with some caution.

Such caution may be justified by the results of a later attempt to replicate these findings in a group of patients in Montreal (the M-HART study: Frasure-Smith *et al.* 1997). The results of this study indicated significantly higher rates of reinfarction among participants in the intervention group than the control group. In retrospect, these findings may have been a consequence of inadequately trained nurses attempting to cope with extremely distressed individuals and perhaps exacerbating rather than moderating their problems. Apparently cheap interventions involving professionals not given adequate specialist training may clearly prove far from cost-effective.

Summary and conclusions

A variety of interventions have been used to influence behaviours that place individuals at risk of disease or that affect the development of disease. As with interventions aimed at quality of life or symptom control, educational programmes can influence risk behaviours, although their impact on behaviour is generally modest. Behavioural programmes of various types have been shown to influence both behaviour and physiological variables underlying the development of disease more consistently. Studies of their impact on disease rates remain sparse; however, those that do exist suggest the potential of psychological interventions to affect the course of disease.

Further reading

Camic, P.M. (ed.) (1998) *Clinical Handbook of Health Psychology: A Practical Guide to Effective Interventions*. Berlin: Hogrefe & Huber.

 # Notes

Chapter 5

1 And non-adherence to antiretroviral medication has particular implications, including the development of drug-resistant viruses that may affect both the health of the individual involved and others who encounter the adapted virus.

Chapter 8

1 An example of this process can be found Price's (1988) conceptualization of Type A behaviour. Through her clinical work with Type A men, Price found a number of common cognitive schemata developed in childhood. As a result of not being valued during childhood, Type A men typically have low self-worth and are highly dependent on the esteem of others. They also have a powerful belief that one is not loved for 'who one is' but for 'what one does'. As a result such individuals find themselves on a treadmill of constantly having to achieve and 'prove' themselves worthy of the positive regard of others around them.

Glossary

Adherence: the degree to which an individual conforms to a prescribed treatment.

Alameda County Study: one of the first epidemiological studies to find a relationship between lifestyle factors and the development of disease.

Angiography: involves injecting radio-opaque dye directly into the cardiac arteries and using X-rays to measure the degree of atheroma within them.

Antigens: include viruses, bacteria, fungi, parasites and cancers.

Appraisal: the process of active consideration of the threat carried by external events.

Atheroma: the build-up of lipid deposits on the artery walls. Contributes to the development of coronary heart disease.

Attributions: perceived causes of events, feelings or actions.

Autogenic training: a form of deep relaxation in which the participant imagines feelings of weight and warmth in the areas of relaxation.

B-cells: a component of the immune system involved in antibody-mediated immunity.

Biofeedback: visual or acoustic representation of muscle tension, usually measured via electrodes placed over the relevant muscle group.

Case-control design: involves comparing individuals who have a disease with matched disease-free controls. Any between-group differences are thought to imply causality.

CD4+ cells: the central organizing aspect of the immune response are the T helper cells, known also as CD4+ cells because of their chemical structure.

Cholesterol: a lipid produced by the body and ingested with food, which may contribute to the development of atheroma.

Client-centred counselling: an unstructured therapeutic approach developed by Carl Rogers. It assumes the central element of therapy is the therapeutic relationship, gained through the therapist providing warmth, empathy, and genuineness.

Clinical audit: monitoring the effectiveness or the process of care and making the results publicly available.

Clinical guidelines: systematically developed and agreed guidelines to aid clinical decision making.

Cognitive-behavioural intervention: a form of therapy based on the assumption that cognitive distortions are central to the development of emotional disorders. Therapeutic change is achieved by changing such distortions by Socratic or behavioural techniques.

Coping effectiveness training: a cognitive-behavioural approach based on identifying the most appropriate coping strategy to use in differing situations, and applying it.

Coronary Heart Disease: restriction of the flow of blood within the coronary arteries as a result of atheromata. May be symptom-free but will eventually result in angina or myocardial infarction.

Coping: the process of reducing distress associated with the appraisals of threat following an environmental event.

Daily hassles: minor events or frustrations that are thought to contribute to the stress process.

Emotion-focused coping: coping focused on directly reducing the negative emotions involved in the stress process.

Emotional disclosure: the reduction of stress through the expression of emotion, often using written means.

Epinephrine: otherwise known as adrenaline. A stress neurotransmitter and hormone.

Fighting spirit: a confrontational behavioural style identified by Derogatis as being prognostic of a good cancer outcome.

Grounded theory: a qualitative technique which involves the development of theory from interviews with relevant individuals, in contrast to theory stemming from prior theoretical models.

Hardiness: a personality characteristic consisting of high levels of commitment, control and willingness to confront challenges. It may be protective against stress.

Health-related behaviour: behaviour which impacts on health.

Hypo/hyperglycaemic episode: unconsciousness as a consequence of abnormally low (hypo) or high (hyper) levels of blood sugar.

Illness representations: cognitive representations of illness. Generally considered to have five dimensions: disease identity, its consequences, causes, timeline, and curability or controllability.

Incidence: the number of new cases of a disease occurring over a specified time period, usually one year.

Irritable bowel syndrome (IBS): disease characterized by bowel pain and alternating diarrhoea and constipation.

Job strain: a function of high job demands, and low autonomy and social support.

Life events: incidents which occur in the environment which can be considered as negative or positive in valence. They are thought to contribute to the stress process.

Longitudinal design: involves measurement of behaviour in cohort of (typically) healthy individuals prior to disease onset followed for a period of several years. Baseline characteristics of those who do and do not develop disease are compared. Any differences on such measures are thought to imply causality.

Lymphocytes: various types of cells within the immune system, including NK cells, T-cells, and B-cells.

Meta-analysis: a quantitative analysis, which combines data from several studies to provide high statistical power.

Morbidity: the development of disease.

Motivational interview: a non-confrontational interview aimed at increasing an individual's motivation to change. Initially developed in the field of addiction, but now more generally used.

Myocardial infarction (MI): an occlusion of one or more of the coronary arteries usually by a blood clot which blocks the artery and prevents blood flow beyond, resulting in death of the cardiac muscle. Otherwise known as a heart attack.

NK cells: cells of the immune system, particularly involved in the body's defence against cancer.

Norepinephrine: otherwise known as noradrenaline. A stress neurotransmitter and hormone.

Operant conditioning: initially studied by Skinner, this approach states that behaviour is directly influenced by its consequences.

Outcome expectancies: the expected outcome of a behaviour.

Parasympathetic nervous system: the arm of the autonomic nervous system which opposes activity and supports feeding, energy storage and reproduction.

Phantom limb pain: pain experienced following amputation of a limb which the individual perceives as originating in the non-existent limb.

Prevalence: the proportion of the population to have a disease at any one time.

Problem-focused coping: coping which involves attempts to reduce stress by changing the potentially stressful situation.

Problem-focused counselling: a structured counselling process that focuses on changing problems in the 'here-and-now'.

Risk factor: a behaviour or physiological state that places an individual at risk of disease.

Self-efficacy: analogous to self-confidence.

Self-management training: a behavioural programme which provides people with the skills to manage a chronic illness.

Serum: blood.

Socio-economic status (SES): position or class, usually measured by education, income or occupation.

Stages of change: usually refers to an atheoretical model of change, with five elements: precontemplation, contemplation, preparation, change, and maintenance or relapse.

Stress: a process involving appraisal of an external event, its associated emotions and the strategies used to moderate any distress experienced.

Stress inoculation training: a three-stage process of coping with stress developed by Meichenbaum: preparation, action and reflection.

Stress management training: a set of cognitive-behavioural procedures to help the individual to cope more effectively with stress.

Sympathetic nervous system: the arm of the autonomic nervous system associated with maintaining or increasing arousal.

T-cells: immune system cells involved in cell-mediated immunity.

Token economies: a process through which patients are rewarded for appropriate behaviours with tokens. These are usually exchanged for desired articles or goods.

Type A behaviour (TAB): an excess of competitiveness, time urgency and easily aroused hostility. Thought to be associated with CHD.

Type C behaviour: a passive and controlled emotional style, thought to be associated with the development of cancer.

Unit of alcohol: measurement of alcohol, the equivalent of half a pint of ordinary strength beer or a single shot of a spirit.

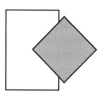

References

Aaronson, N.K. (1993) The EORTC QLQ-C300: a quality of life instrument for use in international clinical trials in oncology (abstract), *Quality of Life Research*, 2: 51.

Abbott, S. (1988) Talking about AIDS. Report for AIDS Action Council, Canberra, *National Bulletin*, August: 24–7.

Adler, N., Boyce, T., Chesney, M. *et al.* (1994) Socio-economic status and health: the challenge of the gradient. *American Psychologist*, 49: 15–24.

Affleck, C., Tennen, H., Croog, S. and Levine, S. (1987) Causal attributions, perceived benefits, and morbidity after a heart attack: an 8-year study, *Journal of Consulting and Clinical Psychology*, 55: 29–35.

Agras, W.S., Southam, M.A. and Taylor, C.B. (1983) Long-term persistence of relaxation-induced blood pressure lowering during the working day, *Journal of Consulting and Clinical Psychology*, 51: 792–4.

Aikens, J.E., Kiolbasa, T.A. and Sobel, R. (1997) Psychological predictors of glycemic change with relaxation training in non-insulin-dependent diabetes mellitus, *Psychotherapy and Psychosomatics*, 66: 302–6.

Ajzen, I. (1985) From intentions to actions: a theory of planned behaviour, in J. Kuhl and J. Beckmann (eds) *Action Control: From Cognition to Behaviour*. Heidelberg: Springer.

Ajzen, I. (1991) The theory of planned behavior, *Organisational Behavior and Human Decision Making*, 50: 179–211.

Ajzen, I. and Fishbein, M. (1980) *Understanding Attitudes and Predicting Social Behavior*. Englewood Cliffs, NJ: Prentice Hall.

Alfredsson, L., Spetz, C-L. and Theorell, T. (1985) Type of occupational and near-future hospitalization for myocardial infarction and some other diagnoses, *International Journal of Epidemiology*, 4: 378–88.

Allison, T.G., Williams, D.E., Miller, T.D. *et al.* (1995) Medical and economic costs of psychologic distress in patients with coronary-artery disease, *Mayo Clinic Proceedings*, 70: 734–42.

Amir, D. (1987) Preventive behaviour and health status among the elderly. *Psychology and Health*, 1: 353–78.

Anderson, R.T., Aaronson, N.K. and Wilkin, D. (1993) Critical review of the international assessments of health-related quality of life, *Quality of Life Research*, 2: 369–95.

Andrykowski, M.A., Brady, M.J. and Henslee-Downey, P.J. (1994) Psychosocial factors predictive of survival after allogeneic bone marrow transplantation for leukemia, *Psychosomatic Medicine*, 56: 432–9.

Antoni, M.H., Baggett, L., Ironson, G. *et al.* (1991) Cognitive behavioral stress management intervention buffers distress responses and immunologic changes following notification of HIV-1 seropositivity, *Journal of Consulting and Clinical Psychology*, 59: 906–15.

Appels, A., Bar, F., Lasker, J. *et al.* (1997) The effect of a psychological intervention program on the risk of a new coronary event after angioplasty: a feasibility study, *Journal of Psychosomatic Research*, 43: 209–17.

Ashton, J. (1992) *Healthy Cities*. Buckingham: Open University Press.

Audrain, J., Boyd, N.R., Roth, J. *et al.* (1997) Genetic susceptibility testing in smoking-cessation treatment: one-year outcomes of a randomized trial, *Addictive Behaviors*, 22: 741–51.

Backett, K. (1990) Studying health in families: a qualitative approach, in S. Cunningham, S. Burly and N. McKeganey (eds) *Readings in Medial Sociology*. London: Routledge.

Baker, A., Heather, N., Wodak, A., Dixon, J. and Holt, P. (1993) Evaluation of a cognitive-behavioural intervention for HIV prevention among injecting drug users. *AIDS*, 7: 247–56.

Baker, A., Kochan, N., Dixon, J. *et al.* (1994) Controlled evaluation of a brief intervention for HIV prevention among injecting drug users not in treatment, *AIDS Care*, 6: 559–70.

Bakker, A.B., Buunk, B.P., Siero, F.W. and VandenEijnden, R.J. (1997) Application of a modified health belief model to HIV preventive behavioral intentions among gay and bisexual men, *Psychology and Health*, 12: 481–92.

Bakwin, H. (1945) Psuedoxia pediatrica, *New England Journal of Medicine*, 232: 691–7.

Bandura, A. (1986) *Social Foundations of Thought and Action: A Social Cognitive Theory*. Englewood Cliffs, NJ: Prentice Hall.

Barefoot, J.C., Dahlstrom, W.G. and Williams, R.B. (1983) Hostility, CHD incidence and total mortality: a 25 year follow-up of 225 physicians, *Psychosomatic Medicine*, 45: 59–63.

Barefoot, J.C., Patterson, J.C., Haney, T.L. *et al.* (1994) Hostility in asymptomatic men with angiographically confirmed coronary artery disease, *American Journal of Cardiology*, 74: 439–42.

Baumgarten, M., Thomas, D., Poulin de Courval, L. and Infante-Rivard, C. (1988) Evaluation of a mutual help network for the elderly residents of planned housing, *Psychology and Aging*, 3: 393–8.

Beck, A.T. (1976) *Cognitive Therapy and the Emotional Disorders*. New York: International Universities Press.

Beck, A.T., Mendelson, M., Mock, J. *et al.* (1961) Inventory for measuring depression, *Archives of General Psychiatry*, 4: 561–71.

Becker, M.H., Haefner, D.P. and Maiman, L.A. (1977) The health belief model in the prediction of dietary compliance: a field experiment, *Journal of Health and Social Behavior*, 18: 348–66.

Beeney, L.J., Bakry, A.A. and Dunn, S.M. (1996) Patient psychological and information needs when the diagnosis is diabetes, *Patient Education and Counseling*, 29: 109–16.

Belar, C. (1997) Clinical health psychology: a specialty for the 21st century, *Health Psychology*, 16: 411–16.

Bennett, P. and Clatworthy, J. (1999) Smoking cessation during pregnancy: testing a psycho-biological model, *Psychology, Health and Medicine*, 4: 319–26.

Bennett, P. and Wilkinson, S. (1985) A comparison of psychological and medical treatment of the irritable bowel syndrome, *British Journal of Clinical Psychology*, 24: 215–16.

Bennett, P., Smith, C., Nugent, Z. and Panter, C. (1991) 'Pssst . . . the really useful guide to alcohol': evaluation of an alcohol education television series, *Health Education Research, Theory and Practice*, 6: 57–64.

Bennett, P., Mayfield, T., Norman, P. *et al.* (1999a) Affective and social cognitive predictors of behavioural change following myocardial infarction, *British Journal of Health Psychology*, 4: 247–56.

Bennett, P., Rowe, A. and Katz, D. (1999b) Adherence with asthma preventive medication: a test of protection motivation theory, *Psychology, Health and Medicine*, 3: 347–54.

Bennett, P., Smith, P. and Gallacher, J.E.J. (1996) Vital exhaustion, neuroticism, and symptom reporting in cardiac and non-cardiac patients, *British Journal of Health Psychology*, 1: 309–13.

Bennett, P.D., Lowe, R., Matthews, V. and Dourali, M. (2000) Stress in nurses: coping, managerial support and work demand, *Stress Medicine*.

Bergner, M., Bobbitt, R.A., Carter, W.B. *et al.* (1981) The Sickness Impact Profile: development and final revision of a health status measure, *Medical Care*, 19: 787–805.

Berkman, L.F. and Syme, S.L. (1979) Social networks host resistance, and mortality: a nine-year follow-up study of Alameda County residents, *American Journal of Epidemiology*, 109: 186–204.

Bibace, R. and Walsh, M.E. (1980) Development of children's concepts of illness, *Pediatrics*, 66: 912–17.

Bien, T.H., Miller, W.R. and Boroughs, J.M. (1993) Motivational interviewing with alcohol patients, *Behavioural and Cognitive Psychotherapy*, 21: 347–56.

Bill-Harvey, D., Rippey, R., Abeles, M. *et al.* (1989) Outcome of an osteoarthritis education program for low-literacy patients taught by indigenous instructors, *Patient Education and Counseling*, 13: 133–42.

Bird, J.E. and Podmore, V.N. (1990) Children's understanding of health and illness, *Psychology and Health*, 4: 175–85.

Bishop, S.D. (1987) Lay conceptions of physical symptoms, *Journal of Applied Social Psychology*, 17: 127–46.

Bisson, J.I., Jenkins, P.L., Alexander, J. and Bannister, C. (1997) Randomised controlled trial of psychological debriefing for victims of acute burn trauma, *British Journal of Psychiatry*, 170: 78–81.

Black, J.L., Allison, T.G., Williams, D.E. *et al.* (1998) Effect of intervention for psychological distress on rehospitalization rates in cardiac rehabilitation patients, *Psychosomatics*, 39: 134–43.

Blaxter, M. (1990) *Health and Lifestyles*. London: Tavistock.

Bloom, J.R., Stewart, S.L., Johnston, M. and Banks, P. (1998) Intrusiveness of illness and quality of life in young women with breast cancer, *Psycho-Oncology*, 7: 89–100.

Blumenhagen, D.W. (1980) Hypertension: a folk illness with a medical name, *Culture, Medicine, and Psychiatry*, 4: 197–227.

Blumenthal, J.A., Jiang, W., Babyak, M.A. *et al.* (1997) Stress management and exercise training in cardiac patients with myocardial ischemia – effects on prognosis and evaluation of mechanisms, *Archives of Internal Medicine*, 157: 2213–23.

Boardway, R.H., Delameter, A.M., Tomakowsky, J. and Gutai, J.P. (1993) Stress management for adolescents with diabetes, *Journal of Pediatric Psychology*, 18: 29–45.

Boer, H. and Seydel, E.R. (1996) Protection motivation theory, in M. Conner and P. Norman (eds) *Predicting Health Behaviour: Research and Practice with Social Cognition Models*. Buckingham: Open University Press.

Borrill, C.S., Wall, T.D., West, M.A. *et al.* (1996) *Mental Health of the Workforce in NHS Trusts. Phase 1. Final Report*. Sheffield: Institute of Work Psychology.

Bowling, A. (1995) *Measuring Disease*. Buckingham: Open University Press.

Bowling, A. (1997) *Measuring Health: A Review of Quality of Life Measurement Scales*. Buckingham: Open University Press.

Brewin, C.B. and Firth-Cozens, J. (1997) Dependency and self-criticism as predictors of depression in young doctors, *Journal of Occupational Health Psychology*, 2: 242–6.

British Medical Association (1998) *Health and Environmental Impact Assessment: An Integrated Approach*. London: Earthscan.

Broman, C.L. (1993) Social relationships and health-related behaviour, *Journal of Behavioral Medicine*, 16: 335–50.

Brooks, G.R. and Richardson, F.C. (1980) Emotional skills training: a treatment program for duodenal ulcer, *Behavior Therapy*, 11: 198–207.

Brown, G. and Harris, T. (1978) *The Social Origins of Depresssion*. London: Tavistock.

Brown, L.K., Schultz, J.R. and Gragg, R.A. (1995) HIV-infected adolescents with hemophilia-adaptation and coping, *Pediatrics*, 96: 459–63.

Brown, S.J., Lieberman, D.A., Gemeny, B.A. *et al.* (1997) Educational video game for juvenile diabetes: Results of a controlled trial, *Medical Informatics*, 22: 77–89.

Brownell, K.D. and Felix, M.R. (1987) Competitions to facilitate health promotions: review and conceptual analysis, *American Journal of Health Promotion*, 2: 28–36.

Budd, R. and Rollnick, S. (1996) The structure of the Readiness to Change Questionnaire: a test of Prochaska and DiClemente's transtheoretical model, *Health Psychology*, 15: 365–76.

Bundy, C., Carroll, D., Wallace, L. and Nagle, R. (1994) Psychological treatment of chronic stable angina pectoris, *Psychology and Health*, 10: 69–77.

Buss, A.H. and Durkee, A. (1957) An inventory for assessing different kinds of hostility, *Journal of Consulting Psychology*, 42: 155–62.

Calnan, M. (1989) Control over health and patterns of health-related behaviour, *Social Science and Medicine*, 29: 131–6.

Calnan, M. (1990) Food and health: a comparison of beliefs and practices in middle-class and working-class households, in S. Cunningham-Burley and N.P. McKeganey (eds) *Readings in Medical Sociology*. London: Routledge.

Cameron, L.D., Leventhal, E.A. and Leventhal, H. (1995) Seeking medical care in response to symptoms and life stress, *Psychosomatic Medicine*, 57: 37–47.

Campbell, E.M., Redman, S., Moffitt, P.S. and Sanson-Fisher, R.W. (1996) The relative effectiveness of educational and behavioral instruction programs for patients with NIDDM: a randomized trial, *Diabetes Educator*, 22: 379–86.

Campbell, L.A., Kirkpatrick, S.E., Berry, C.C. *et al.* (1992) Psychological preparation of mothers of pre-school children undergoing cardiac catherization, *Psychology and Health*, 7: 175–85.

Carey, S. (1985) *Conceptual Changes in Childhood*. Cambridge, MA: MIT Press.

Carver, C.S., Scheier, M.F. and Weintraub, J.K. (1989) Assessing coping strategies: a theoretically based approach, *Journal of Personality and Social Psychology*, 56: 267–83.

Cassell, E.J. (1982) The nature of suffering and the goals of medicine, *New England Journal of Medicine*, 396: 639–45.

Chaitchik, S., Kreitler, S., Shaked, S. *et al.* (1992) Doctor–patient communication in a cancer ward, *Journal of Cancer Education*, 7: 41–54.

Chesney, M.A. and Folkman, S. (1994) Psychological impact of HIV disease and implications for intervention, *Psychiatric Clinics of North America*, 17: 163–82.

Chesney, M.A., Hecker, M.H. and Black, G.W. (1988) Coronary-prone components of type A behavior in the WCGS: a new methodology, in B.K. Houston and C.R. Snyder (eds) *Type A Behavior Pattern: Research, Theory, and Intervention*. New York: Wiley.

Cinciprini, P.M., Lapitsky, L.G., Wallfisch, A. *et al.* (1994) An evaluation of a multicomponent treatment program involving scheduled smoking and relapse prevention procedures: initial findings, *Addictive Behaviors*, 19: 13–22.

Cohen, S., Frank, E., Doyle, W.J., Skoner, D.P., Rabin, B.S., Gwaltney, J.M. Jr. (1998) Types of stressors that increase susceptibility to the common cold in healthy adults. *Health Psychology*, 17: 214–23.

Cohen, S., Tyrell, D.A. and Smith, A.P. (1993) Life events, perceived stress, negative affect and susceptibility to the common cold, *Journal of Personality and Social Psychology*, 64: 131–40.

Colby, S.M., Monti, P.M., Barnett, N.P. *et al.* (1998) Brief motivational interviewing in a hospital setting for adolescent smoking: a preliminary study, *Journal of Consulting and Clinical Psychology*, 66: 574–8.

Cole, S.W., Kemeny, M.E., Taylor, S.E. and Visscher, B.R. (1996) Elevated physical health risk among gay men who conceal their homosexual identity, *Health Psychology*, 15: 23–5.

Collins, J.A. and Rice, V.H. (1997) Effects of relaxation intervention in phase II cardiac rehabilitation: replication and extension, *Heart and Lung*, 26: 31–44.

Conner, M. and Sparks, P. (1996) The theory of planned behaviour and health behaviours, in M. Conner and P. Norman (eds) *Predicting Health Behaviour. Research and Practice with Social Cognition Models*. Buckingham: Open University Press.

Cook, W.W. and Medley, D.M. (1954) Proposed hostility and pharasaic-virtue scales for the MMPI, *Journal of Applied Psychology*, 38: 414–18.

Cornuz, J., Zellweger, J-P., Mounoud, C. *et al.* (1997) Smoking cessation counseling by residents in an outpatient clinic, *Preventive Medicine*, 26: 292–6.

Council, J.R., Ahern, D.K., Follick, M.J. and Kline, C.L. (1988) Expectancies and functional impairment in chronic low back pain, *Pain*, 33: 323–31.

Crown, S., Crown, J.M. and Fleming, A. (1975) Aspects of the psychology and epidemiology of rheumatoid disease, *Psychological Medicine*, 5: 291–9.

Cullen, I. (1979) Urban social policy and problems of family life: the use of an extended diary method to inform decision analysis, in C. Harris (ed.) *The Sociology of the Family: New Directions in Britain*, Sociological Review Monograph 28. University of Keele.

Dancey, C.P., Taghavi, M. and Fox, R.J. (1998) The relationship between daily stress and symptoms of irritable bowel: a time-series approach, *Journal of Psychosomatic Research*, 44: 537–45.

Davey Smith, G., Carroll, D., Rankin, S. and Rowan, D. (1992) Socioeconomic differentials in mortality: evidence from Glasgow graveyards, *British Medical Journal*, 305: 1554–7.

Davey Smith, G., Dorling, D., Gordon, D. and Shaw, M. (1999) The widening health gap: what are the solutions? *Critical Public Health*, 9: 151–70.

Davidson, A.R. and Morrison, D.M. (1983) Predicting contraceptive behavior from attitudes: a comparison of within-versus-across subjects procedures, *Journal of Personality and Social Psychology*, 45: 997–1009.

Dean, C. and Surtees, P.G. (1989) Do psychological factors predict survival in breast cancer? *Journal of Psychosomatic Research*, 33: 651–9.

Decker, T.W. and Cline-Elsen, J. (1992) Relaxation therapy as an adjunct in radiation oncology, *Journal of Clinical Psychology*, 48: 388–93.

Decker, B.D. and Evans, R.G. (1989) Efficacy of a minimal contact version of a multimodal smoking cessation program, *Addictive Behaviors*, 14: 487–91.

De Haes, J.C.J.M., Van Knippenberg, F.C.E. and Neijt, J.P. (1990) Measuring psychological and physical distress in cancer patients: structure and application of the Rotterdam Symptom Checklist, *British Journal of Cancer*, 62: 1034–8.

Denollet, J. (1993) Sensitivity of outcome assessment in cardiac rehabilitation, *Journal of Consulting and Clinical Psychology*, 61: 686–95.

Denollet, J. (1994) Health complaints and outcome assessment in coronary heart disease, *Psychosomatic Medicine*, 56: 463–74.

DeRidder, D., Depla, M., Severens, P. and Malsch, M. (1997) Beliefs on coping with illness: a consumer's perspective, *Social Science and Medicine*, 44: 553–9.

Derogatis, L.R., Abeloff, M.D. and Melisaratos, N. (1979) Psychological coping mechanisms and survival time in metastatic breast cancer, *Journal of the American Medical Association*, 242: 1504–8.

DeVellis, B.M., Blalock, S.J., Hahn P.M. *et al.* (1988) Evaluation of a problem-solving intervention for patients with arthritis. *Patient Education and Counselling*, 11: 29–34.

DiClemente, C.C., Prochaska, J.O., Fairhurst, S.K. *et al.* (1991) The process of smoking cessation: an analysis of precontemplation, contemplation, and preparation stages of change, *Journal of Consulting and Clinical Psychology*, 59: 295–304.

Digiusto, E. and Bird, K.D. (1995) Matching smokers to treatment: self-control versus social support, *Journal of Consulting and Clinical Psychology*, 63: 290–5.

Dimigen, G. and Ferguson, K. (1993) An investigation into the relationship of children's cognitive development and their concepts of illness, *Psychologia*, 36: 97–102.

Dolcini, M.M., Coates, T.J., Catania, J.A. *et al.* (1995) Multiple sexual partners and their psychosocial correlates: the population-based AIDS in Multiethnic Neighbourhoods (AMEN) Study, *Health Psychology*, 14: 22–31.

Donovan, J.L. and Blake, D.R. (1992) Patient non-compliance: deviance or reasoned decision making, *Social Science and Medicine*, 34: 507–13.

Douglas, M. and Nicod, M. (1974) Taking the biscuit: the structure of British meals, *New Society*, 30: 744–7.

Dunkel-Schetter, C., Feinstein, L., Taylor, S.E. and Falke, R. (1992) Patterns of coping with cancer and their correlates, *Health Psychology*, 11: 79–87.

Dzewaltowski, D.A., Noble, J.M. and Shaw, J.M. (1990) Physical activity participation: social cognitive theory versus the theories of reasoned action and planned behavior, *Journal of Sport and Exercise Psychology*, 12: 388–405.

Eagly, A.H. and Chaiken, S. (1993) *The Psychology of Attitudes*. Orlando, FL: Harcourt Brace Jovanovich.

Echabe, A.E., Guillen, C.S. and Ozamiz, J.A. (1992) Representations of health, illness and medicines: coping strategies and health promoting behaviour, *British Journal of Clinical Psychology*, 31: 339–49.

Egan, G. (1990) *The Skilled Helper: Models, Skills, and Methods for Effective Helping*. Monterey, CA: Brooks Cole.

Eisenberg, D.M., Delbanco, T.L., Berkey, C.S. *et al.* (1993) Cognitive behavioral techniques for hypertension: are they effective? *Annals of Internal Medicine*, 118: 964–72.

Eiser, C. (1989) Children's concepts of illness: toward an alternative to the 'stage' approach, *Psychology and Health*, 3: 93–101.

Elford, J. and Cockcroft, A. (1991) Compulsory HIV antibody testing, universal precautions and the perceived risk of HIV: a survey among medical students and consultant staff at a London teaching hospital, *AIDS Care*, 3: 151–8.

Elkin, A.J. and Rosch, P.J. (1990) Promoting mental health at work, *Occupational Medicine State of the Art Review*, 5: 739–54.

Elmer, P.J., Grimm, R., Laing, B. *et al.* (1995) Lifestyle intervention: results of the treatment of mild hypertension study (TOMHS), *Preventive Medicine*, 24: 378–88.

Elwyn, G., Edwards, A. and Kinnersley, P. (1999) Shared decision-making in primary care: the neglected second half of the consultation, *British Journal of General Practice*, 49: 477–82.

Endler, N.S., Parker, J.D.A. and Summerfeldt, L.J. (1998a) Coping with health problems: developing a reliable and valid multidimensional measure, *Psychological Assessment*, 10: 195–205.

Endler, N.S., Courbasson, C.M.A. and Fillion, L. (1998b) Coping with cancer: the evidence for the temporal stability of the French-Canadian version of the Coping with Health Injuries and Problems (CHIP), *Personality and Individual Differences*, 25: 711–17.

Erdman, R.A. (1982) *Heart Patients Psychological Questionnaire*. Lisse: Swets & Zeitlinger.

Evans, D.G.R., Blair, V., Greenhalgh, R. *et al.* (1994) The impact of genetic counselling on risk perception in women with a family history of breast cancer, *British Journal of Cancer*, 70: 934–8.

Evans, D.L., Leserman, J., Perkins, D.O. *et al.* (1997) Severe life stress as a predictor of early disease progression in HIV infection, *American Journal of Psychiatry*, 154: 630–4.

Everson, S.A., Goldberg, D.E., Kaplan, G.A. *et al.* (1996) Hopelessness and risk of mortality and incidence of myocardial infarction and cancer, *Psychosomatic Medicine*, 58: 113–24.

Everson, S.A., Kauhanen, J., Kaplan, G.A. *et al.* (1997) Hostility and increased risk of mortality and acute myocardial infarction: the mediating role of behavioral risk factors, *American Journal of Epidemiology*, 146: 142–52.

Fallowfield, L.J., Baum, M. and Maguire, G.P. (1986) Effects of breast conservation on psychological morbidity associated with diagnosis and treatment of early breast cancer, *British Medical Journal*, 293: 1331–4.

Family Heart Study Group (1994) Randomised controlled trial evaluating cardiovascular screening and intervention in general practice: principal results of British family heart study, *British Medical Journal*, 308: 313–20.

Farquhar, J.W., Maccoby, N., Wood, P.D. *et al.* (1977) Community education for cardiovascular health, *Lancet*, 1: 1192–8.

Farquhar, J.W., Fortmann, S.P., Flora, J.A. *et al.* (1990) Effects of community-wide education on cardiovascular disease risk factors: the Stanford Five-City Project, *Journal of the American Medical Association*, 264: 359–65.

Fawzy, F.I., Fawzy, N.W., Hyun, C.S. *et al.* (1993) Malignant melanoma: effects of an early structured psychiatric intervention, coping, and affective state on recurrence and survival 6 years later, *Archives of General Psychiatry*, 50: 681–9.

Fawzy, I., Namir, S. and Wolcott, D. (1989) Group intervention with newly diagnosed AIDS patients, *Psychiatry and Medicine*, 7: 35–46.

Faymonville, M.E., Mambourg, P.H., Joris, J. *et al.* (1997) Psychological approaches during conscious sedation. Hypnosis versus stress reducing strategies: a prospective randomized study, *Pain*, 73: 361–7.

Fielding, R. (1987) Patients' beliefs regarding the causes of myocardial infarction: implications for information giving and compliance, *Patient Education and Counseling*, 9: 121–34.

Firth-Cozens, J. and Morrison, I.M. (1989) Sources of stress and ways of coping in junior house doctors, *Stress Medicine*, 5: 121–6.

Fitzpatrick, R., Newman, S., Lamb, R. and Shipley, M. (1989) A comparison of measures of health status in rheumatoid arthritis, *British Journal of Rheumatology*, 28: 201–6.

Folkman, S. and Lazarus, R.S. (1988) *Manual of the Ways of Coping Questionnaire*. Palo Alto, CA: Consulting Psychologists Press.

Folkman, S., Lazarus, R.S., Dunkelschetter, C. *et al.* (1986) Dynamics of a stressful encounter – cognitive appraisal, coping, and encounter outcomes, *Journal of Personality and Social Psychology*, 50: 992–1003.

Fordyce, W.E. (1982) A behavioural perspective on chronic pain. *British Journal of Clinical Psychology*, 21: 313–20.

Forester, B., Kornfeld, D.S., Fleiss, J.L. and Thompson, S. (1993) Group psychotherapy during radiotherapy: effects on emotional and physical distress, *American Journal of Psychiatry*, 150: 1700–6.

Forsen, A. (1991) Psychosocial stress as a risk for breast cancer, *Psychotherapy and Psychosomatics*, 55: 176–85.

Frasure-Smith, N., Lesperance, F., Prince, R.H., *et al.* (1997) Randomised trial of home-based psychosocial nursing intervention for patients recovering from myocardial infarction, *Lancet*, 350: 473–9.

Frasure-Smith, N. and Prince, R. (1985) The ischemic heart disease life stress monitoring program: impact on mortality, *Psychosomatic Medicine*, 47: 431–45.

Frasure-Smith, N., Lesperance, F. and Talajic, M. (1993) Depression following myocardial infarction, *Journal of the American Medical Association*, 270: 1819–25.

Friedman, M. and Powell, L.H. (1984) The diagnosis and quantitative assessment of Type A behavior: introduction and description of the videotaped structured interview, *Integrative Psychiatry*, 2: 123–31.

Friedman, M., Thoresen, C.E., Gill, J.J. *et al.* (1986) Alteration of type A behavior and its effect on cardiac recurrences in post myocardial infarction patients:

summary results of the recurrent coronary prevention project, *American Heart Journal*, 112: 653–65.

Friedman, S., Vila, G., Timsit, J. *et al.* (1998) Anxiety and depressive disorders in an adult insulin-dependent diabetic mellitus (IDDM) population: relationships with glycaemic control and somatic complications, *European Psychiatry*, 13: 295–302.

Fries, J.F., Fries, S.T., Parcell, C.L. and Harrington, H. (1992) Health risk changes with a low-cost individualized health promotion program: effects at up to 30 months, *American Journal of Health Promotion*, 6: 364–71.

Gallacher, J., Hopkinson, J., Bennett, P. and Yarnell, J. (1997) Stress management in the treatment of angina, *Psychology and Health*, 12: 523–32.

Gatchel, R.J., Polatin, P.B., Mayer, T.G. *et al.* (1998) Use of the SF-36 health status survey with a chronically disabled back pain population: strengths and limitations, *Journal of Occupational Rehabilitation*, 8: 237–46.

Gellert, G.A., Maxwell, R.M. and Siegel, B.S. (1984) Survival of breast cancer patients receiving adjunctive psychosocial support therapy: a 10-year follow-up study, *Journal of Clinical Oncology*, 11: 66–9.

Geyer, S. (1991) Life events prior to manifestation of breast cancer: a limited prospective study covering eight years before diagnosis, *Journal of Psychosomatic Research*, 35: 355–63.

Gifford, A.L., Laurent, D.D., Gonzales, V.M. *et al.* (1998) Pilot randomized trial of education to improve self-management skills of men with symptomatic HIV/AIDS, *Retrovirology*, 18: 136–44.

Glanz, K., Sorensen, G. and Farmer, A. (1996) The health impact of worksite nutrition and cholesterol intervention programs, *American Journal of Health Promotion*, 10: 453–70.

Glasgow, R.E., Hollis, J.F., Ary, D.V. and Boles, S.M. (1993) Results of a year-long incentives-based worksite smoking-cessation program, *Addictive Behaviors*, 18: 455–64.

Glasgow, R.E., Terborg, J.R., Hollis, J.F. *et al.* (1995) Take Heart: results from the initial phase of a work-site wellness program, *American Journal of Public Health*, 85: 209–16.

Glasgow, R.E., Toobert, D.J. and Hampson, S.E. (1996) Effects of a brief office-based intervention to facilitate diabetes dietary self-management, *Diabetes Care*, 19: 835–42.

Godding, P.R. and Glasgow, R.E. (1985) Self-efficacy and outcome expectations as predictors of controlled smoking status, *Cognitive Therapy and Research*, 9: 583–90.

Goldberg, D.P. and Williams, P. (1988) *A User's Guide to the General Health Questionnaire*. Windsor: NFER/Nelson.

Goldman, S.L., Whitneysaltiel, D., Granger, J. and Rodin, J. (1991) Children's representations of everyday aspects of health and illness, *Journal of Pediatric Psychology*, 16: 747–66.

Gollwitzer, P.M. (1993) Goal achievement: the role of intentions, in W. Stroebe and M. Hewstone (eds) *European Review of Social Psychology*, Volume 4. Chichester: Wiley.

Gomel, M., Oldenburg, B., Lemon, J. *et al.* (1993) Pilot study of the effects of a workplace smoking ban on indices of smoking, cigarette craving, stress and other health behaviours, *Psychology and Health*, 8: 223–39.

Green, S.B. (1997) Does assessment of quality of life in comparative cancer trials make a difference? A discussion, *Controlled Clinical Trials*, 18: 306–10.

Greenfield, S., Kaplan, S.H., Ware, J.E., Jr *et al.* (1988) Patients' participation in medical care: effects on blood sugar control and quality of life in diabetes, *Journal of General Internal Medicine*, 3: 448–57.

Greer, S. (1991) Psychological response to cancer and survival, *Psychological Medicine*, 21: 40–9.

Greer, S. and Morris, T. (1975) Psychological attributes of women who develop breast cancer: a controlled study, *Journal of Psychosomatic Research*, 19: 147–53.

Gruber, B.L., Hersh, S.P., Hall, N.R. *et al.* (1993) Immunological responses of breast cancer patients to behavioral interventions, *Biofeedback and Self Regulation*, 18: 1–22.

Hall, S.M., Tunstall, C., Rugg, D. *et al.* (1985) Nicotine gum and behavioral treatment in smoking cessation, *Journal of Consulting and Clinical Psychology*, 53: 256–8.

Harrison, J.A., Mullen, P.D. and Green, L.W. (1992) A meta-analysis of studies of the health belief model with adults, *Health Education Research, Theory and Practice*, 7: 107–16.

Hatch, M.C., Wallenstein, S., Beyea, J. *et al.* (1991) Cancer rates after the Three Mile Island nuclear accident and proximity to the plant, *American Journal of Public Health*, 81: 719–24.

Hathaway, D. (1986) Effect of preoperative instruction on postoperative outcomes – a metaanalysis, *Nursing Research*, 35: 269–75.

Hausenblas, H.A., Carron, A.V. and Mack, D.E. (1997) Application of the theories of reasoned action and planned behavior to exercise behavior: a meta-analysis, *Journal of Sport and Exercise Psychology*, 19: 36–51.

Haynes, G. and Feinleib, M. (1980) Women, work, and coronary heart disease: prospective findings from the Framingham heart study, *American Journal of Public Health*, 70: 133–41.

Hearnshaw, H., Baker, R. and Robertson, N. (1994) Multi-disciplinary audit in primary health care teams: facilitation by audit support staff, *Quality in Health Care*, 2: 164–8.

Hebert, J.R., Harris, D.R., Sorensen, G. *et al.* (1993) A work-site nutrition intervention: its effects on the consumption of cancer-related nutrients, *American Journal of Public Health*, 83: 391–3.

Heckhausen, H. (1991) *Motivation and Action*. Berlin: Springer.

Heijmans, M.J. (1998) Coping and adaptive outcome in chronic fatigue syndrome: importance of illness cognitions, *Journal of Psychosomatic Research*, 45: 39–51.

Heijmans, M. and deRidder, D. (1998) Assessing illness representations of chronic illness: explorations of their disease-specific nature, *Journal of Behavioral Medicine*, 21: 485–503.

Heim, E., Augustiny, K., Blaser, A. and Burki, C. (1987) Coping with breast cancer: a longitudinal prospective study, *Psychotherapy and Psychosomatics*, 48: 44–59.

Hein, H.O., Suadicani, P. and Gyntelberg, F. (1992) Ischaemic heart disease incidence by social class and form of smoking: the Copenhagen male study – 17 years follow-up, *Journal of Internal Medicine*, 231: 477–83.

Heller, R.F., Knapp, J.C., Valenti, L.A. and Dobson, A.J. (1993) Secondary prevention after acute myocardial infarction, *American Journal of Cardiology*, 72: 759–62.

Herzlich, C. (1973) *Health and Illness: A Social Psychological Analysis*. London: Academic Press.

Hill, P. (1999) Patient Care Development Programme. Unpublished document, Royal United Hospitals, Bath.

Hinton, J. (1999) The progress of awareness and acceptance of dying assessed in cancer patients and their caring relatives, *Palliative Medicine*, 13: 19–35.

Hobfoll, S.E. (1989) Conservation of resources: a new attempt at conceptualising stress, *American Psychologist*, 44: 513–24.

Hogbin, B. and Fallowfield, L.J. (1989) Getting it taped: the 'bad news' consultation with cancer patients, *British Journal of Hospital Medicine*, 41: 330–3.

Holland, J.C., Morrow, G.R. and Schmal, A. (1991) A randomized clinical trial of alprazolam versus progressive muscle relaxation in cancer patients with anxiety and depressive symptoms, *Journal of Clinical Oncology*, 9: 1004–11.

Holmes, T.H. and Rahe, R.H. (1967) The Social Readjustment Scale, *Journal of Psychosomatic Research*, 2: 213–18.

Horne R. (1997) Representations of medication and treatment: advances in theory and measurement, in K.J. Petrie and J.A. Weinman (eds) *Perceptions of Health and Illness*. Chur, Switzerland: Harwood.

Houston, D.M. and Allt, S.K. (1997) Psychological distress and error making among junior house officers, *British Journal of Health Psychology*, 2: 141–51.

Hunt, S.M. (1984) Nottingham Health Profile, in N.K. Wenger, M.E. Mattson, C.D. Furberg *et al.* (eds) *Assessment of Quality of Life in Clinical Trials of Cardiovascular Therapies*. New York: Le Jacq.

Ibbotson, T., Maguire, P., Selby, P. *et al.* (1994) Screening for anxiety and depression in cancer patients: the effects of disease and treatment, *European Journal of Cancer*, 30: 37–40.

Ingham, R. and van Zessen, G. (1997) Towards an alternative model of sexual behaviour: from individual properties to interactional processes, in L. van Camphoudt, M. Cohen, G. Guizzardi, and D. Hausser (eds) *Sexual Interactions and HIV Risk: New Conceptual Perspectives in European Research*. London: Taylor & Francis.

Irvine, J., Johnston, D.W., Jenner, D.A. and Marie, G.V. (1986) Relaxation and stress management in the treatment of essential hypertension, *Journal of Psychosomatic Research*, 30: 437–50.

Isen, A.M., Rosenzweig, A.S. and Young, M.J. (1991) The influence of positive affect on clinical problem solving, *Medical Decision Making*, 11: 221–7.

Jacobs, D.R., Luepker, R.V., Mittelmark, M.B. *et al.* (1986) Community-wide prevention strategies: evaluation design of the Minnesota Heart Health Program, *Journal of Chronic Diseases*, 39: 775–88.

Jacobson, B. (1981) *The Lady Killers: Why Smoking is a Feminist Issue*. London: Pluto Press.

Janz, N. and Becker, M.H. (1984) The health belief model: a decade later, *Health Education Quarterly*, 11: 1–47.

Jay, I., Elliott, C.H., Fitzgibbons, I. *et al.* (1995) A comparative study of cognitive behavior therapy versus general anesthesia for painful medical procedures in children, *Pain*, 62: 3–9.

Jensen, M.P., Karoly, P. and Braver, S. (1986) The measurement of clinical pain intensity: a comparison of six methods, *Pain*, 27: 117–26.

Johansson, C., Dahl, J., Jannert, M., Melin, L. and Andersson, G. (1998) Effects of a cognitive-behavioral pain-management program, *Behaviour Research and Therapy*, 36: 915–30.

Johnson, D.L. (1988) Primary prevention of behaviour problems in young children: the Houston Parent-Child Development Center. In R.H. Price, E.L. Cowen, R.P. Lorion and J. Ramos-McKay (eds) *14 ounces of prevention: a casebook for practitioners*. Washington DC: American Psychological Association.

Johnson, N.A. and Heller, R.F. (1998) Prediction of patient nonadherence with home-based exercise for cardiac rehabilitation: the role of perceived barriers and perceived benefits, *Preventive Medicine*, 27: 56–64.

Johnston, M. and Vogele, C. (1993) Benefits of psychological preparation for surgery: a meta-analysis, *Annals of Behavioral Medicine*, 15: 245–56.

Julkunen, J., Salonen, R., Kaplan, G.A. *et al.* (1994) Hostility and the progression of carotid atherosclerosis, *Psychosomatic Medicine*, 56: 519–25.

Kahneman, D. and Tversky, A. (1979) Prospect theory: an analysis of decision under risk, *Econometrica*, 47: 263–91.

Kalichman, S.C., Nachimson, D., Cherry, C. and Williams, E. (1998) AIDS treatment advances and behavioral prevention setbacks: preliminary assessment of reduced perceived threat of HIV-AIDS, *Health Psychology*, 17: 546–50.

Kanner, A.D., Coyne, J.C., Schaefer, C. and Lazarus, R.S. (1981) Comparison of two modes of stress measurement: daily hassles and uplifts versus major life events, *Journal of Behavioral Medicine*, 4: 1–39.

Karasek, R. and Theorell, T. (1990) *Stress, Productivity and the Reconstruction of Working Life*. New York: Basic Books.

Katz, R.C., Ashmore, J., Barboa, E. *et al.* (1998) Knowledge of disease and dietary compliance in patients with end-stage renal disease, *Psychological Reports*, 82: 331–6.

Keel, P.J., Bodoky, C., Gerhard, U. and Muller, W. (1998) Comparison of integrated group therapy and group relaxation training for fibromyalgia, *Clinical Journal of Pain*, 14: 232–8.

Keesling, B. and Friedman, H.S. (1995) Interventions to prevent skin cancer: experimental evaluation of information and fear appeals, *Psychology and Health*, 10: 477–90.

Kelley, J.A., St Lawrence, J.S., Brasfield, T.L. *et al.* (1990) Psychological factors that predict AIDS high-risk versus AIDS precautionary behavior, *Journal of Consulting and Clinical Psychology*, 58: 225–37.

Kelley, J.A., Murphy, D.A., Washington, C.D. and Wilson, T.S. (1994) The effects of HIV/AIDS intervention groups for high-risk women in urban clinics, *American Journal of Public Health*, 84: 1918–22.

Kelley, J.E., Lumley, M.A. and Leisen, J.C.C. (1997) Health effects of emotional disclosure in rheumatoid arthritis patients, *Health Psychology*, 16: 331–40.

Kessler, R.C., Foster, C., Joseph, J. *et al.* (1991) Stressful life events and symptom onset in HIV-infection, *American Journal of Psychiatry*, 148: 733–8.

Kiecolt-Glaser, J.K., Garner, W., Speicher, C.E. *et al.* (1984) Psychosocial modifiers of immunocompetence in medical students, *Psychosomatic Medicine*, 46: 7–14.

Kiecolt-Glaser, J.K., Glaser, R., Williger, D. *et al.* (1985) Psychosocial enhancement of immunocompetence in geriatric population, *Health Psychology*, 4: 25–41.

King, C. and Kennedy, P. (1999) Coping effectiveness training for people with spinal cord injury: preliminary results of a controlled trial, *British Journal of Clinical Psychology*, 38: 5–14.

Kinmonth, A.L., Woodcock, A., Griffin, S., Spiegal, N. and Campbell, M.J. (1968) Randomised controlled trial of patient centred care of diabetes in general practice: impact on current wellbeing and future disease risk. The Diabetes Care From Diagnosis Research Team. *British Medical Journal*, 317: 1202–8.

Klesges, R.C., Cigrang, J. and Glasgow, R.E. (1989) Worksite smoking modification programes: a state-of-the-art review and directions for future research, in M. Johnston and T. Marteau (eds) *Applications in Health Psychology*. New Jersey: Transaction Publishers.

Koffman, D.M., Lee, J.W., Hopp, J.W. and Emont, S.L. (1998) The impact of including incentives and competition in a workplace smoking cessation program on quit rates, *American Journal of Health Promotion*, 13: 105–11.

Koh, K.B. and Lee, B.K. (1998) Reduced lymphocyte proliferation and interleukin-2 production in anxiety disorders, *Psychosomatic Medicine*, 60: 479–83.

Koikkalainen, M., Lappalainen, R. and Mykkanen, H. (1996) Why cardiac patients do not follow the nutritionist's advice: barriers in nutritional advice perceived in rehabilitation, *Disability and Rehabilitation*, 13: 619–23.

Kreuter, M.W. and Stretcher, V.J. (1996) Do tailored behavior change messages enhance the effectiveness of health risk appraisal? Results from a randomized trial, *Health Education Research, Theory and Practice*, 11: 97–105.

Kristensen, T.S. (1995) The demand–control–support model: methodological challenges for future research, *Stress Medicine*, 11: 17–26.

Kubler-Ross, A. (1969) *On Death and Dying*. New York: Macmillan.

Kune, G.A., Kune, S., Watson, L.F. and Bahnson, C.B. (1991) Personality as a risk factor in large bowel cancer: data from the Melbourne Colorectal Cancer Study, *Psychological Medicine*, 21: 43–60.

Kvien, T.K., Kaasa, S. and Smedstad, L.M. (1998) Performance of the Norwegian SF-36 Health Survey in patients with rheumatoid arthritis. II. A comparison of the SF-36 with disease-specific measures, *Journal of Clinical Epidemiology*, 51: 1077–86.

Lahad, A., Heckbert, S.R., Koepsell, T.D. *et al.* (1997) Hostility, aggression and the risk of nonfatal myocardial infarction in postmenopausal women, *Journal of Psychosomatic Research*, 43: 183–95.

Lampic, C., Von Essen, L., Peterson, V.W. *et al.* (1996) Anxiety and depression in hospitalized patients with cancer: agreement in patient–staff dyads, *Cancer Nursing*, 19: 419–28.

Langewitz, W., Wossmer, B., Iseli, J. and Berger, W. (1997) Psychological and metabolic improvement after an outpatient teaching program for functional intensified insulin therapy, *Diabetes Research and Clinical Practice*, 37: 157–64.

Latimer, P.R. (1979) Irritable bowel syndrome: a behavioural model, *Behaviour Research and Therapy*, 19: 140–2.

Lau, R.R. and Hartman, K.A. (1983) Common sense representations of common illnesses, *Health Psychology*, 2: 167–86.

Lazarus, R.S. (1991) *Emotion and Adaptation*. New York: Oxford University Press.

Lazarus, R.S. and Folkman, S. (1984) *Stress, Appraisal, and Coping*. New York: Springer.

Lefebvre, M.F. (1981) Cognitive distortion and cognitive errors in depressed psychiatric low back pain patients, *Journal of Consulting and Clinical Psychology*, 49: 517–25.

Lekander, M., Furst, C.J., Rotstein, S. *et al.* (1997) Immune effects of relaxation during chemotherapy for ovarian cancer, *Psychotherapy and Psychosomatics*, 66: 185–91.

Lerman, C., Biesecker, B., Benkendorf, J.L. *et al.* (1997) Controlled trial of pretest education approaches to enhance informed decision making for BRCA1 gene testing, *Journal of the National Cancer Institute*, 89: 148–57.

Leventhal, H., Benyamini, Y., Brownlee, S. *et al.* (1997) Illness representations: theoretical foundations, in K.J. Petrie and J.A. Weinman (eds) *Perceptions of Health and Illness*. Chur: Harwood.

Leventhal, H., Easterling, D.V., Coons, H., Luchterhand, C. and Love, R.R. (1986) Adaptation to chemotherapy treatments, in B. Anderson (ed.) *Women With Cancer*. New York: Springer-Verlag.

Lewin, B., Robertson, I.H., Irving, J.B. and Campbell, M. (1992) Effects of self-help post-myocardial-infarction rehabilitation on psychological adjustment and use of health services, *Lancet*, 339: 1036–40.

Lewis, B., Mann, J.I. and Mancini, M. (1986) Reducing the risks of coronary heart disease in individuals and the population. *Lancet*, i: 956–9.

Ley, P. (1988) *Communicating with Patients: Improving Communication, Satisfaction, and Compliance*. London: Chapman & Hall.

Ley, P. (1997) Compliance among patients, in A. Baum, S. Newman, J. Weinman, R. West and C. McManus (eds) *Cambridge Handbook of Psychology, Health and Medicine*. Cambridge: Cambridge University Press.

Lichtenstein, E. and Glasgow, R.E. (1992) Smoking cessation: what have we learned over the past decade? *Journal of Consulting and Clinical Psychology*, 60: 518–27.

Lim, L.L.Y., Johnson, N.A., O'Connell, R.L. and Heller, R.F. (1998) Quality of life and later adverse health outcomes in patients with suspected heart attack, *Australian and New Zealand Journal of Public Health*, 22: 540–6.

Lin, N., Ensel, W.M., Simeone, R.S. and Kuo, W. (1979) Social support, stressful life events, and illness: a model and empirical test, *Journal of Health and Social Behavior*, 20: 108–19.

Lindberg, G., Rastam, L., Gullberg, B. and Eklund, G.A. (1992) Low serum cholesterol concentration and short-term mortality from injuries in men and women, *British Medical Journal*, 305: 277–9.

Lindstrom, I., Ohlund, C., Eek, C. *et al.* (1992) The effect of graded activity on patients with subacute low back pain: a randomized prospective clinical study with an operant-conditioning behavioral approach, *Physical Therapy*, 72: 279–90.

Linegar, J., Chesson, C. and Nice, D. (1991) Physical fitness gains following simple environmental change, *American Journal of Preventive Medicine*, 7: 298–310.

Liossi, L. and Hatira, P. (1999) Clinical hypnosis versus cognitive behavioral training for pain management with pediatric cancer patients undergoing bone marrow aspirations, *International Journal of Clinical and Experimental Hypnosis*, 47: 104–16.

Lorig, K. (1996) *Patient Education: A Practical Approach*. Newbury Park, CA: Sage.

Lorig, K. and Holman, H. (1993) Arthritis self-management studies: a twelve-year review, *Health Education Quarterly*, 20: 17–28.

Lorig, K.R., Sobel, D.S., Stewart, A.L. *et al.* (1999) Evidence suggesting that a chronic disease self-management program can improve health status while reducing hospitalization – a randomized trial, *Medical Care*, 37: 5–14.

Lovallo, W.R. (1997) *Stress and Health: Biological and Psychological Interactions*. Thousand Oaks, CA: Sage.

Lundberg, U., de Chateau, P., Winberg, J. and Frankenhauser, M. (1981) Catecholamine and cortisol excretion patterns in three year old children and their parents, *Journal of Human Stress*, 7: 3–11.

Lupton, D. and Chapman, S. (1995) 'A healthy lifestyle might be the death of you': discourses on diet, cholesterol control and heart disease in the press and among the lay public, *Sociology of Health and Illness*, 17: 477–94.

Lutgendorf, S.K., Antoni, M.H., Ironson, G. *et al.* (1997) Cognitive-behavioral stress management decreases dysphoric mood and herpes simplex virus-type 2 antibody titers in symptomatic HIV-seropositive gay men, *Journal of Consulting and Clinical Psychology*, 65: 31–43.

Mackinnon, A., Jorm, A.F., Christensen, H. *et al.* (1999) A short form of the Positive and Negative Affect Schedule: evaluation of factorial validity and invariance across demographic variables in a community sample, *Personality and Individual Differences*, 27: 405–16.

Maes, S. and Schlosser, M. (1987) The role of cognition and coping in health behaviour outcomes of asthmatic patients, *Current Psychological Research and Reviews*, 6: 79–90.

Maes, S., Leventhal, H. and deRidder, D.T.D. (1996) Coping with chronic diseases, in M. Zeidner and N.S. Endler (eds) *Handbook of Coping: Theory, Research, Applications*. New York: Wiley.

Maes, S., Kittel, F., Scholten, H. and Verhoeven, C. (1998) Effects of the Brabantia-project, a Dutch wellness-health programme at the worksite, *American Journal of Public Health*, 88: 1037–41.

Maguire, P., Fairbairn, S. and Fletcher, C. (1986) Consultation skills of young doctors. I: Benefits of feedback training as students persist, *British Medical Journal*, 292: 1573–6.

Maisiak, R., Austin, J. and Heck, L. (1996) Health outcomes of two telephone interventions for patients with rheumatoid arthritis or osteoarthritis. *Arthritis and Rheumatism*, 39: 1391–9.

Malow, R.M., McPherson, S., Klimas, N. *et al.* (1998) Adherence to complex combination antiretroviral therapies by HIV-positive drug abusers, *Psychiatric Services*, 49: 1021–2.

Mansfield, C. (1995) Attitudes and behaviours towards clinical guidelines: the clinicians' perspective, *Quality in Health Care*, 4: 250–5.

Marcus, A.C., Crane, L.A., Kaplan, C.P. *et al.* (1992) Improving adherence to screening follow-up among women with abnormal pap smears – results from a large clinic-based trial of 3 intervention strategies, *Medical Care*, 30: 216–30.

Marcus, B.H., Emmons, K.M., SimkinSilverman, L.R. *et al.* (1998) Evaluation of motivationally tailored vs standard self-help physical activity interventions at the workplace, *American Journal of Health Promotion*, 12: 246–53.

Marmot, M.G., Shipley, M.J. and Rose, G. (1984) Inequalities in health – specific explanations of a general pattern? *Lancet*, i: 1003–6.

Marshall, J., Penckofer, S. and Llewellyn, J. (1986) Structured postoperative teaching and knowledge and compliance of patients who had coronary artery bypass surgery, *Heart and Lung*, 15: 76–82.

Marteau, T.M. (1989) Framing of information: its influence upon decisions of doctors and patients, *British Journal of Social Psychology*, 28: 89–94.

Marteau, T.M. and Bekker, H. (1992) The development of a short-form of the state scale of the Spielberger State Trait Anxiety Inventory (STAI), *British Journal of Clinical Psychology*, 31: 301–6.

Mays, V.M. and Cochran, S.D. (1988) Issues in the perception of AIDS risk and risk reduction activities by Black and Hispanic/Latino women. *American Psychologist*, 43: 949–57.

McCranie, E.W., Watkins, L.O., Brandsma, J.M. and Sisson, B.D. (1986) Hostility, coronary heart disease (CHD) incidence and total mortality: lack of association in a 25-year follow-up study of 478 physicians, *Journal of Behavioral Medicine*, 9: 119–25.

McGee, H.M., O'Boyle, C.A., Hickey, A. *et al.* (1991) Assessing the quality of life of the individual: the SEIQoL with a healthy and a gastro-enterology unit population, *Psychological Medicine*, 21: 749–59.

McGee, H.M., Hevey, D. and Horgan, J.H. (1999) Psychosocial outcome assessments for use in cardiac rehabilitation service evaluation: a 10-year systematic review, *Social Science and Medicine*, 48: 1373–93.

McNeil, B.J., Pauker, S.G., Sox, H.C. and Tversky, A. (1982) On the elicitation of preferences for alternative therapies, *New England Journal of Medicine*, 306: 1259–62.

Mead, H. (1934) *Mind, Self and Society*. Chicago: University of Chicago Press.

Meehl, P.E. (1954) *Clinical versus Statistical Prediction: A Theoretical Analysis and Review of the Evidence*. Minneapolis: University of Minneapolis Press.

Meichenbaum, D. (1985) *Stress Inoculation Training*. New York: Pergamon.

Melzack, R. (1975) The McGill pain questionnaire: major properties and scoring mechanisms, *Pain*, 1: 277–99.

Melzack, R. (1996) Gate control theory: On the evolution of pain concepts. *Pain Forum*, 5: 128–38.

Melzack, R. and Wall, P.D. (1965) Pain mechanisms: A new theory. *Science*, 150, 971–9.

Mendez, F.J. and Belendez, M. (1997) Effects of a behavioral intervention on treatment adherence and stress management in adolescents with IDDM, *Diabetes Care*, 20: 1370–5.

Meyer, D., Leventhal, H. and Gutmann, M. (1985) Common-sense models of illness: the example of hypertension, *Health Psychology*, 4: 115–35.

Meyerowitz, B.E. and Chaiken, S. (1987) The effect of message framing on breast self-examination attitudes, intentions and behaviour, *Journal of Personality and Social Psychology*, 52: 500–10.

Meyerowitz, S., Jacob, R.R. and Hess, D.W. (1968) Monozygotic twins discordant for rheumatoid arthritis: a genetic, clinical, and psychological study, *Arthritis and Rheumatism*, 11: 1–21.

Miller, T.Q., Smith, T.W., Turner, C.W. *et al.* (1996) Meta-analytic review of research on hostility and physical health, *Psychological Bulletin*, 119: 322–48.

Miller, W. and Rollnick, S. (1991) *Motivational Interviewing: Preparing People to Change Addictive Behavior*. New York: Guilford Press.

Montgomery, C., Lydon, A. and Lloyd, K. (1999) Psychological distress among cancer patients and informed consent, *Journal of Psychosomatic Research*, 46: 241–5.

Moorey, S. and Greer, S. (1989) *Psychological Therapy for Patients with Cancer: A New Approach*. Oxford: Heinemann Medical.

Moorey, S., Greer, S., Watson, M. *et al.* (1994) Adjuvant psychological therapy for patients with cancer: outcome at one year, *Psycho-Oncology*, 3: 39–46.

Moos, R.H. and Schaefer, A. (1984) The crisis of physical illness: an overview and conceptual approach, in R.H. Moos (ed.) *Coping with Physical Illness: New Perspectives*, Volume 2. New York: Plenum Press.

Moos, R.H. and Schaefer, J.A. (1997) Health-care environments. In A. Baum, S. Newman, J. Weinman, R. West and C. McManus (eds) *Cambridge handbook of Psychology, Health and Medicine.* Cambridge: Cambridge University Press.

Morgan, M. and Watkins, C.J. (1988) Managing hypertension: beliefs and responses to medication among cultural groups, *Sociology of Health and Illness*, 10: 561–78.

Myrtek, M., Kaiser, A., Rauch, B. and Jansen, G. (1997) Factors associated with work resumption: a 5 year follow-up with cardiac patients, *International Journal of Cardiology*, 59: 291–7.

Nabiloff, B.D., Munakata, J., Chang, L. and Mayer, E.A. (1998) Toward a biobehavioral model of visceral hypersensitivity in irritable bowel syndrome, *Journal of Psychosomatic Research*, 45: 485–93.

Neaton, J.D., Blackburn, H., Jacobs, D. *et al.* (1992) Serum cholesterol and mortality findings for men screened in the Multiple Risk Factor Intervention Trial, *Archives of Internal Medicine*, 152: 1490–500.

Nerenz, D.R. and Leventhal, H. (1983) Self-regulation theory in chronic illness, in T.G. Burish and L.A. Bradley (eds) *Coping with Chronic Disease.* New York: Academic Press.

Newton, C.R. and Barbaree, H.E. (1987) Cognitive changes accompanying headache treatment: the use of a thought-sampling procedure, *Cognitive Therapy and Research*, 11: 635–52.

Nicassio, P.M., Radojevic, V., Weisman, M.H. *et al.* (1997) A comparison of behavioral and educational interventions for fibromyalgia, *Journal of Rheumatology*, 24: 2000–7.

Nicholas, M.K., Wilson, P.H. and Goyen, J. (1991) Operant-behavioural and cognitive-behavioral treatment for chronic low back pain. *Behaviour Research and Therapy*, 29: 225–38.

Nicholas, M.K., Wilson, P.H. and Goyen, J. (1992) Comparison of cognitive-behavioral group treatment and an alternative non-psychological treatment for chronic low back pain. *Pain*, 48: 339–47.

Nichols, K.A. (1984) *Psychological Care in Physical Illness.* London: Croom Helm.

Norman, P., Bennett, P., Murphy, S. and Tudor-Smith, C. (1998) Health locus of control and health behaviour, *Journal of Health Psychology*, 3: 171–80.

Normandeau, S., Kalnins, I., Jutras, S. and Hanigan, D. (1998) A description of 5- to 12-year old children's conception of health within the context of their daily life, *Psychology and Health*, 13: 883–96.

Novaco, R.W. (1975) *Anger Control: The Development and Evaluation of an Experimental Treatment.* Lexington, MA: D.C. Heath.

Nutbeam, D., Smith, C., Murphy, S. and Catford, J. (1993) Maintaining evaluation designs in a long term community based health promotion programme: Heartbeat Wales case study, *Journal of Epidemiology and Community Health*, 47: 127–33.

O'Boyle, C.A., McGee, H., Hickey, A. *et al.* (1992) Individual quality of life in patients undergoing hip replacement, *Lancet*, 339: 1088–91.

O'Donnell, L.N., Doval, A.S., Duran, R. and O'Donnell, C. (1995) Video-based sexually transmitted disease patient education: its impact on condom acquisition, *American Journal of Public Health*, 85: 817–22.

Office of National Statistics (1999) *Social Trends 29*. London: The Stationery Office.

Oldenburg, B., Gomel, M., Owen, N. *et al.* (1989) Evaluation of the effectiveness of worksite health promotion programs, *Community Health Studies*, 13: 360–8.

Oldenburg, B. and Harris, D. (1996) The workplace as a setting for promoting health and preventing disease, *Homeostasis in Health and Disease*, 37: 226–32.

Oldridge, N., Streiner, D., Hoffmann, R. and Guyatt, G. (1995) Profile of mood states and cardiac rehabilitation after acute myocardial infarction, *Medicine and Science in Sports and Exercise*, 27: 900–5.

O'Leary, A., Shoor, S., Lorig, K. and Holman, H.R. (1988) A cognitive behavioral treatment for rheumatoid arthritis, *Health Psychology*, 7: 527–44.

Orbell, S., Hodgkins, S. and Sheeran, P. (1997) Implementation intentions and the theory of planned behavior, *Personality and Social Psychology*, 23: 945–54.

Ornish, D., Brown, S.E., Scerwitz, L.W., Bilings, J.H., Armstrong, W.T., Ports, T.A., McLanahan, S.M., Kirkeeide, R.L., Brand, R.J. and Gould, K.L. (1990) Can life-style changes reverse coronary heart disease? The lifestyle heart trial. *Lancet*, 336, 470–76.

Ornish, D.M., Brown, S.E., Scherwitz, L.W. *et al.* (1990) Can lifestyle changes reverse coronary heart disease? The Lifestyle Heart Trial, *Lancet*, 336: 129–33.

Ornish, D.M., Scherwitz, L.W., Doody, R.S. *et al.* (1983) Effects of stress management training and dietary changes in treating ischaemic heart disease. *Journal of the American Medical Association*, 249: 54–9.

Orth-Gomer, K. and Johnsson, J.V. (1987) Social network interaction and mortality: a six year follow-up study of a random sample of the Swedish population, *Journal of Chronic Diseases*, 40: 949–57.

Orth-Gomer, K. and Unden, A-L. (1990) Type A behavior, social support, and coronary risk: interaction and significance for mortality in cardiac patients, *Psychosomatic Medicine*, 52: 59–72.

Ostberg, O. (1973) Inter-individual differences in circadian fatigue patterns of shiftworkers, *British Journal of Industrial Medicine*, 30: 341–51.

Owen, N., Ewins, A.L. and Lee, C. (1989) Smoking cessation by mail: a comparison of standard and personalized correspondence course formats, *Addictive Behaviors*, 14: 355–63.

OXCHECK Study Group (1994) Effectiveness of heart checks conducted by nurses in primary care: results of the OXCHECK Study after one year, *British Medical Journal*, 308: 3008–12.

Paffenbarger, R.S., Hyde, R.T., Wing, A.L. and Hsiech, C.C. (1986) Physical activity, all cause mortality and longevity of college alumni, *New England Journal of Medicine*, 314: 605–13.

Parker, J.C., Smarr, K.L., Buckelew, S.P. *et al.* (1995) Effects of stress management on clinical outcomes in rheumatoid arthritis, *Arthritis and Rheumatism*, 12: 1807–18.

Parle, M., Jones, B. and Maguire, P. (1996) Maladaptive coping and affective disorders in cancer patients, *Psychological Medicine*, 26: 736–44.

Payne, A. and Blanchard, E.B. (1995) A controlled comparison of cognitive therapy and self-help support groups in the treatment of irritable bowel syndrome, *Journal of Consulting and Clinical Psychology*, 63: 779–86.

Pennebaker, J.W. (1992) *The Psychology of Physical Symptoms*. New York: Springer.

Pennebaker, J.W. and Seagal, J.D. (1999) Forming a story: the health benefits of narrative, *Journal of Clinical Psychology*, 55: 1243–54.

Perez, M.G., Feldman, L. and Caballero, F. (1999) Effects of a self-management educational program for the control of childhood asthma, *Patient Education and Counselling*, 36: 47–55.

Perri, M.G., Martin, A.D., Leermakers, E.A. *et al.* (1997) Effects of group-versus home-based exercise in the treatment of obesity, *Journal of Consulting and Clinical Psychology*, 65: 278–85.

Persky, V.W., Kempthorne-Rawson, J. and Shekelle, R.B. (1987) Personality and risk of cancer: 20 year follow-up of the Western Electric Study, *Psychosomatic Medicine*, 49: 435–49.

Peto, R. and Lopez, A.D. (1990) Worldwide mortality from current smoking patterns, in B. Durston and K. Jamrozik (eds) *Tobacco and Health 1990: The Global War. Proceedings of the Seventh World Conference on Tobacco and Health*. Perth: Health Department of Western Australia.

Petrie, K.J., Weinman, J., Sharpe, N. and Buckley, J. (1996) Role of patients' view of their illness in predicting return to work and functioning after myocardial infarction: longitudinal study, *British Medical Journal*, 312: 1191–4.

Petty, R. and Cacioppo, J. (1986) The elaboration likelihood model of persuasion, in L. Berkowitz (ed.) *Advances in Experimental Social Psychology*, Volume 19. Orlando, FL: Academic Press.

Pill, R., Stott, N.C.H., Rollnick, S.R. and Rees, M. (1998) A randomized controlled trial of an intervention designed to improve the care given in general practice to Type II diabetic patients: patient outcomes and professional ability to change behaviour, *Family Practice*, 15: 229–35.

Price, V.A. (1988) Research and clinical issues in treating Type A behavior, in B.K. Houston and C.R. Synder (eds) *Type A Behavior Pattern: Research, Theory, and Practice*. New York: Wiley.

Prochaska, J.O. and DiClemente, C.C. (1986) Toward a comprehensive model of change, in W.R. Miller and N. Heather (eds) *Treating Addictive Behaviors: Processes of Change*. New York: Plenum Press.

Prochaska, J.O., Velicer, W., Guadagnoli, E. *et al.* (1991) Patterns of change: dynamic typology applied to smoking cessation, *Multivariate Behavioral Research*, 26: 83–107.

Pruitt, B.T., Waligora-Serafin, B., McMahon, T. *et al.* (1993) An educational intervention for newly-diagnosed cancer patients undergoing radiotherapy, *Psycho-Oncology*, 2: 55–62.

Puska, P., Nissinen, A., Tuomilehto, J. *et al.* (1985) The community-based strategy to prevent coronary heart disease: conclusions from the ten years of the North Karelia Project, *Annual Review of Public Health*, 6: 147–93.

Radojevic, V., Nicassio, V. and Weisman, M.H. (1992) Behavioral intervention with and without family support for rheumatoid arthritis, *Behavior Therapy*, 23: 13–20.

Rahn, A.N., Mose, S., ZandeerHeinz, A. *et al.* (1998) Influence of radiotherapy on psychological health in breast cancer patients after breast conserving surgery, *Anticancer Research*, 18: 2271–3.

Ramirez, A.J., Craig, T.K., Watson, J.P. *et al.* (1989) Stress and relapse of breast cancer, *British Medical Journal*, 298: 291–3.

Reddy, D.M., Fleming, R. and Adesso, V.J. (1992) Gender and health, in S. Maes, H. Leventhal and M. Johnston (eds) *International Review of Health psychology*, Volume 1. Chichester: Wiley.

Redman, S., Sanson Fisher, R., Kreft, S. *et al.* (1995) Is the Australian National Heart Foundation programme effective in reducing cholesterol levels among general practice patients? *Health Promotion International*, 10: 293–303.

Reid, J.C., Klachko, D.M., Kardash, C.A.M. *et al.* (1995) Why people don't learn from diabetes literature: influence of text and reader characteristics, *Patient Education and Counseling*, 25: 31–8.

Reynolds, P. and Kaplan, G.A. (1990) Social connections and risk for cancer: prospective evidence from the Alameda County Study, *Behavioral Medicine*, 16: 101–10.

Richards, J., Fisher, P. and Conner, F. (1989) The warnings on cigarette packages are ineffective, *Journal of the American Medical Association*, 261: 45.

Ridgeway, V. and Mathews, A. (1982) Psychological preparation for surgery: a comparison of methods, *British Journal of Clinical Psychology*, 21: 271–80.

Rigby, K., Brown, M., Anganostou, P. *et al.* (1989) Shock tactics to counter AIDS: the Australian experience, *Psychology and Health*, 3: 145–59.

Ringdal, G.I. and Ringdal, K. (1993) Testing the EORTC quality-of-life questionnaire on cancer-patients with heterogenous diagnoses, *Quality of Life Research*, 2: 129–40.

Roberts, F.D., Newcomb, P.A., Trentham-Diet, A. and Storer, B.E. (1996) Self-reported stress and risk of breast cancer, *Cancer*, 77: 1089–93.

Rogers, C.R. (1967) *The Therapeutic Relationship and its Impact*. Madison, WI: University of Wisconsin Press.

Rogers, R.W. (1983) Cognitive and physiological processes in fear appeals and attitude change: a revised theory of protection motivation, in J.T. Cacioppo and R.E. Petty (eds) *Social Psychophysiology: A Source Book*. New York: Guilford Press.

Rokicki, L.A., Holroyd, K.A., France, C.R. *et al.* (1997) Change mechanisms associated with combined relaxation/EMG biofeedback training for chronic tension headache, *Applied Psychophysiology and Biofeedback*, 22: 21–44.

Rose, G., Heller, R.F., Tunstall-Pedoe, H. and Christie, D.G.S. (1980) Heart Disease Prevention Project: a randomized controlled trial in industry, *British Medical Journal*, 280: 747–51.

Ross, M.G. and Lappin, B.W. (1967) *Community Organization: Theory, Principles and Practice*. New York: Harper & Row.

Roter, D.L. (1977) Patient-participation in the patient-provider interaction: The effects of patient question-asking on the quality of the interaction, satisfaction and compliance, *Health Education Monographs*, 5: 281–330.

Rotter, J.B. (1966) Generalised expectancies for internal and external control of reinforcement. *Psychological Monographs*, 80, 609, 1–28.

Russell, M.A., Wilson, C. and Baker, C.D. (1979) Effect of general practitioners' advice against smoking, *British Medical Journal*, 2: 231–5.

Sallis, J.F., Haskell, W.L., Fortmann, S.P., Wood, P.D. and Vranizan, K.M. (1986) Moderate-intensity physical activity and cardiovascular risk factors: the Stanford Five-City Project. *Preventive Medicine*, 15: 561–8.

Savage, R. and Armstrong, D. (1990) Effect of a general practitioner's consulting style on patient satisfaction, *British Medical Journal*, 301: 968–70.

Scheier, M.F. and Carver, C.S. (1985) Optimism, coping, and health: assessment and implications of generalized outcome expectancies, *Health Psychology*, 4: 219–47.

Scheier, M.F., Carver, C.S. and Bridges, M.W. (1994) Distinguishing optimism from neuroticism (and trait anxiety, self-mastery, and self-esteem): a re-evaluation of the Life Orientation Test, *Journal of Personality and Social Psychology*, 67: 1063–78.

Schiaffino, K.M. and Revenson, T.A. (1992) The role of perceived self-efficacy, perceived control and causal attributions in adaptation to rheumatoid arthritis, *Personality and Social Psychology Bulletin*, 18: 709–18.

Schiaffino, K.M., Shawaryn, M.A. and Blum, D. (1998) Examining the impact of illness representations on psychological adjustment to chronic illnesses, *Health Psychology*, 17: 262–8.

Schmidt, L.R. (1997) Hospitalization in children, in A. Baum, S. Newman, J. Weinman, R. West and C. McManus (eds) *Cambridge Handbook of Psychology, Health and Medicine*. Cambridge: Cambridge University Press.

Schwartz, S. and Griffin, T. (1986) *Medical Thinking: The Psychology of Medical Judgement and Decision Making*. New York: Springer.

Schwarzer, R. (1992) Self-efficacy in the adoption and maintenance of health behaviors: theoretical approaches and a new model, in R. Schwarzer (ed.) *Self-efficacy: Thought Control of Action*. Washington, DC: Hemisphere.

Selye, H. (1956) *The Stress of Life*. New York: McGraw-Hill.

Shaffer, J.W., Graves, P.L., Swank, R.T. and Pearson, T.A. (1987) Clustering of personality traits in youth and the subsequent development of cancer among physicians, *Journal of Behavioral Medicine*, 10: 441–7.

Shaper, A.G., Wannamethee, G. and Walker, M. (1994) Alcohol and coronary heart disease: a perspective from the British Regional Heart Study, *International Journal of Epidemiology*, 23: 482–94.

Sheeran, P. and Orbell, S. (1998) Do intentions predict condom use? Meta-analysis and examination of six moderator variables, *British Journal of Social Psychology*, 37: 231–50.

Siegel, K., Schrimshaw, E.W. and Dean, L. (1999) Symptom interpretation and medication adherence among late middle-age and older HIV-infected adults, *Journal of Health Psychology*, 4: 247–57.

Siegrist, J., Peter, R., Junge, A. *et al.* (1990) Low status control, high effort at work and ischemic heart disease: prospective evidence from blue collar men, *Social Science and Medicine*, 35: 1127–34.

Silver, B.V. and Blanchard, E.B. (1978) Biofeedback and relaxation training in the treatment of psychophysiological disorders: or are the machines really necessary? *Journal of Behavioral Medicine*, 1: 217–39.

Sinzato, R., Fukino, O., Tamai, H. *et al.* (1985) Coping behaviors of severe diabetics, *Psychotherapy and Psychosomatics*, 43: 447–68.

Skinner, B.F. (1953) *Science and human behaviour*. New York: Macmillan.

Slama, K., Redman, S., Perkins, J. *et al.* (1990) The effectiveness of two smoking cessation programmes for use in general practice: a randomised clinical trial, *British Medical Journal*, 300: 1707–9.

Slenker, S.E., Price, J.H. and O'Connell, J.K. (1985) Health locus of control of joggers and non-exercisers, *Perceptual and Motor Skills*, 61: 323–8.

Smith, C.A. and Lazarus, R.S. (1993) Appraisal components, core relational themes, and the emotions, *Cognition and Emotion*, 7: 233–69.

Smith, T.W., Pope, K., Rhodewalt, F. and Poulton, J.L. (1989) Optimism, neuroticism, coping, and symptom reports: an alternative interpretation of the Life Optimism Test, *Journal of Personality and Social Psychology*, 56: 640–8.

Sobo, E.J. (1993) Inner-city women and AIDS: the psycho-social benefits of unsafe sex, *Culture, Medicine and Psychiatry*, 17: 455–85.

Sorensen, G., Stoddard, A., Hunt, M.K. *et al.* (1998) The effects of a health promotion health protection intervention on behavior change: the WellWorks study, *American Journal of Public Health*, 88: 1685–90.

Spiegel, D. and Bloom, J.R. (1983) Group-therapy and hypnosis reduce metastatic breast-carcinoma pain, *Psychosomatic Medicine*, 45: 333–9.

Spiegel, D. and Kato, P.M. (1996) Psychosocial influences on cancer incidence and progression, *Harvard Review of Psychiatry*, 4: 10–25.

Spiegel, D., Bloom, J.R. and Yalom, I.D. (1981) Group support for patients with metastatic cancer: a randomized prospective outcome study, *Archives of General Psychiatry*, 38: 527–33.

Spielberger, C.D., Jacobs, G., Russell, S. and Crane, R. (1983) Assessment of anger: the State-Trait Anger Scale, in J.N. Butcher and C.D. Spielberger (eds) *Advances in Personality Assessment*, Volume 2. Hillsdale, NJ: Lawrence Erlbaum.

Spielberger, C.D., Johnson, E.H., Russell, S.F. *et al.* (1985) The experience and expression of anger: construction and validation of an anger expression scale, in M.A. Chesney and R.H. Rosenman (eds) *Anger and Hostility in Cardiovascular and Behavioral Disorders*. Washington, DC: Hemisphere.

Stamler, R., Stamler, J., Gosch, F.C. *et al.* (1989) Primary prevention of hypertension by nutritional-hygienic means: final report of a randomized, controlled trial, *Journal of the American Medical Association*, 262: 1801–7.

Stansfeld, S.A., Bosma, H., Hemingway, H. and Marmot, M.G. (1998) Psycho-social work characteristics and social support as predictors of SF-36 health functioning: the Whitehall II study, *Psychosomatic Medicine*, 60: 247–55.

Stevens, V.J. and Hollis, J.F. (1989) Preventing smoking relapse, using an individually tailored skills-training technique, *Journal of Consulting and Clinical Psychology*, 57: 420–4.

Stiff, J., McCormack, M., Zook, E. *et al.* (1990) Learning about AIDS and HIV transmission in college-age students, *Communication Research*, 17: 743–53.

Stoate, H. (1989) Can health screening damage your health?, *Journal of the Royal College of General Practitioners*, 39: 193–5.

Strauss, A. and Corbin, J. (1990) *Basics of Qualitative Research. Grounded Theory Procedures and Techniques*. Newbury Park, CA: Sage.

Stretcher, V.J. and Rosenstock, I.M. (1997) The health belief model, in A. Baum, S. Newman, J. Weinman, R. West and C. McManus (eds) *Cambridge Handbook of Psychology, Health and Medicine*. Cambridge: Cambridge University Press.

Sturges, J.W. and Rogers, R.W. (1996) Preventive health psychology from a developmental perspective: an extension of protection motivation theory, *Health Psychology*, 15: 158–66.

SuperioCabuslay, E., Ward, M.M. and Lorig, K.R. (1996) Patient education interventions in osteoarthritis and rheumatoid arthritis: a meta-analytic comparison with nonsteroidal antiinflammatory drug treatment, *Arthritis Care and Research*, 9: 292–301.

Sutton, S.R. (1996) Can 'stages of change' provide guidance in the treatment of addictions? A critical examination of Prochaska and DiClemente's model, in G. Edwards and C. Dare (eds) *Psychotherapy, Psychological Treatments, and the Addictions*. Cambridge: Cambridge University Press.

Tadmor, C.S. (1988) The perceived personal control preventive intervention for a caesarean birth population, in R.H. Price, E.L. Cowen, R.P. Lorion and J. Ramos-McKay (eds) *14 Ounces of Prevention: A Casebook for Practitioners*. Washington, DC: American Psychological Association.

Tang, P.C. and Newcomb, C. (1998) Informing patients: a guide for providing patient health information, *Journal of the American Medical Informatics Association*, 5: 563–70.

Tattersall, M.H., Butow, P.N., Griffin, A-M. and Dunn, S.M. (1994) The take-home message: patients prefer consultation audiotapes to summary letters, *Journal of Clinical Oncology*, 12: 1305–11.

Taylor, C.B., Bandura, A., Ewart, C.K. *et al.* (1985) Exercise testing to enhance wives' confidence in their husbands' cardiac capability soon after clinically uncomplicated acute myocardial infarction, *American Journal of Cardiology*, 55: 635–8.

Taylor, R., Kirby, B., Burdon, D. and Caves, R. (1998) The assessment of recovery in patients after myocardial infarction using three generic quality-of-life measures, *Journal of Cardiopulmonary Rehabilitation*, 18: 139–44.

Taylor, S.E., Lichtman, R.R. and Wood, J.V. (1984) Attributions, beliefs about control, and adjustment to breast cancer, *Journal of Personality and Social Psychology*, 46: 499–502.

Telch, C.F. and Telch, M.J. (1986) Group coping skills instruction and supportive group therapy for cancer patients: a comparison of strategies, *Journal of Consulting and Clinical Psychology*, 54: 802–8.

Temoshok, L. (1987) Personality, coping style, emotion and cancer: toward an integrative model, *Social Science and Medicine*, 20: 833–40.

Temoshok, L. (1990) On attempting to articulate the biopsychosocial model: psychological–psychophysiological homeostasis, in H.S. Friedman (ed.) *Personality and Disease*. New York: Wiley.

Tjemsland, L., Soreide, J.A., Matre, R. and Malt, U.F. (1997) Preoperative psychological variables predict immunological status in patients with operable breast cancer, *Psycho-Oncology*, 6: 311–20.

Tooth, L.R., McKenna, K.T. and Maas, F. (1998) Pre-admission education/counselling for patients undergoing coronary angioplasty: impact on knowledge and risk factors, *Australian and New Zealand Journal of Public Health*, 22: 583–8.

Triandis, H.C. (1977) *Interpersonal Behaviour*. Monterey, CA: Brooks Cole.

TubianaRufi, N., Moret, L., Czernichow, P. and Chwalow, J. (1998) The association of poor adherence and acute metabolic disorders with low levels of cohesion and adaptability in families with diabetic children, *Acta Paediatrica*, 87: 741–6.

Turk, D.C., Rudy, T.E. and Salovey, P. (1986) Implicit models of illness, *Journal of Behavioral Medicine*, 9: 453–74.

Turner, J.A. and Jensen, M.P. (1993) Efficacy of cognitive therapy for chronic low back pain, *Pain*, 52: 169–77.

Tversky, A. and Kahneman, D. (1981) The framing of decisions and the psychology of choice, *Science*, 211: 453–8.

Urrows, S., Affleck, G., Tennen, H. and Higgins, P. (1994) Unique clinical and psychological correlates of fibromyalgia tender points and joint tenderness in rheumatoid arthritis, *Arthritis and Rheumatism*, 37: 1513–20.

Vagero, D. and Lahelma, E. (1998) Women, work and mortality: an analysis of female labor participation, in K. Orth-Gomer, M.A. Chesney and N.K. Wegner (eds) *Women, Stress, and Heart Disease*. Hillsdale, NJ: Lawrence Erlbaum.

Vaillant, G.E. (1998) Natural history of male psychological health. XIV: Relationship of mood disorder vulnerability and physical health, *American Journal of Psychiatry*, 155: 184–91.

Valanis, B., McNeil, V. and Driscoll, K. (1991) Staff members' compliance with their facility's antineoplastic drug handling policy, *Oncology Nursing Forum*, 18: 571–6.

Vazquez, M.I. and Buceta, J.M. (1993) Effectiveness of self-management programmes and relaxation training in the treatment of bronchial asthma: relationships with trait anxiety and emotional attack triggers, *Journal of Psychosomatic Research*, 37: 71–81.

Vidmar, P.M. and Rubinson, L. (1994) The relationship between self-efficacy and exercise compliance in a cardiac population, *Journal of Cardiopulmonary Rehabilitation*, 14: 246–54.

Vlaeyen, J.W., Haazen, I.W., Schuerman, J.A. *et al.* (1995) Behavioural rehabilitation of chronic low back pain: comparison of an operant treatment, an operant-cognitive treatment and an operant-respondent treatment, *British Journal of Clinical Psychology*, 34: 95–118.

Wadden, T.A. (1984) Relaxation therapy for essential hypertension: specific or nonspecific effects, *Journal of Psychosomatic Research*, 28: 53–61.

Wallston, K.A. (1991) The importance of placing measures of health locus of control beliefs in a theoretical context, *Health Education Research, Theory and Practice*, 6: 251–2.

Wallston, K.A. and Smith, M.S. (1994) Issues of control and health: the action is in the interaction, in G. Penny, P. Bennett and M. Herbert (eds) *Health Psychology: A Lifespan Perspective*. London: Harwood.

Wallston, K.A., Wallston, B.S. and DeVellis, R. (1978) Development of multi-dimensional health locus of control (MHLC) scale, *Health Education Monographs*, 6: 160–70.

Ware, J.E., Snow, K.K., Kosinski, M. and Gandek, B. (1993) *SF-36 Health Survey: Manual and Interpretation Guide*. Boston, MA: The Health Institute, New England Medical Center.

Warwick, I., Aggleton, P. and Homans, H. (1988) Constructing commonsense – young people's beliefs about AIDS, *Sociology of Health and Illness*, 10: 213–33.

Watson, D., Clark, L. and Tellegen, A. (1988) Development and validation of brief measures of Positive and Negative Affect: the PANAS scales, *Journal of Personality and Social Psychology*, 54: 1063–70.

Watson, M., Lloyd, S., Davidson, J. *et al.* (1999) The impact of genetic counselling on risk perception and mental health in women with a family history of breast cancer, *British Journal of Cancer*, 79: 868–74.

Wegner, D.M., Schneider, D.J., Carter, S.R. and White, T.L. (1987) Paradoxical effects of thought suppression, *Journal of Personality and Social Psychology*, 53: 5–13.

Weinman, J., Petrie, K.J., Moss-Morris, R. and Horne, R. (1996) The Illness Perception Questionnaire: a new method for assessing the cognitive representation of illness, *Psychology and Health*, 11: 431–45.

Weisse, C., Turbiasz, A. and Whitney, D. (1995) Behavioural training and AIDS risk reduction: overcoming barriers to condom use, *AIDS Education and Prevention*, 7: 50–9.

Wellings, K., Field, J., Johnson, A.M. and Wadsworth, J. (1994) *Sexual Behaviour in Britain: The National Survey of Sexual Attitudes and Lifestyles*. Harmondsworth: Penguin.

West, R., Edwards, M. and Hajek, P. (1998) A randomized controlled trial of a 'buddy' system to improve success at giving up smoking in general practice, *Addiction*, 93: 1007–11.

WHOQOL Group (1998) The World Health Organization Quality of Life Assessment (WHOQOL): development and general psychometric properties, *Social Science and Medicine*, 46: 1569–85.

Whorwell, P.J., Prior, A. and Colgan, S.M. (1987) Hypnotherapy in severe irritable bowel syndrome, *Gut*, 27: 37–40.

Wilkinson, M. (1992) Income distribution and life expectancy, *British Medical Journal*, 304: 165–8.

Williams, R.B., Barefoot, J.C., Califf, R.M. *et al.* (1992) Prognostic importance of social resources among patients with CAD, *Journal of the American Medical Association*, 267: 520–4.

Williams, S., Michie, S. and Pattani, S. (1998) *Improving the Health of the NHS Workforce: Report of the Partnership on the Health of the NHS Workforce*. London: Nuffield Trust.

Wilson, J.F. (1981) Behavioural preparation for surgery: benefit or harm? *Journal of Behavioral Medicine*, 4: 79–102.

Wilson, J.F., Moore, R.W., Randolph, S. and Hanson, B.J. (1982) Behavioral preparation of patients for gastrointestinal endoscopy: information, relaxation, and coping style. *Journal of Human Stress*, 8, 13–23.

World Bank (1993) *World Development Report 1993: Investing in Health*. Oxford: Oxford University Press.

World Health Organization (1991) *Supportive Environments for Health: The Sundsvall Statement*. Geneva: WHO.

Wrisley, D. and Rubenfire, M. (1988) Ineffectiveness of standardized dietary counseling in hypercholesterolemic patients with coronary disease, *Journal of Cardiopulmonary Rehabilitation*, 8: 226–30.

Zautra, A.J., Hoffman, J., Potter, P. *et al.* (1997) Examination of changes in interpersonal stress as a factor in disease exacerbations among women with rheumatoid arthritis, *Annals of Behavioral Medicine*, 19: 279–86.

Zigmond, A.S. and Snaith, R.P. (1983) The Hospital Anxiety and Depression Scale, *Acta Psychiatrica Scandinavica*, 67: 361–70.

Index

PSYCHOLOGY AND HEALTH PROMOTION

Paul Bennett and Simon Murphy

- What part do behavioural and psychological factors play in the health of an individual?
- Which theories contribute to health promotion at the individual and community level?
- How effective are such interventions in improving people's health?

Psychology and Health Promotion is the first book to set out in clear and authoritative terms the role of psychological theory in health promotion. It adopts both structuralist and social regulation models of health and health promotion, considering the significance of psychological processes in each case. The authors examine how behaviour and the social environment may contribute to health status and how psychological processes may mediate the effect of environmental conditions. They go on to consider the theory underlying interventions that are aimed at individuals and large populations, and the effectiveness of attempts to change both individual behaviour and the environmental factors that may contribute to ill-health.

This highly approachable volume is structured as a textbook and includes a summary and further reading at the end of each chapter, as well as a substantial bibliography. It is designed to provide an invaluable resource for advanced undergraduate and postgraduate courses in health psychology, clinical psychology and social psychology as well as students and practitioners in health and social welfare, including health promotion.

Contents

192pp   0 335 19765 5 (Paperback)   0 335 19766 3 (Hardback)